Racism and Resistance

SUNY series in African American Studies

John R. Howard and Robert C. Smith, editors

Racism and Resistance

Essays on Derrick Bell's Racial Realism

Edited by

TIMOTHY JOSEPH GOLDEN

Published by State University of New York Press, Albany

© 2022 State University of New York

All rights reserved

Printed in the United States of America

No part of this book may be used or reproduced in any manner whatsoever without written permission. No part of this book may be stored in a retrieval system or transmitted in any form or by any means including electronic, electrostatic, magnetic tape, mechanical, photocopying, recording, or otherwise without the prior permission in writing of the publisher.

For information, contact State University of New York Press, Albany, NY
www.sunypress.edu

Library of Congress Cataloging-in-Publication Data

Name: Golden, Timothy Joseph, editor.
Title: Racism and resistance : essays on Derrick Bell's racial realism /
   [edited by] Timothy Joseph Golden.
Description: Albany : State University of New York Press, 2022. | Series:
   SUNY series in African American studies | Includes bibliographical
   references and index.
Identifiers: LCCN 2021024226 | ISBN 9781438485973 (hardcover : alk. paper) |
   ISBN 9781438485980 (ebook) | ISBN 9781438485966 (pbk. : alk. paper)
Subjects: LCSH: Racism—United States. | United States—Race relations. |
   African Americans—Civil rights.
Classification: LCC E184.A1 R3266 2021 | DDC 305.800973—dc23
LC record available at https://lccn.loc.gov/2021024226

10 9 8 7 6 5 4 3 2 1

To the memory of my brother,
Marshall Golden
Thank you, "Brother Fred," for always resisting
Until "the wheels fall off"

Contents

Foreword   ix
   Tommy J. Curry

Preface   xix

Acknowledgments   xxvii

Introduction: I Want My Ham   1
   Timothy J. Golden

Part I
Racial Realism, Religion, and the Negro Problem

Chapter 1
The Last Decade of Derrick Bell's Thought   29
   George H. Taylor

Chapter 2
Derrick Bell and the "Negro Problem"   55
   Bill E. Lawson

Part II
Racial Realism and Legal Theory

Chapter 3
From Psychology to Resistance: Racial Realism and American Legal Realism   85
   Timothy J. Golden

Chapter 4
A Rock and a Hard Place: Interest Convergence for the
Racial-Religious Minority   119
Audra Savage

Part III
Racial Realism and Hope

Chapter 5
The Authority of Hope: Hopeful Illusions in *Brown v. Board of Education* and Beyond   145
Vincent Lloyd

Chapter 6
Between Hope and a White Body: The Challenge of Racial Realism and Interracial Love   171
Desirée H. Melton

Part IV
Racial Realism and Theology

Chapter 7
Rethinking Hope: The Importance of Radical Racial Realism for Womanist Theological Thought   195
Keri Day

Chapter 8
Liberalism, Christendom, and Narrative: Paradox and Indirect Communication in Derrick Bell and Søren Kierkegaard   215
Timothy J. Golden

Epilogue: Critical Race Theory as Paradox: The Propositional and the Poetic   253
Timothy J. Golden

Contributors   265

Index   269

Foreword

"He Reminds Us That":
The Philosophical Urgency of Recovering
the Work of Derrick Bell

Tommy J. Curry

America is burning and the symbols of Black progress are being shown to be little more than the illusions of the past, or chimeras unable to sustain, much less support, the demands of Black life or provide the conditions necessary for the realization of Black freedom in the United States.[1] The cherished humanism of liberal political thought and many reformist programs in Black and ethnic studies refuse the souls of Black folk.[2] Black people in America remain outsiders—peering into the world as tragic figures forced to observe their ostracization, extrication, and lethal extermination at the hands of whites. The reality of Black death and the ongoing failure of American democracy demonstrates that the subjugation of Black people in the United States is not accidental, meaning that it does not appear as an abnormality but rather as an abiding repetition, a feature orienting white citizens toward the promise of America as a white republic. The realization of the failures of post–civil rights integrationism and the enduring legacy of white supremacy demands new thinking and thinkers to make sense of this moment. The idols of old must fall, as do all idols.

Our Philosophical Commitments and Reactionary Optimism

Despite the undeniable failure of integration and multiculturalism, race theory in philosophy continues to endorse a dilapidated hope in liberal democracy that ignores the historic and systemic racism of American society.[3] Current theories about race focus on its socially constructed nature—its contingency rather than the actual effect(s) racism has had and continues to have on the lives of Black people in America. In philosophy, the tendency to privilege "race" over "racism" is particularly worrisome, as current writings on the question of race remain dedicated to fulfilling the unrealized promises of integration. Despite the work of scholars outside of philosophy such as Michelle Alexander's concrete articulation of the "New Jim Crow," or the maintenance of America's racial caste system through mass incarceration,[4] or Barbara J. Field's interrogation of the historical complexity that emerges from the ideological limitations of the race construct in analyzing American racism, our present-day philosophical engagements with race propagate a conceptually simplistic view that sees race as a problem able to be solved through dialogue and interracial understanding. Ignoring the various social and legal manifestations of anti-Black racism that show the regression of race relations in America, rather than progress,[5] this dogma calls for a peaceful coexistence between Blacks and whites in which the long-denied humanity of Black people are recognized in exchange for Blacks interiorizing America's liberal creed of (racial) equality, (Black) individuality, and (African American) faith.

Academic theories of democracy and race tend to privilege the desired political outcomes as evidence of the cultural and ethical possibilities of American democracy as political theory, rather than the repetitive vacillations of repressive political dictum and its cessation. When Barack Obama was president, the celebrated theories of American democratic potentiality suggested a resolution between democracy and anti-Black racism was possible given the core commitments of liberal theory. Works in Black philosophy and race theory such as Tommie Shelby's *We Who Are Dark: The Philosophical Foundations of Black Solidarity*, Elizabeth Anderson's *The Imperative of Integration*, and Eddie Glaude's *In a Shade of Blue: Pragmatism and the Politics of Black America* follow this mode of political declaration that privileges the idea that integration and racial coexistence are the *only* democratic means of dealing with the racial inequalities that persist in the United States. Despite the role that Black Power–style nationalism, and radical (systemic) critiques of white supremacy have historically had throughout the twentieth century, "Black philosophers primarily rely on the promises of American liberalism and the hopes of democracy in the post–civil rights era to fundamentally change the racial context of the United States and remedy individual attachments to racial loyalties."[6]

Instead of dealing with the seeming permanence of American racism and theorizing from this actuality, Black pundits choose to place their hopes in instrumental reforms. Unable to demand concrete political rights or direct sustain political movements against white racial dominance, Black Americans have remained reactionary. The present intersectional mode of Black politics urges coalitions and funding from white liberals and the democratic national platform. Black activists are demanding the representation of Black women in candidates such as Senator Kamala Harris, and lecturing the Black community on its need to vote for Joe Biden, not because a Biden and Harris ticket will actually help Black people economically but because it would replace the horror of Donald Trump. Despite almost eight years of Black Lives Matter protest and organizing, the number of deaths of Black men has not decreased. Black men remain roughly 96 percent of all Blacks killed by police, and in the later quarter of 2020 are 99 percent (145 of 146) of the people shot by police in the United States.[7] Rather than reacting against the liberal conceptualization of American race relations as gradual and naturally progressing toward the resolution of anti-Black racism, the dominant mode of Black political thought and protest seeks to revise Black experience and the tyranny constraining Black political being into the triumphalism of Black representation.[8] While people are dying, the bourgeois class of Black political pundits and opinionmakers are urging Black Americans to retreat into the hope of a new symbol, an anyone-but-Trump idol, a ticket that supported segregation, and disproportionately convicted poor Black people, but is undeniably not Donald Trump.[9]

Following this logic, the election of President Donald Trump and the concurrent rise of neo-fascism and white ethno-nationalism is merely a moment, a historical interruption in the teleological character of American democracy. The disproportionate targeting of Black men by police has persisted throughout American history. The violence we witnessed under President Trump is not new—it is simply now more public. Trump's election provided a political platform and national audience for the politics that were often covert and institutional—the aversions toward Blacks demonstrated in boardrooms, juries, hiring committees, and politics. By offering white supremacists a public, an audience with a shared vision and political platform, Trump made visible what has always been present but denied.

Black political theory is often the product of biography, the belief that because Black political theorists have often explained their rise within the academy as an act of faith in education, socioeconomic mobility, and democratic principles, it follows that anti-Black racism can be ameliorated in this way. The belief that they, Black theorists, are that exceptional class of thinkers who can abstract away from the world and think freely without the bounds and boundaries of Blackness allows many of our conceptualizations to roam freely above the world without regard. As identity or sociopolitical constraint, there is an imagined freedom from Blackness *in theory*, a distance in the theorist's ability to think outside of *being* Black. This cherished optimism, however, is reactionary. It does not arise from the demonstrable facts about the world, or the Black condition, but manifests itself as the only viable option among chaos and impending death. The inability to think beyond the confines of the political systems and disciplinary concepts of our time does not actually provide evidence to support the possibility of change. In actuality, it is in this uncertainty that one should realize that optimism, the faith in the ideals of the system actively oppressing Black people to remedy that oppression, is an entailment of the program designed to preserve itself. This reactionary optimism dulls our senses and burdens Black political theory with counterfactuals as its basis. Black oppression is explained as looming, but resolvable; Black death is normal, but not essential; and Black thought must remain democratic and hopeful. These axioms dictate an approach to Black reality that Derrick Bell sought to remedy through realism and requires intellectual and spiritual courage.

Despite the actual political reality before racialized Americans, theory insists that history does not offer evidence against the dominant liberal ethos of American democratic governance. Even today, American political thinkers dealing with the race question are motivated by the Pyrrhic successes of *Brown versus the Board of Education* and the civil rights era,[10] choosing to read into historic Black works contemporary ideas of integrationism and racial ethics, as if the insights of Black authors who wrote during slavery and Reconstruction illuminate current racial issues in America only insofar as they enrich the racial success stories of liberalism and the possibility of racial amelioration under American democracy. If Black political theory is to move beyond the current apologetic revisionism of historic Black thinkers—a revisionism set on depicting even the most adamant nationalists as closet integrationists—Black political theory must begin to exert new energies toward theorizing about the political and social inequality that Blacks currently endure, which means both creating a discussion in Black social political philosophy open to the possibility of permanent racial inequality in the United States, and engaging in a more diligent and earnest reading of Black resistance outside of the *political aims* of American liberalism and integration's racial moralizations. It is my hope that the introduction of Derrick Bell's work into the Black political arena hastens the detaching of decades-old optimism and faith in systems that not only oppress but bring death onto Black Americans.

The Contributions of Golden's Edited Work on Bell

There are no philosophy books published on the work of Derrick Bell because most people who write on Derrick's work publish in law journals. While there has been a sustained effort to center Bell's work and theory by myself and others in philosophy, this collected edition is the first engaged reflection with Derrick Bell's corpus as political theory.[11] This is why the edition is needed. But it reminds us that Derrick Bell anticipated the inevitable failure of the symbols of our era. He insisted that we expect that Obama and the celebrations of representation would fade once it was no longer in the interest of a critical mass of whites to behave as if it were. Bell's work offers us tremendous resources for thinking about the contingency of Black rights and life in the United States that is pessimistic but still rich in resistance and revolutionary potential.

Derrick Bell understood that racism was programmatic and systematic. He cannot be reduced to his analysis of racial realism or the provocative thesis that racism is permanent. The insight of Bell revolves around the profound insights he had into the very structure and operation of racism. Extending the insights of his mentor and friend Judge Robert L. Carter, Bell insisted that desegregation missed the actual core of Black inequality in the United States, which was white supremacy.[12] Bell was adamant that "we have never understood that the essence of the racism we contended against was not simply that we were exploited in slavery, degraded by segregation, and frustrated by the unmet promises of equal opportunity. The essence of racism in America was the hope that we who were [B]lack would not exist."[13] This reality however did not, and does not, demand Black acquiescence.[14] Bell believed that the realization that the system was committed to Black subjugation, and the law could not be used to sustain Black civil rights gains, was freeing.[15] He was of the opinion that the need to resist, to struggle against one's oppressor, would be energized by the truth, and that this reality of American race relations, no matter how bleak to some, was necessary to inspire Black Americans to think beyond the moral rhetoric of equality and the platitudes of democratic faith.

Golden's book is a welcomed attempt to center Derrick's work both philosophically and academically. This book will be remembered as a definitive work in Bell studies for the richness and care Golden takes in attending to the diversity within Bell's thought. Very few philosophers have seriously engaged, much less published, on Derrick Bell's work. Despite his relatively recent death, Derrick Bell has not been afforded the proper regard within philosophy as a political theorist or serious race thinker despite multiple philosophy departments throughout the country claiming to specialize and support Critical Race Theory as an area of study and critical philosophies of race as a specialization.[16] This edited book will be formative in reintroducing Derrick Bell's political theory and is a trailblazing collection of works that show why now more than ever Derrick Bell's voice should be heard again.

Notes

1. Calvin Warren, "Black Nihilism and the Politics of Hope," *CR: The New Centennial Review* 15.1 (2015): 215–248.

2. Calvin Warren, *Ontological Terror: Blackness, Nihilism, and Emancipation* (Durham, NC: Duke University Press, 2018).

3. "White-on-black oppression is systemic and has persisted over several centuries without the broad and foundational racial transformations that many social analysts suggest should have happened. While some significant changes have certainly taken place, systemic racism today retains the numerous basic features that perpetuate the racial views, proclivities, actions and intentions of many earlier white generations, including white founders like Thomas Jefferson. Because of its power and centrality in this still racially hierarchical society, white-on-black oppression has shaped considerably all other types of racial oppression that whites later developed within this still white controlled society. . . . In addition, white-on-black oppression is an independent social reality that cannot be reduced to other social realities such as class stratification, though all major forms of oppression do interact and intersect with it historically" (Joe R. Feagin, *Systemic Racism*. New York: Routledge, 2006, 7). For an historical explanation of

racial development in the United States, see Joe R. Feagin, *Racist America* (New York: Routledge, 2001).

4. Michelle Alexander, *The New Jim Crow: Mass Incarceration in the Age of Colorblindness* (New York: The New Press, 2010).

5. The murder of Black men in the United States continues to be seen as normal. Black men are identified as thugs, and their deaths are seen as justifiable consequences of the thug life (*Newsweek*, "The Search for Thugs," November 10, 2007). For a discussion of the continuing murder of Black men, see Cyril Josh Barker, "Oct 22 Coalition Holds Anti-Police Brutality Rally," *New York Amsterdam News*, Oct 25–27, 2007, 3; Alton H. Maddox Jr., "The Sean Bell Fiasco in Black and White," *New York Amsterdam News*, March 8, 2007, 12–28. For a discussion of the racial inequality involved in the Jena Six case, see Michael Eric Dyson, "It's Not Only the Jena Six, You Could Be Next," *Ebony*, December 2007, 58. For a discussion of the tragedy that befell Megan Williams, see Francie Latour, "Hell on Earth," *Essence*, November 2007, 210, 214, 242.

6. Tommy J. Curry, "Who K(new): The Nation-ist Contour of Racial Identity in the Thought of Martin R. Delany and John E. Bruce," *Journal of Pan-African Studies* 1 (2007): 43.

7. John Muyskens and Joe Fox, "Fatal Force." The *Washington Post* Fatal Force database shows that 1,195 Black people were killed between January 2015 and December 2019. Black men were 1,148 of those killed, or roughly 96 percent.

8. Tommy J. Curry, "He Never Mattered: Poor Black Males and the Dark Logic of Intersectional Invisibility," in *The Movement for Black Lives: Philosophical Perspectives*, eds. Michael Choli, Alex Madva, Benjamin Yost, and Brandon Hogan (Oxford: Oxford University Press, 2020).

9. Janell Ross, "Joe Biden Didn't Just Compromise with Segregationists," NBCnews.com, June 25, 2019, www.nbcnews.com/news/nbcblk/joe-biden-didn-t-just-compromise-segregationists-he-fought-their-n1021626; Michael Finnegan, "California's Tough on Crime Past Haunts Kamala Harris," *Los Angeles Times*, October 24, 2019, www.latimes.com/politics/story/2019-10-24/kamala-harris-california-crime, and Lara Bazelon, "Kamala Harris' Criminal Justice Record Killed Her Presidential Run," TheAppeal.org, December 4, 2019, https://theappeal.org/kamala-harris-criminal-justice-record-killed-her-presidential-run

10. Integration has failed on several fronts. The historical work in this area has convincingly demonstrated that *Brown v. Board* (1954) was nothing more than a political agenda pushed to increase American soft power during the Cold War era; see Mary Dudziak, "Desegregation as a Cold War Imperative," *Stanford Law Review* FSD241 (1988): 61; Mary Dudziak, *Cold War Civil Rights: Race and the Image of American Democracy* (Princeton, NJ: Princeton University Press, 2002). The idea of racial equality is fundamentally bankrupt; see Derrick Bell, *And We Are Not Saved: The Elusive Quest for Racial Justice* (New York: Basic Books, 1987); Derrick Bell, *Faces at the Bottom of the Well: The Permanence of Racism* (New

York: Basic Books, 1992). And desegregation worsened the education and economic viability of Black communities; see Derrick Bell, *Silent Covenants: Brown v. Board of Education and the Unfilled Hopes for Racial Reform* (New York: Oxford, 2004). For a discussion on the errant belief that education and multicultural associations through education are the barometer of racial progress, see Tommy J. Curry, "Saved by the Bell: Racial Realism as Pedagogy," *Philosophical Studies in Education* 39 (2008): 35–46.

11. See Curry, "Saved by the Bell," 35–46; "Shut Your Mouth When You're Talking to Me: Silencing the Idealist School of Critical Race Theory through a Culturalogic Turn in Jurisprudence," *Georgetown Law Journal of Modern Critical Race Studies* 3.1 (2012): 1–38; "Back to the Woodshop: Black Education, Imperial Pedagogy, and Post-Racial Mythology under the Reign of Obama," *Teacher's College Record* 117.14 (2015): 27–52; and Tommy J. Curry and Gwenetta D. Curry, "Critical Race Theory and the Demography of Death and Dying," in *Critical Race Theory in the Academy*, ed. Vernon Farmer and Evelyn Shephard-Wynn (Charlotte, NC: Information Age Publishing, 2020), 89–106. See also Jessica Otto, "Derrick Bell's Paradigm of Racial Realism: An Overlooked and Unappreciated Theorist," *Radical Philosophy Review* 20.2 (2017): 243–264.

12. Robert L. Carter, "The Warren Court and Desegregation," *Michigan Law Review* 67 (1968): 237–248, and "The U.S. Supreme Court and the Issue of Racial Discrimination since 1940," *Presence Africaine* (1959): 177–195, and "The Effects of Segregation and the Consequences of Desegregation: A Social Science Statement," *Journal of Negro Education* 22.1 (1953): 68–76.

13. Derrick Bell, *Gospel Choirs: Psalms of Survival in an Alien Land Called Home* (New York: Basic Books, 1996), 23.

14. Derrick Bell, "Racial Remediation: A Historical Perspective on Current Conditions," *Notre Dame Lawyer* 52 (1976–77): 5–29.

15. Derrick Bell, *Faces at the Bottom of the Well: The Permanence of Racism* (New York: Basic Books, 1992).

16. See Tommy J. Curry, "Will the Real CRT Please Stand Up: The Dangers of Philosophical Contributions to CRT," *The Crit: A Journal in Critical Legal Studies* 2.1 (2009): 1–47, and "Canonizing the Critical Race Artifice: An Analysis of Philosophy's Gentrification of Critical Race Theory," in *The Routledge Companion to the Philosophy of Race*, eds. Paul Taylor, Linda Alcoff, and Luvell Anderson (New York: Routledge Press, 2017), 349–361.

Works Cited

Alexander, Michelle. *The New Jim Crow: Mass Incarceration in the Age of Color-Blindness*. New York: The New Press, 2010.

Barker, Cyril Josh. "Oct 22 Coalition Holds Anti-Police Brutality Rally," *New York Amsterdam News*, Oct 25–27, 2007.
Bell, Derrick. *Silent Covenants:* Brown v. Board of Education *and the Unfilled Hopes for Racial Reform*. New York: Oxford, 2004.
———. *Gospel Choirs: Psalms of Survival in an Alien Land Called Home*. New York: Basic Books, 1996.
———. *Faces at the Bottom of the Well: The Permanence of Racism*. New York: Basic Books, 1992.
———. *And We Are Not Saved: The Elusive Quest for Racial Justice*. New York: Basic Books, 1987.
———. "Racial Remediation: A Historical Perspective on Current Conditions." *Notre Dame Lawyer* 52 (1976–77): 5–29.
Carter, Robert L. "The Warren Court and Desegregation," *Michigan Law Review* 67 (1968): 237–248
———. "The U.S. Supreme Court and the Issue of Racial Discrimination since 1940," *Presence Africaine* (1959): 177–195.
———. "The Effects of Segregation and the Consequences of Desegregation: A Social Science Statement," *Journal of Negro Education* 22.1 (1953): 68–76.
Curry, Tommy J., and Gwenetta D Curry. "Critical Race Theory and the Demography of Death and Dying," in *Critical Race Theory in the Academy*, ed. Vernon Farmer and Evelyn Shephard-Wynn. Charlotte, NC: Information Age Publishing, 2020. 89–106.
Curry, Tommy J. "He Never Mattered: Poor Black Males and the Dark Logic of Intersectional Invisibility," in *The Movement for Black Lives: Philosophical Perspectives*, ed. Michael Cholbi, Alex Madva, Benjamin Yost, and Brandon Hogan. Oxford: Oxford University Press, 2020.
———. "Canonizing the Critical Race Artifice: An Analysis of Philosophy's Gentrification of Critical Race Theory," in *The Routledge Companion to the Philosophy of Race*, ed. Paul Taylor, Linda Alcoff, and Luvell Anderson. New York: Routledge Press, 2017. 349–361.
———. "Back to the Woodshop: Black Education, Imperial Pedagogy, and Post-Racial Mythology under the Reign of Obama," *Teacher's College Record* 117.14 (2015): 27–52.
———. "'Shut Your Mouth When You're Talking to Me': Silencing the Idealist School of Critical Race Theory through a Culturalogic Turn in Jurisprudence," *Georgetown Law Journal of Modern Critical Race Studies* 3.1 (2012): 1–38.
———. "Will the Real CRT Please Stand Up: The Dangers of Philosophical Contributions to CRT," *The Crit: A Journal in Critical Legal Studies* 2.1 (2009): 1–47.
———. "Saved by the Bell: Racial Realism as Pedagogy," *Philosophical Studies in Education* 39 (2008): 35–46.

———. "Who K(new): The Nation-ist Contour of Racial Identity in the Thought of Martin R. Delany and John E. Bruce," *Journal of Pan-African Studies* 1 (2007): 43.

Dudziak, Mary. *Cold War Civil Rights: Race and the Image of American Democracy.* Princeton, NJ: Princeton University Press, 2002.

———. "Desegregation as a Cold War Imperative," *Stanford Law Review* FSD241 (1988): 61

Dyson, Michael Eric. "It's Not Only the Jena Six, You Could Be Next," *Ebony* (December 2007): 58.

Feagin, Joe R. *Systemic Racism*. New York: Routledge, 2006.

———. *Racist America*. New York: Routledge, 2001.

Finnegan, Michael. "California's Tough on Crime Past Haunts Kamala Harris," *Los Angeles Times*, October 24, 2019.

Latour, Francie. "Hell on Earth," *Essence* (November 2007): 210, 214, 242.

Maddox Jr., Alton H. "The Sean Bell Fiasco in Black and White," *New York Amsterdam News*, March 8, 2007.

Muyskens, John, and Joe Fox. "Fatal Force," *The Washington Post*.

Otto, Jessica. "Derrick Bell's Paradigm of Racial Realism: An Overlooked and Unappreciated Theorist," *Radical Philosophy Review* 20.2 (2017): 243–264.

Ross, Janell. "Joe Biden Didn't Just Compromise with Segregationists," NBCnews.com, June 25, 2019. www.nbcnews.com/news/nbcblk/joe-biden-didn-t-just-compromise-segregationists-he-fought-their-n1021626

Warren, Calvin. *Ontological Terror: Blackness, Nihilism, and Emancipation*. Durham, NC: Duke University Press, 2018.

———. "Black Nihilism and the Politics of Hope," *CR: The New Centennial Review* 15.1 (2015): 215–248.

Preface

This book was conceived in October of 2011, not long after Derrick Bell's death. My former professor, colleague, and now friend, Bill E. Lawson had been encouraging me to read Bell as a philosopher since 2007, and, inspired by Bell's courageous life and work, I decided to assemble an array of scholars across the fields of philosophy, law, theology, and rhetoric to pay tribute to Bell through an analysis of one of the most compelling yet puzzling accounts of American racism which is found in Bell's notion of racial realism: racism is a permanent feature of American life, yet we must resist it at every turn. Bell called it "salvation through struggle." He writes: "We reject any philosophy that insists on measuring life's success on the achieving of specific goals—overlooking the process of living. More affirmatively and as a matter of faith, we believe that, despite the lack of linear progress, there is satisfaction in the struggle itself."[1] So Bell asks us to maintain hope in the face of despair—a daunting task indeed. Bell's view is somewhat aporetic and raises a host of questions. How does one strive for the unattainable without succumbing to despair? What does it mean to claim victory not in the achievement of one's goal, but rather in the attempt to achieve it, even while knowing that it is impossible? By conceding racism's permanence, are we not also conceding the fight against it? Bell's racial realism provokes these and many other questions that the contributors of this book explore in detail. I am deeply grateful for their contributions.

The more I reflected on Lawson's encouragement to read Bell philosophically, the more I began to understand the nature of Bell's racial realism not only as a fundamentally inductive claim based on experience but also as a deeply moral claim with philosophical implications that reached from affinities with the existentialist tradition—Bell himself mentions Camus, and I have an essay in this volume on Bell and Kierkegaard—and Christian theology, as in the work of George Taylor, to affinities with some of the most basic cosmological and moral problems of Western philosophy, as I describe below in my discussion of Bell and the pre-Socratic, Milesian philosopher, Anaximander. Reading Bell philosophically, one can see that Bell is not only working within a rich tradition of Black American intellectual history (as he is in dialogue with both Ralph Bunche[2] and Martin Delany[3]) but also that Bell is grappling with deep philosophical, moral, and theological problems at the core of human life—problems worthy of some brief commentary here.

One might think that Derrick Bell and Anaximander are two thinkers whose intellectual paths would never cross. After all, not only are they chronologically separated by more than two millennia, their subject matter is different (Anaximander was a pre-Socratic thinker who engaged in the sort of cosmological speculation at the foundation of Western philosophy, while Bell was a twentieth and twenty-first-century African American legal theorist and educator who confronted what he argued was the intractable problem of anti-Black racism in America). And yet despite these vast differences in both era and subject matter, there is, I think, a remarkable affinity between the two.

Both thinkers present different versions of what philosophers have called the "long since" argument. Anaximander, in response to Thales, his Milesian predecessor, argued that Thales was incorrect about his claim that all is water because of the coexistence of opposites: water was cold and wet, fire was hot and dry, and yet they can coexist. But if Thales was right about water, it would have "long since" consumed the other elements of fire, earth, and air. And since water has not consumed them, there must be another unseen force regulating all four of the elements. Anaximander calls this unseen force *apeiron*, and claims that it is the infinite origin of all the elements. *Apeiron* ensures a perpetual cycle of injustice in nature, such that the summer is unjust in its extreme hotness and dryness and the winter is unjust in its extreme of coldness and wetness. In the winter, when the extremes of coldness and wetness predominate, *apeiron* has consumed the extreme hotness and dryness of summer, and vice versa. And in the fall and spring, there are refreshing but brief "just" periods of moderation as the extremities of summer and winter transition into the boundless *apeiron* for their cyclical punishment. Simplicius, a commentator on pre-Socratic thought, writes that Anaximander says that the *arkhē* is neither water nor any of the other things called elements, but some other nature which is *apeiron*, out of which come to be all the heavens and the worlds in them. The things that are perish into the things from which they come to be, according to necessity, for they pay penalty and retribution to each other for their injustice in accordance with the ordering of time.[4]

What one sees in Anaximander's account of nature is a perpetual cycle of injustice—the extremes of summer and winter—that is briefly interrupted by the "just" moderation of fall and spring. For Anaximander, justice is never permanent and will always be brief; we know through a study of nature and through experience that injustice is the predominant force and that justice, though predictable, is transitory.

Bell makes a similar claim with his thesis of racial realism. Akin to the ephemeral nature of justice in Anaximander's account of fall and spring, Bell, in his quintessential articulation of racial realism, points out that the most "herculean efforts" to attain full equality for Black people in America "will produce no more than temporary 'peaks of progress,' short-lived victories that slide into irrelevance as racial patterns adapt in ways that maintain white dominance."[5] It is these temporary "peaks of progress" that Bell references which, I argue, correspond to the moderation of fall and spring in Anaximander's cosmological account. Bell, unlike Anaximander, is not engaged in a study of nature, but rather in a study of American history, legal theory, and politics that yields a similar result to Anaximander's portrait of the cosmos: injustice in the form of anti-Black racism is the predominant feature of American political life, which is only briefly interrupted with noticeable but temporary just results. At bottom, Bell's argument, like Anaximander's, has at its core a "long since" quality to it: considering the many "herculean efforts" to overcome American anti-Black racism, racism, were it not permanent, should have "long since" been overcome, even as water should have "long since" overcome fire.

One may object here and argue that Bell and Anaximander argue *ad ignorantium*, that is, they commit the fallacy of assuming something to be true (in Anaximander's case, the regularity of nature, and in Bell's case, the permanence of racism) because it has yet to be proven false. But such an objection can be made about almost any inductive claim. For example, one can argue that just because the sun has never *failed to rise* that the claim that it *will rise tomorrow* is an *ad ignorantium* claim. If one were to defend this claim, however, one would point to the various astronomical and mathematical calculations and argue that at the current rotational and revolutionary speed of the Earth around the Sun that, while not guaranteed (again, an inherent feature of *all* inductive arguments) there is a strong likelihood that the sun will indeed rise tomorrow and one can thus plan accordingly. For Bell and Anaximander, their argument is similar: the dynamics between injustice and justice, both in nature and in American legal, social, and political life have been such that one can predict, not with certainty, but rather with considerable assurance that racism in America will persist in a similar fashion to the way that one can predict the sunrise; not with an astronomical, mathematical, and scientific certainty, but rather, for Bell, at least, with sort of moral assurance after a careful study of the historical, legal, social, and political evidence that enables us, just as in the case of tomorrow's predicted sunrise, to plan accordingly.

Indeed, even in the most cursory surveys of American social, political, and legal history one sees strong evidence of what Bell called "herculean efforts" to eliminate racism that, time and again, have failed. Consider that America was founded twice: once in 1776 when chattel slavery was the law of the land, and again nearly one hundred years later when the Reconstruction Amendments of 1865, 1868, and 1870 ended chattel slavery, ensured citizenship rights to freedmen, and guaranteed freedmen the right to vote, respectively. Then consider that the Reconstruction Amendments were insufficient; nineteenth- and twentieth-century federal civil rights laws had to buttress them, and even then, the United States Supreme Court nullified such laws, due to abstract legal doctrines such as federalism, ruling that they were unconstitutional intrusions on state power. Indeed, this often applied to the Reconstruction Amendments themselves, as in the *Slaughterhouse Cases*. Mary Frances Berry, in her important text *Black Resistance, White Law*, points out that the policy of federal inaction, preventing intervention in state-level racial violence, was an important part of how the United States Supreme Court maintained white supremacy. Add to this history the countless number of affirmative action programs, beginning with initiatives such as the Freedmen's Bureau, that failed because of abstract, ahistorical notions of "equality" in our legal, cultural, and political discourse, a variety of other failed social and political initiatives, and a current world in which voter suppression, mass incarceration, and police brutality persist, and we are living with all of the injustice of summer's sweltering heat and winter's frigid cold. There are times in between these injustices when we behold the social and cultural popularity of the Black Lives Matter movement, when the first African American is elected President of the United States, when the first African American woman is elected Vice President of the United States, when the President nominates and the Senate confirms the first Black woman to serve on the United States Supreme Court, when there is a presidential pardon of an African American unjustly convicted, or when a national police reform bill or a voting rights bill is pending in Congress. But these are, like the moderate warmth and coolness of spring and fall, transitory moments of hope rather than genuine, enduring change for justice. As Bell argues throughout his corpus, initiatives such as these are so laden with the interests of wealthy and influential whites that their effects, while seemingly positive, are nullified when the interests of wealth and influence cease to converge with the interests of Blacks. So in the end, "justice" appears for a moment, only to soon fade in the face of injustice, as nature dictates.

Two more points of comparison between Bell and Anaximander are important here. First, for Anaximander, the perpetuity of injustice is not incidental—it is a constituent and permanent feature of the natural world. Similarly, for Bell, anti-Black racism and its attendant injustices are not aberrations in America, but rather are conditions legislated into the fabric of—and are perhaps even necessary for—America to thrive. There is no escaping them. Indeed, as Bell has argued, contrary to Gunnar Myrdal's anomaly thesis, justice is the exception and injustice is the rule. Second, both Anaximander and Bell conclude something almost mystical from the natural order and from the American political order, respectively. For Anaximander, since water cannot be the first principle of all things because if it were it would have long since consumed fire, the first principle of all things must be *apeiron*, an infinite, theological, and deeply moral force that regulates injustice. And for Bell, if racism is permanent because our best efforts would have long since eliminated it, there must be something greater at work that we do not see—something that controls the world, and something that, in Bell's case, can at least motivate us to deal with the intractable problem of injustice through the power of moral struggle in the form of resistance to racism.

Consider the following fragment from Anaximander, as Aristotle recounts it:

> This [the infinite, *apeiron*] does not have an *arkhē*, but this seems to be the *arkhē* of the rest, and to contain all things and steer all things, as all declare who do not fashion other causes aside from the infinite [the *apeiron*] . . . and this is the divine. For it is deathless and indestructible, as Anaximander and most of the natural philosophers say.[6]

Compare this statement from Bell:

> The world is moved by diverse powers and pressures creating cross currents that unpredictably, yet with eerie precision, determine the outcome of events. Often invisible in their influence, these forces shape our destinies, furthering or frustrating our ambitions and goals. The perfection for which we strive is elusive precisely because we are caught up in the myriad of manifestations of perfection itself.[7]

Anaximander writes of an *arkhē*, that is, an origin of all things that itself has no origin. This infinite is not only said to "contain all things" but also to "steer all things." This mystical entity, which Anaximander refers to as "*apeiron*," is considered "divine," thus giving it a theological dimension. *Apeiron*, as Anaximander calls it, is the infinite force that ensures a perpetual seasonal cycle. Similarly, Bell writes of "invisible" "forces" that "shape our destinies, furthering or frustrating our ambitions and goals." What are we to make of these mystical notions of "invisible forces"? For Bell, the invisible force that shapes our destiny is found deep inside us, inside the hearts and minds of people like Mrs. Biona McDonald, whose indefatigable spirit of resistance in the face of anti-Black racism led her to conclude that she "lives to harass white folks." And it is, I think, the relative strength or weakness of this invisible force within us that will either "further" or "frustrate" our spirit while we grapple with anti-Black racism, as Bell writes.

This book is thus aptly titled *Racism and Resistance*. It is a book not only about Bell's thesis concerning the permanence of racism but also about Bell's demand that we have the necessary courage to continually resist it. It is this juxtaposition of racism and resistance that inspired the reflections in the pages that follow, and that I hope will inspire both further philosophical and cross-disciplinary scholarly reflection on a thinker of Bell's high caliber for a long time to come.

Notes

1. Derrick Bell, *Faces at the Bottom of the Well: The Permanence of Racism* (New York: Basic Books, 1992), 98.
2. See Bell's Discussion of Ralph Bunche in Derrick Bell, *Race, Racism and American Law* (Frederick, MD: Aspen Publishers, 2008), 1–8.
3. See Bill E. Lawson's discussion of Bell and Martin Delany in "Frederick Douglass and American Social Progress: Does Race Matter at the Bottom of the Well?" in *Frederick Douglass: A Critical Reader*, eds. Bill E. Lawson and Frank M. Kirkland (Malden, MA: Blackwell Publishers, 1999), 356–391, 374–378.
4. Simplicius, "Commentary on Aristotle's Physics," *A Pre-Socratics Reader: Selected Fragments and Testimonia*, ed. Patricia Curd, trans. Richard McKirahan (Indianapolis, IN: Hackett Publishing, 2011), 16–17.
5. Bell, *Faces at the Bottom of the Well*, 12.
6. Aristotle, "Physics," *The Complete Works of Aristotle*, ed. Jonathan Barnes, trans. R. P. Hardie and R. K. Gaye (Princeton, NJ: Princeton University Press, 1984), 203b10–15.
7. Derrick Bell, *Silent Covenants:* Brown v. Board of Education *and the Unfulfilled Hopes for Racial Reform* (New York: Oxford University Press, 2004), x.

Works Cited

Aristotle. "Physics," *The Complete Works of Aristotle*, ed. Jonathan Barnes, trans. R. P. Hardie and R. K. Gaye. Princeton, NJ: Princeton University Press, 1984.

Bell, Derrick. *Race, Racism and American Law*. Frederick, MD: Aspen Publishers, 2008.

———. *Silent Covenants:* Brown v. Board of Education *and the Unfulfilled Hopes for Racial Reform*. New York: Oxford University Press, 2004.

———. *Faces at the Bottom of the Well: The Permanence of Racism*. New York: Basic Books, 1992.

Lawson, Bill E. "Frederick Douglass and American Social Progress: Does Race Matter at the Bottom of the Well?," in *Frederick Douglass: A Critical Reader*, ed. Bill E. Lawson and Frank M. Kirkland. Malden, MA: Blackwell Publishers, 1999.

Simplicius. "Commentary on Aristotle's Physics," *A Pre-Socratics Reader: Selected Fragments and Testimonia*, ed. Patricia Curd, trans. Richard McKirahan. Indianapolis, IN: Hackett Publishing, 2011.

Acknowledgments

Human error makes expressions of gratitude a risky proposition. There is always a likelihood of omitting people who should be included on your list. So in advance, I ask those unnamed here to forgive me. I want to first thank the State University of New York Press for accepting this book for publication and for the anonymous reviewers who expressed their confidence in this project and gave such strong constructive criticism. My editors, Michael Rinella and Eileen Nizer, have demonstrated a patient professionalism that is nothing short of extraordinary as this book has made it through the long journey to publication. Thank you, Michael and Eileen. I am also grateful to each of the contributors for their remarkable patience with and confidence in this project—without you, this book simply could not be. So thank you.

Special thanks are also due to three of my fine colleagues, all first-rate philosophers who I am so fortunate to know and from whom I continue to learn. I want to thank Bill E. Lawson, who inspired me to begin philosophically reading Bell in 2007. Bill, our many conversations about Bell have pushed my thinking in directions I never thought I would take. Thank you. I am also grateful to Tommy J. Curry for our many conversations about Bell's work. Tommy, the insights into Bell that I gained from our discussions have made me a better interpreter of Bell by situating him within the much broader tradition of Black intellectual history—a history that, as you so persuasively point out, is often overlooked in the interest of novel but problematic interpretations of Black thinkers that can—and often do—dilute their ideas.[1] I am forever indebted to you for awakening me from my "dogmatic slumber." Your groundbreaking work in Critical Race Theory and Black Male Studies has redirected my thinking in a constructive way. Again, thank you, Tommy. I likewise owe a debt of gratitude to George Yancy, who has helped me to think of Bell as an existentialist—the subject of my next monograph. George, our discussions about Bell have inspired me to dig deeper into his work and produce more literature on this extraordinary thinker as a philosopher in the tradition of Black existentialism, a tradition in which you have played a pivotal role in founding. Thank you, George.

I am also thankful to my colleagues in the Department of History and Philosophy at Walla Walla University and my students. Greg Dodds, my department chair, Terrie Aamodt, and Hilary Dickerson—all historians—Monique Roddy, an archaeologist, and Linda Emmerson, my fellow philosopher. Each of you have all inspired me to take the study of history seriously, which philosophers often neglect to do. Terrie, our many conversations about American Reconstruction have generated my burgeoning and now rather strong interest in American legal history, which is essential for understanding Bell. For that, Terrie, I say thank you. And my thanks to each of you for being such good colleagues, peers, and friends. I have learned and continue to learn so much from each of you. To my students, every time I teach Bell's work in African American Philosophy or Critical Race Theory, I learn as much—probably more—about Bell from you as you learn from me. Thank you for being such engaged readers and careful interpreters of Bell's work, especially my former student, Jack Stinson, who wrote his senior thesis on Bell's work in Critical Race Theory as part of his interest in the United States Supreme Court's Reconstruction jurisprudence. It was a joy to supervise your work, Jack. It was well done, and best wishes to you in your career as an attorney. All of my students and colleagues have made me a better scholar, and to all of them I am forever grateful.

And then there is my family and friends, whom I must also gratefully acknowledge. My parents, James B. Golden Sr. and Margaret Catherine Golden are gone, but I am certainly grateful to them both for my life and the beautiful family into which they brought me. My sisters and brothers, Joyce, Jimmy, Debbie, Marshall, Rita, and Dennis, have all supported me throughout some difficult circumstances in my life in recent years, and I am so grateful to each of you for the love and care you have shown and continue to show me. Thank you, and I love each of you more than I can say. To my friends, Keith Davidson, Jason Hall, Adia Taliaferro, Tameka Lafayette, Donald Cantrell, Dwayne Wyre, Jim and Anita Trotman, Aaron and Nicky Scott, Charles and Michelle Cammack, Maurits and Katherine Hughes, Larry and Ina Farrell, Steven L. Garner, James and Jacqueline Winston, and Marissa and Dwayne Leslie, without your love, support and encouragement, this book would not be possible. I can only hope to be as good a friend to each of you as each of you has been to me. Thank you, and my love for each of you knows no bounds.

Lastly, chapter 5 of this book is reprinted here in revised form with permission of New York University Press. It has previously appeared in *Religion, Law, USA*, eds. Joshua Dubler and Isaac Weiner (New York: New York University Press, 2019), 265–282. And portions of chapter 4 are reprinted here with permission of *Utah Law Review*. These portions were originally published in the article, "The Religion of Race: The Supreme Court as Priests of Racial Politics," *Utah Law Review* 2021 (2021): 569, 576–79, 589. These permissions are gratefully acknowledged.

Note

1. For an excellent discussion of Curry's work in this regard, see his essays "On Derelict and Method: The Methodological Crisis of Africana Philosophy's Study of African Descended People under an Integrationist Milieu," *Radical Philosophy Review* 14.2 (2011): 139–164, "The Derelictical Crisis of African American Philosophy: How African American Philosophy Fails to Contribute to the Study of African Descended People," *Journal of Black Studies* 42.3 (2011): 314–333, "Concerning the Under-specialization of Race Theory in American Philosophy: An Essay Outlining Ignored Bibliographic Sources Addressing the Aforementioned Problem," *Pluralist* 5.1 (2010): 44–64, and "Deliberate Misreadings: Derelictical Avoidance, William H. Ferris, and the Need to Expand the Geography of Black Nationalism to Comprehend The African Abroad," in *The Philosophical Treatise of William H. Ferris: Selected Readings from The African Abroad or, his Evolution in Western Civilization*, ed. Tommy J. Curry (Lanham, MD: Rowman and Littlefield, 2016), 1–18.

Works Cited

Curry, Tommy J. "Deliberate Misreadings: Derelictical Avoidance, William H. Ferris, and the Need to Expand the Geography of Black Nationalism to Comprehend The African Abroad," in *The Philosophical Treatise of William H. Ferris: Selected Readings from The African Abroad or, His Evolution in Western Civilization*, ed. Tommy J. Curry. Lanham, MD: Rowman and Littlefield, 2016. 1–18.

———. "On Derelict and Method: The Methodological Crisis of Africana Philosophy's Study of African Descended People under an Integrationist Milieu," *Radical Philosophy Review* 14.2 (2011): 139–164.

———. "The Derelictical Crisis of African American Philosophy: How African American Philosophy Fails to Contribute to the Study of African Descended People," *Journal of Black Studies* 42.3 (2011): 314–333.

———. "Concerning the Under-specialization of Race Theory in American Philosophy: An Essay Outlining Ignored Bibliographic Sources Addressing the Aforementioned Problem," *Pluralist* 5.1 (2010): 44–64.

Introduction

I Want My Ham

TIMOTHY J. GOLDEN

"And because white people have never experienced the lower end of the stick of racism, they can't fully recognize when it is and isn't happening . . . yet they have so much to say about whether or not it still exists. The victim blaming of unarmed black bodies shows that white people aren't really tired of racism. White people are tired of "talking" about racism. They want us to shut up about it. They want us to pretend like it's not happening. They want us to look at Barack Obama, Michael Jordan, and Oprah Winfrey and believe that everything is okay with us because those three made it . . . therefore . . . we should be able to as well. We've had a black president, so racism must be over."

—"Superiority Fantasy," *Hands Up*[1]

"He gonna give me my ham. He gonna give me my ham. I want my ham. He gonna give me my ham."

—*Two Trains Running*[2]

Just three years before his death, as Derrick Bell was preparing the sixth edition of his landmark text *Race, Racism, and American Law* for publication, the United States was on the verge of a major historical moment: the nomination and election of the first African American President of the United States. Bell wrote about this during Barack Obama's presidential campaign in 2008, candidly observing what he thought an Obama presidency would mean for Black people in America: "It is unlikely, even if Senator Obama survives the many challenges to his nomination and election that this historical first will alter significantly the racial barriers that most people of color face."[3] Such statements about racism in America were familiar refrains for Bell, and until he died in 2011, so many of his theoretical insights proved accurate. For example, one can argue—as Bell himself did in 2010—that the election of Barack Obama is a classic example of Bell's theory of interest convergence: the notion that what appears to be racial progress for African Americans actually would not happen but for the need to also further some coexisting and, in the view of whites at least, more important white interest. So, Bell's argument goes, notions of racial "progress" are badly misguided and are mere racial symbols—trinkets that, as Bell's fictional character, Jesse B. Semple points out, are more an expression of white influence than Black progress:

> From the Emancipation Proclamation on, the Man been handing us a bunch of bogus freedom checks he never intends to honor. He makes you work, plead, and pray for them, and then when he has you either groveling or threatening to tear his damn head off, he lets you have them as though they were some kind of special gift. As a matter of fact, regardless of how great the need is, he only gives *you* when it will do *him* the most good! And before you can cash them in . . . the Man has called the bank and stopped payment or otherwise made them useless—except, of course, as symbols.[4]

Again, the 2008 American presidential election is an example of what Jesse B. Semple calls a racial "symbol," and an example of Bell's theory of interest convergence. Some historical detail will be useful here. Recall that the 2008 presidential election between Senator Barack Obama and the late Senator John McCain was rather close, and the gap did not begin to widen until the Wall Street financial collapse shortly after Labor Day, as the fall election season intensified. Upper class and upper-middle-class whites began to bleed large sums of money from their retirement accounts because of profligate Wall Street spending. The financial collapse was so bad that reports surfaced of many people—most of them white—who retired toward the end of the Clinton presidency, some as millionaires, needing to return to work. So attention in the presidential election quickly turned to which of the two candidates was more competent to stop the bleeding. As Senator McCain proclaimed that "the fundamentals of the economy are strong," and Governor Sarah Palin waxed not so eloquently about how she could keep an eye on Russia from Alaska, the American electorate began to see Obama's opposition as incompetent to deal with the financial crisis, and their attention turned to the junior Senator from Illinois, whose intellect and competence they thought would be the best prescription for the financial crisis facing the nation. And the financial crisis was not the only crisis facing America. There were wars in Afghanistan and Iraq, the economy was steadily losing jobs, and the American auto industry was on the brink of total collapse. Juxtaposing the relative competence and skill of the two candidates, the American people made their choice, electing Barack Hussein Obama the 44th President of the United States of America on Tuesday, November 4, 2008.

When President-elect Obama took the stage in Chicago the night of the election to give his victory speech, I was watching on live television from Memphis, Tennessee. I was a graduate student studying philosophy at the University of Memphis, and I could not help but think, as I watched Obama say that "change has come to America," that maybe he was right. After all, just across town was the National Civil Rights Museum at the Lorraine Motel where Dr. Martin Luther King Jr. was assassinated. Dr. King's dream for America, along with the hopes and dreams of so many other African Americans, was perhaps embodied in the candidacy of the now President-elect, the child of an American white mother and a Kenyan father, and married to an African American woman from the south side of Chicago. Maybe, just maybe, I thought, this moment in time would be the change that President Obama proclaimed had come to America.

But my rapture in this historical moment was short lived. I began to think of how the National Civil Rights Museum across town stood as a monument to battles for racial equality in America still being fought to that very day, with little sustainable progress. I thought of how Dr. King's challenge to America's symbiotic triad of racism, militarism, and poverty left him dead from an assassin's bullet on the terrace at the Lorraine Motel on April 4, 1968; and how this America was the same America that elected Barack Obama just a little more than forty years later on November 4, 2008. It was then that I thought that the election of Barack Obama had less to do with America turning the corner on race relations and more with which candidate could best aid the American economy in a time of crisis—an economy whose white participants were in dire need of help from what they thought would be competent, intelligent, and otherwise strong leadership. So it is that in that very moment, as I watched Obama make his victory speech, I saw his election as a classic case of Bell's notion of interest convergence: the financial interests of upper-class and upper-middle-class whites coincidentally converged with the hopes and dreams of African Americans—hopes and dreams that were longstanding because they were long deferred. What for many was a turning point, I, inspired by Bell, understood as a mere racial symbol—a symbol that, as Bell predicted when he wrote the preface to *Race, Racism, and American Law*, would do little to nothing to help the plight of African Americans and other people of color in the United States.

And throughout the Obama presidency, Bell could not have been more correct in his assessment. Indeed, socially and politically speaking, things seemed to worsen for African Americans during Obama's tenure in the White House. From court decisions that curtailed voting rights[5] to a spate of police and vigilante violence directed at African Americans, the Obama presidency, in stark contrast to initiating a new era of so-called "post-racial" politics that marked an end to racism, showed that racism in America is alive and well. What was especially troubling about the police killings was that so many of them were captured on video and widely disseminated through electronic and social media. This transformed the tragic loss of human life at the hands of state actors into a spectacle. Aggravating this spectacle was a complete lack of legal accountability for the killings, as police officers who undisputedly killed unarmed African Americans were routinely put on some sort of administrative leave only to be unindicted, or, after immense public pressure brought the cases to trial, acquitted. This lack of accountability has done little to promote African American confidence in the American criminal justice system. Add to these realities the election of President Trump, who stirred up racial resentment of African Americans from disaffected whites during his 2016 presidential campaign, and the behavior of today's America demonstrates racial attitudes that hearken back to the post-Reconstruction era, when newly freed black slaves could be arrested for vagrancy pursuant to the Black Codes. This point is not far-fetched, as whites have recently been using emergency police services as a means of social control of African Americans. Whether it is innocently waiting for a business colleague in a Starbucks in Philadelphia, peacefully having a barbeque in a public park in Oakland, or a little girl selling water to raise money for a trip to Disneyland in San Francisco, African Americans have been reported to police for the most innocuous of ordinary activities.

Among the most bizarre of these incidents involving police and African Americans is the case of Byron Ragland. Mr. Ragland is a nine-year veteran of the U.S. Air Force and court-appointed supervisor of noncustodial parents during court-ordered visitation hours. Mr. Ragland's job as an employee of the court system requires his in-person supervision. In November 2018, while supervising a noncustodial parental visit at a yogurt shop in the Seattle area, the owner called the police after his employees reported Mr. Ragland as looking suspicious because he had not bought anything and was looking at his cell phone and would periodically look up at them. When the police arrived, they asked Ragland to "move along," despite the fact that his job—again, a job with the legal system—required him to be there. Consider the maddening, absurd, and oppressive relationship between African Americans and the American legal system that Mr. Ragland's situation represents: the legal system that demanded Mr. Ragland's *presence in the yogurt shop* for court-appointed supervision is the same legal system that demanded Mr. Ragland's *absence from the yogurt shop* because the employees were "uncomfortable." Mr. Ragland thus had to solve the problem of how to be both present in and absent from the exact same location at the exact same time. After all, it is what "the law" required of him. Such Kafkaesque, existentialist notions of the absurd as depicted in Mr. Ragland's case abound in African American life because of the ongoing influence of white supremacy and its entrenchment in American law, politics, and culture. So much for the Obama presidency ushering in a new era of "post-racial" politics and culture, a notion that is laughable considering America's current racial climate. Hence Bell's robust criticism of the social and political foundations of American law, its connection to—and perhaps its dependence upon—racism.

Voting Rights, Criminal Justice, and the Permanence of Racism

Aside from the racist social dysfunction at the level of the quotidian that leads some whites to engineer police interventions to exert social control over Black people, African Americans face deep structural inequities in myriad areas of both constitutional and civil rights. Bell's landmark text,

Race, Racism and American Law provides a comprehensive treatment of race and the law in the areas of education, employment discrimination, criminal justice, voting rights, housing, interracial relationships, public facilities, and protest. Bell presents a detailed historical treatment of the law and its state of affairs in each of these areas of law as it existed in 2008, the year that the sixth edition of *Race, Racism, and American Law* was published. Since I cannot duplicate such a treatise-length, detailed treatment of each of these areas in this introduction, I want to emphasize some recent (within the last decade) legal developments in the area of voting rights, and, with some discussion of the American constitutional doctrine of federalism, connect voting rights to certain historical trends in the administration of criminal justice as it relates to African Americans. These trends are arguably inconsistent with the original aims and purposes of the United States Department of Justice, which was a product of American Reconstruction intended to enforce laws prohibiting white racial violence against newly freed slaves (freedmen). My aim here is to provide some explanatory force to Bell's claim that racism is permanent and his claim—consistent with Ralph Bunche—that reliance on civil rights litigation alone has proven and will continue to prove itself ineffective in the pursuit of racial equality in America.

The Fifteenth Amendment of the United States Constitution secured the right to vote for freedmen and was ratified in 1870. As if this "second founding" of America was not embarrassing enough (slaves had no voting rights secured in the 1787 Constitution that emerged from the Philadelphia convention), the embarrassment only worsened in the United States Supreme Court's Reconstruction jurisprudence, which left African Americans with only nominal voting rights for nearly a hundred years, from 1870 to 1965. Throughout this ninety-five year time period, the Supreme Court, in the *Slaughterhouse Cases*,[6] *United States v. Cruikshank*,[7] and the *Civil Rights Cases*[8] helped to secure the legacy of chattel slavery through its doctrine of federalism, allowing for extensive and unchecked state autonomy, enabling southern states to not only deny Black suffrage but also to enact Black codes, Jim Crow, and to practice lynching with impunity. Such judicial complicity in and outright support of white racial domination began in the *Slaughterhouse Cases*, decided in 1873, which, on one hand, declared that both the Thirteenth and Fourteenth Amendments applied exclusively to freedmen—and not to the Louisiana butchers who brought their constitutional claims to court—but, on the other hand, ruled that the constitutional protections of these amendments only applied to actions of the federal government—not to the actions of state government. According to Justice Miller, the Thirteenth and Fourteenth Amendments were only enforceable against a federal depravation of such rights as access to ports and waterways, international travel, and the right to run for federal office. But such rights had no real practical implications for freedmen. Indeed, historian Eric Foner points out that few of such rights "were of pressing concern to the majority of black Americans."[9] Foner continues, summing up the duality of the decision in the *Slaughterhouse Cases* as it related to African Americans: "Thus, in the guise of affirming the freedmen's status as national citizens," the *Slaughterhouse Cases* "severely limited the rights for which they could claim federal protection."[10] The *Slaughterhouse Cases*, then, achieved a jurisprudential sleight of hand that was truly remarkable: the Supreme Court managed to secure protection for freedmen from the actions of the federal government that was plainly unnecessary, as the federal government was actively trying to help freedmen through the robust federal legislative and executive protections of Reconstruction, while the Court provided freedmen virtually no constitutional protection from the actions of state governments, which were aggressively out to harm freedmen in southern states through the proliferation of Black Codes, Jim Crow, the denial of suffrage, and lynching. The stage was thus set for *United States v. Cruikshank* in 1876. The *Cruikshank* case declared that federal indictments against white defendants charging them with violations of the constitutional rights of African Americans were deficient in that they failed to allege violations of enforceable federal rights pursuant to the terms of the Enforcement Act of 1870. In the *Cruikshank* case, then, the Court reasoned that the alleged violations of federal constitutional rights in the indictment—a predicate for the application of the Enforcement Act—were not violations of federal rights at all because, consistent with the ruling in the *Slaughterhouse Cases*, the rights alleged to have been violated were only enforceable against the federal government, not state governments or private citizens. So, the Court dismissed the indictments. The *Cruikshank* decision resulted in the exoneration of otherwise culpable whites who participated in the notorious Colfax massacre on April 13, 1873, in Louisiana that left nearly 100 African Americans dead. Then came the *Civil Rights Cases*, an 1883 decision, declaring that the Civil Rights Act of 1875, which was intended to protect freedmen from private acts of racial discrimination—what the Civil Rights Act of 1964 eventually did some eighty-one years later—was an unconstitutional assertion of federal power over private individuals. So troublesome was the decision in the

Civil Rights Cases for African Americans that it led Black journalist, T. Thomas Fortune, just four days after the decision, to write:

> The colored people of the United States feel to-day as if they had been baptized in ice water . . . Public meetings are being projected far and wide to give expression to the common feeling of disappointment and apprehension for the future . . . Having declared that colored men have no protection from the government in their political rights, the Supreme Court now declares that we have no civil rights—declares that railroad corporations are free to force us into smoking cars or cattle cars; that hotel keepers are free to make us walk the streets at night; that theatre managers can refuse us admittance to their exhibitions for amusement of the public—it has reaffirmed the infamous decision . . . of Chief Justice Taney that a "black man has no rights that a white man is bound to respect."[11]

Fortune's reference to Chief Justice Taney is significant, for Taney wrote the majority opinion in *Dred Scott v. Sandford*, which claimed that Blacks were never intended to be American citizens because they were brought to America as slaves. Taney thus concluded that Blacks had no cognizable legal rights, constitutional or statutory. Although *Dred Scott* is universally condemned today, in theory at least, for its anti-Black views, Bell argues that its widespread disregard in contemporary legal education impedes our understanding of the depths of American anti-Black racism. Bell writes that because law students are so poorly informed about cases like *Dred Scott*, "students receive little background as to how much of politics and how little of morality" was poured into seemingly valiant efforts such as the Constitution's Reconstruction Amendments.[12] According to Bell, despite the Reconstruction Amendments' theoretical voiding of *Dred Scott*, "As black gains slipped away in the 1870s, The Supreme Court and the lower courts confirmed what blacks had feared, that the citizenship they had been granted . . . was citizenship in name only."[13] Bell was right, for although the Reconstruction Amendments "voided" *Dred Scott*, they ultimately brought nothing to African Americans except a reaffirmation of that decision in practice despite its rejection in theory; hence Fortune's and the Black community's consternation in the wake of the Supreme Court's decision in the *Civil Rights Cases*.

Next in this line of restrictive Supreme Court jurisprudence was *Plessy v. Ferguson* and the infamous "separate but equal" doctrine, which ensured that the Fourteenth Amendment—an Amendment ratified to help freedmen—would guarantee their social and political inferiority for the foreseeable future. Through these restrictive interpretations of both the Reconstruction Amendments and the congressional authority to enforce them, the Supreme Court enabled a reign of terror on African Americans that lasted from the end of Reconstruction until deep into the twentieth century. Jim Crow, lynching, and the denial of suffrage under state law would be the status quo in the American south for nearly one hundred years until President Lyndon Johnson signed the Civil Rights Act into law in July of 1964 and the Voting Rights Act into law in August of 1965. To put this status quo into greater historical perspective, recall that Medgar Evers was assassinated for registering Black voters in Mississippi in 1963. And, as I discuss below, much of this social and political oppression arguably persists today in the forms of mass incarceration, state-sanctioned police violence against Black people that occurs with seeming impunity—as did lynching—and voter suppression efforts, not just in southern states, but in states throughout the union.

What did the Voting Rights Act of 1965 actually do? It contained a preclearance provision (§5) that required southern states with a history of racial discrimination in voting determined by a formula in §4(b) to submit any plans for changes in their voting laws to the Department of Justice for approval. This was the standard for forty-eight years, from 1965 until 2013, when the United States Supreme Court, in *Shelby County, Alabama v. Holder*, declared the 2006 Congressional renewal of the preclearance provision of §5 under the constraints of §4b of the Voting Rights Act of 1965 unconstitutional. Writing for a five member majority, Chief Justice John Roberts reasoned that the formula of §4(b) used to determine which states had to comply with the preclearance requirements of §5 was outdated in that it failed to account for the changed political circumstances between 1965 and 2013. But it was the very application of the formula in §4(b) that led to the changed circumstances in the first place. Justice Ruth Bader Ginsburg points this out in the first sentence of her dissenting opinion in the *Shelby County* case, when she wrote that "In the Court's view, the very success of §5 of the Voting Rights Act demands its dormancy."[14] The nullification of §4(b) has, for all practical purposes, resulted in the nullification of §5 because the two sections work together: §4(b) determined which states needed to comply with the preclearance requirements of §5. So without §4(b), §5 can never be applied. Not surprisingly, the constitutional challenge to the law came from Alabama, a southern state with a history of denying the franchise to African Americans. Although the Court struck down the pre-clearance provision based on what it considered to be an outdated formula from the 1960s, Chief Justice Roberts's majority opinion was laden with language suggesting that Congress exerted too much federal power over state autonomy. For example, as the opinion opens, Chief Justice Roberts refers to the Voting Rights Act as "extraordinary," and as "strong medicine." To his credit, Chief Justice Roberts recognized that the enforcement of the Fifteenth Amendment was a failure, that voting rights litigation was "slow and expensive," and that "Voter registration of African-Americans barely improved" since the ratification of the Fifteenth Amendment and before the Voting Rights Act of 1965. Chief Justice Roberts writes:

> In the 1890s, Alabama, Georgia, Louisiana, Mississippi, North Carolina, South Carolina, and Virginia began to enact literacy tests for voter registration and to employ other methods designed to prevent African-Americans from voting. Congress passed statutes outlawing some of these practices and facilitating litigation against them, but litigation remained slow and expensive, and the States came up with new ways to discriminate as soon as existing ones were struck down. Voter registration of African-Americans barely improved.[15]

But conspicuously absent from Chief Justice Roberts's recitation of the legal history of voting rights for African Americans is the complicity of the Supreme Court in the denial of African American suffrage. The Chief Justice never mentions the *Slaughterhouse Cases* and how they laid the foundation for restrictive interpretations of the Reconstruction Amendments based on limited federal authority over state law, effectively both allowing for state-sponsored literacy tests and immunizing such racist practices from appellate review based on principles of federalism, as I have been discussing here. Aside from this omission in the Chief Justice's opinion, his restrictive view of federal power, as its earlier iterations have done, can be profoundly injurious to African American suffrage. As the Court's Reconstruction jurisprudence indicates, such a view of federalism has a troubling history in its application in cases involving African

American constitutional and civil rights. And failing to acknowledge this troubling history and engage with it more than Chief Justice Roberts does in his opinion not only reflects poorly on the Court's ability to come to grips with its own role in maintaining American chattel slavery's social and political vestiges of Black inferiority but also is an erasure of a history that, if not both remembered and resisted, may repeat itself; federalism is an integral part of this history.

Why is federalism so significant? And what is its impact on racism and American law, specifically on voting rights? Legal historian and constitutional scholar Mary Frances Berry points out in her important text, *Black Resistance White Law* that the policy of federal inaction as it relates to racial violence against African Americans is a "pattern of constitutional interpretation, which has been successfully utilized to maintain the continued social, economic, and political subordination of black people."[16] Berry also points out that the concept of federalism, "the division of power and responsibility between the central and local governments, which arrived in America with the first colonists, has become a handy philosophical tool for maintaining white superiority."[17] Berry writes:

> Federalism as a policy has been advanced to explain national noninterference when state agencies refused to protect nonconforming blacks from white violence intended to keep them in their place; and then, it has been cited to explain the compulsory use of national force when state agencies found themselves unable to successfully ward off black attacks on white persons or their property.[18]

Berry's observation that federalism was a theory that "arrived in America with the first colonists" is significant, for following federalism's arrival with the colonists was an implementation of federalism that established an enduring connection between American constitutional law and the maintenance of white supremacy. Consider W.E.B. Du Bois's essay *The Suppression of the African Slave Trade*, in which he observes that northern delegates to the Philadelphia Convention of 1787 relied on notions of federalism to maintain chattel slavery. Du Bois points out that there was a series of moral arguments against slavery that were made during the debates at the Philadelphia Convention, but these arguments were to no avail, as they were overcome by arguments grounded in both federalism and those grounded in rank expediency. Du Bois writes:

> The difficulty of the whole argument from the moral standpoint, lay in the fact that it was completely checkmated by the obstinate attitude of South Carolina and Georgia . . . In such a dilemma the Convention listened not unwillingly to the *non possumus* arguments of the States' Rights advocates. The "morality and wisdom" of slavery, declared Ellsworth of Connecticut, "are considerations belonging to the States themselves;" let every State "import what it pleases;" the Confederation has not "meddled" with the question, why should the Union? It is a dangerous symptom of centralization, cried Baldwin of Georgia; the "central States" wish to be the "vortex for everything," even matters of "a local nature." The national government said Gerry of Massachusetts, had nothing to do with slavery in the States; it had only to refrain from giving direct sanction to the system.[19]

Du Bois's observations not only bolster Berry's point about federalism being a "handy philosophical tool" that maintains white supremacy but they also show that the constitutional doctrine of federalism and white supremacy in the form of American chattel slavery are inextricably linked at the founding of the American constitutional republic. The depth of a connection such as this ought not to be dismissed, as it has serious implications for the social and political oppression of African Americans throughout American history and into the present day.

Considering this link between the maintenance of white supremacy and the constitutional doctrine of federalism, one may raise serious questions about the efficacy of using the legal system to bring an end to the social and political oppression of African Americans, as Bell has done. Many will point to *Brown v. Board of Education* as a victory against racial oppression, but Bell has argued at length that *Brown* is a classic illustration of interest convergence. Moreover, before Bell, Bunche argued against the use of the American legal system as an effective strategy against racism because of the Supreme Court's penchant for abstraction when it comes to the cases involving the political and civil rights of African Americans. Bunche wrote at length about how the Supreme Court, in specific voting rights cases, rather than consider concrete realities, resorted to a form of legal reasoning that was, in his view, way off in the "dialectical stratosphere," instead of securing voting rights for African Americans based on their concrete political realities. Bell cites Bunche's work in *Race, Racism, and American Law*, and Berry is reasoning in a manner similar to both Bunche and Bell when she writes of federalism and its role in maintaining white supremacy. In *Black Resistance White Law*, Berry is interested in the invocation of federalism in two ways that are oppressive toward African Americans: first, as a doctrine of inaction when African Americans are the victims of white racial violence, and second, as a doctrine of action when considered necessary to quell any perceived Black "rebellion." Consistent with Berry's thesis, what results from this sort of inconsistent and arguably bad-faith adherence to federalism as a legal doctrine is, on one hand, a voting rights policy that limits federal action to protect African American suffrage, and, on the other hand, a criminal justice policy that asserts federal authority, through the Department of Justice, to criminalize African Americans with a variety of legal practices that are arguably inconsistent with the purposes of the Department of Justice, founded in 1870, to help protect freedmen from white racial violence.

Berry's thesis from *Black Resistance White Law* is shown in the hands-off approach with states as it relates to voting rights for African Americans in the wake of the *Shelby County* decision as compared with federal criminal justice policy of the Reagan Administration Justice Department and moving forward into the twenty-first century.[20] Again, the concept of federalism embraces a hands-off approach from the federal government that allows states to maintain racist practices of disenfranchisement against African Americans. But in criminal justice administration, the federal government has been hands-on, and what a heavy federal hand it has been! Beginning the in the mid-1980s, federal mandatory minimum sentencing and mandatory sentencing enhancements in the Federal Sentencing Guidelines, which effectively divested federal judges of discretion in sentencing, led to the phenomenon that Michelle Alexander has referred to as "mass incarceration"—a new form of institutional racism that, while not directly attributable to race, nevertheless has the same effects as Jim Crow, exemplified in the exclusion of Black people from jury service, voting, housing, and other important civil rights. Interestingly, the same Department of Justice that was founded to protect African Americans—the most vulnerable members of American society—was the same Justice Department whose criminal justice policy executed a new Jim Crow. A corollary of Berry's argument, then, is that abstract, formalist, applications of law (i.e., legal principles of federalism) become little more than euphemisms for the juridical maintenance of white domination as federalist principles are applied in ways that allow for state deprivations of African American voting rights in the name of "federalism," while a vigorous enforcement of federal law will be considered essential as a means of social control over African Americans in the name of criminal justice administration, again, all from a federal Justice Department that was founded to protect African Americans from racial violence. Berry, it seems, was correct. And it is this sort of uneven enforcement of federal law that I contend helps explain Bell's claim about the permanence of racism.

Racism is permanent not only because of an uneven adherence to the constitutional "principle" of federalism but also because of the political muck and mire of public policy. Consider the notion of "voter suppression." This phrase has been popularized since the *Shelby County Alabama* decision because that decision paved the way for not only southern states with a history of racial discrimination in voting to do as they please but also other states. Meanwhile, the John Lewis Voting Rights Advancement Act, introduced as a Senate Bill in 2020 by Senator Patrick Leahy of Vermont, has arguably changed the formula from §4(b) of the Voting Rights Act in a manner that would pass constitutional muster, thus enabling the application of the preclearance provisions of §5. But the Senate bill has taken a backseat to several other domestic legislative initiatives such as COVID-19 relief, infrastructure legislation, and now, inflation reduction and climate change. Moreover, despite adjusting the coverage formula of §4(b) so as to help it pass constitutional muster under the *Shelby County Alabama* case, recent restrictive interpretations of the Voting Rights Act portend even greater difficulty to secure the franchise in federal law for African Americans.[21] It is not far-fetched to be concerned that if voting rights legislation and police reform legislation are not enacted—and soon—the pre-1965 status quo will prevail, and that America will find itself entrenched in the mire of slavery's legacy deeper than ever before. But this should not be surprising, because, as Bell repeatedly claimed, American anti-Black racism has a way of reasserting itself at every turn. So here we are, in the twenty-first century, more than one-hundred fifty years after the ratification of the Fifteenth Amendment, and African Americans have had the right to vote secured in law for a grand total of forty-eight years, which is both shocking and untenable. It is in this historical and legal context; a context thoroughly infused with anti-Black racism and white supremacy, that Bell's claim that racism is a permanent fixture of American social and political life rings true.

The expanse of Bell's oeuvre is impressive. It is indeed worthy of extensive scholarly treatment in law, philosophy, social and political theory, and theology. Moreover, Bell's discussion of racism in America and his trenchant critique of liberalism as a handmaiden in maintaining the structural and material conditions of white supremacy such that white supremacy is made "legal" is so extensive that to discuss both in one book—and *a fortiori*, one introduction to a book—is a task far beyond what I can do here. Indeed, any scholarly endeavor that purports to be a comprehensive treatment of Bell's work ought to be a multivolume treatise, which, though on my long-term research agenda, is not my goal here. Instead, this volume has the much more modest aim of providing a serious scholarly treatment of one aspect of Bell's thought, namely his thesis of Racial Realism. The other contributors and I attempt to accomplish this narrow task through this collection of essays concentrated on various interpretations of Bell's theory of Racial Realism along legal, philosophical, rhetorical, and theological lines.

Structure and Chapter Summaries

There are four parts to this book. Each part has two chapters related more broadly to different aspects of Bell's racial realism. Part I, "Racial Realism, Religion, and the Negro Problem," lays the groundwork for racial realism as discussed throughout the remainder of the book. The first chapter lays the foundation for the essays in the book that discuss Bell and theology (Keri Day's essay on Bell and womanist theology, my essay on Bell and Kierkegaard, and Vincent Lloyd's essay on Bell's view of the *Brown* decision and theological hope). And the second chapter gives the permanence thesis of racial realism an explanatory force that lays the foundation for the essays on legal theory (Audra Savage's essay on interest convergence and the racial-religious minority, and my essay on Bell's Racial Realism as situated in and moving beyond the American Legal Realist tradition), and hope (Desiree Melton's essay on hope and interracial relationships). Part I thus provides a broader background for the discussion of the more detailed aspects of racial realism and its connection to other disciplinary and conceptual frameworks.

George Taylor, the author of chapter 1, "The Last Decade of Derrick Bell's Thought," taught a course called "Race, Religion, and the Law" with Bell at the University of Pittsburgh School of Law in the fall of 2006. This chapter discusses the substantive themes of that course. Taylor argues that the themes of the course that he co-taught with Bell—race, religion, and law—give insight into the themes most prominent in the last decade of

Bell's thought. Taylor also draws from some of Bell's later work, *Ethical Ambition* and *Silent Covenants*, and some later unpublished speeches to show that Bell's interest in religion in the last decade of his thought extends more generally to a theme that Bell engaged throughout his work: the conclusion that racism itself is an article of faith that includes religion but is not limited to it. On this point, Taylor engages Bell's reading of African American theologians George Kelsey and Howard Thurman to conclude that Bell's understanding of racism as an article of faith not only helps to explain racism's resiliency and its permanence, but also provides, in Taylor's words, "a missive of continuing vitality for the struggles toward racial justice in the changing landscapes of today and tomorrow." For Taylor, we can thus better appreciate the uniqueness of Bell's enduring contribution both to the methodology of critical race theory and to critical race theory itself.

In chapter 2, "Derrick Bell and the 'Negro Problem,'" Bill E. Lawson aims to situate Bell's "racism is permanent" thesis in the context of the "Negro Problem," which is the problem of what to do with African Americans whose labor can no longer be legally forced. In other words, what is to be done with newly freed slaves? Lawson links Bell's position with the American historical problem of what to do with the Negro. He reads Bell's view on the permanence of racism as Bell's response to how Bell believes America has attempted to solve the "Negro Problem," and how that attempt has helped to cause the permanence of racism. Viewed in this way, Racial Realism problematizes our understanding of public policy initiatives designed to achieve social equality. The intransigence of anti-Black racism in America results from a tragically false but profoundly influential belief that Black people are inferior, a belief that Lawson asserts is at the foundation of racism's permanence because of its connection to the Negro Problem, or what to do with Black people, who are good for nothing but forced labor because of their inferiority. Lawson concludes his essay with the insight that what has prevented the oppression of Black people from being a "fait accompli" is the resistance that all people of good will—Black and white—have offered against that oppression. But despite our best efforts at resistance, the belief in Black inferiority stemming from the Negro problem abides, and it is in this context that Bell develops his theory of racial realism.

Part II, "Racial Realism and Legal Theory," has a chapter on Bell's Racial Realism and American Legal Realism and a chapter on an analysis of interest convergence as applied to the hybrid case of racial-religious minorities. Both essays explore resources that Racial Realism brings to bear on the analysis of adjudication. Chapter 3, "From Psychology to Resistance: Racial Realism and American Legal Realism," presents my analysis of Racial Realism in both its descriptive and normative dimensions. In this chapter, I situate Bell's Racial Realism within the broader tradition of American Legal Realism and argue that Racial Realism extends beyond it. I read Bell with Brian Leiter to conclude that Racial Realism's reliance on social science data and folk psychology puts him squarely within the American Legal Realist tradition. I then go further to argue that Racial Realism transcends a descriptive account of adjudication—where realists argue that judges simply base their decisions on the stimulus of the facts of a case rather than on any a priori notion of law. Instead, I submit that Bell's Racial Realism is a culturally informed understanding of Black subjectivity rich in African American thought that accounts for the permanence of racism through an incessant and trenchant critique of liberalism's abstract reliance on "rights" and "equality," both of which cause American law to support power relations that maintain white dominance. Responding to the permanence of racism, Racial Realism prescribes an ethic of resistance to anti-Black racism that is as perpetual as institutionalized racism itself.

A major reason for Bell's Racial Realism is his notion that genuine racial progress in American law is illusory because African Americans benefit from law and the political process only when their interests converge with those of white Americans. This insight, known as Bell's theory of interest convergence, is taken up in chapter 4, "A Rock and a Hard Place: Interest Convergence for the Racial-Religious Minority," where Audra Savage examines interest-convergence theory in the hybrid case of minorities who are both racial and religious. Through a study of the religious practices of the Yoruba-based Santeria, Savage argues that the Supreme Court decision in *Church of the Lukumi Babalu Aye, Inc. v. City of Hialeah*, despite its unanimity, is not actually a robust affirmation of constitutional rights for a racial-religious minority, but rather only a decision that does not adversely affect the interests of white Christians. Savage points out through a critical discussion of First Amendment Free Exercise jurisprudence that Bell's notion of interest convergence helps one to "better appreciate the fragility of rights for the racial-religious minority."

Part III, "Racial Realism and Hope," addresses questions of hope in the context of the permanence of racism; that is, what is hope and what sort of hope may one have? The first essay in part III considers hope in the rhetoric of U.S. Supreme Court decisions and the second presents an argument for hope in interracial relationships. In chapter 5, "The Authority of Hope: Hopeful Illusions in *Brown v. Board of Education* and Beyond," Vincent Lloyd analyzes hope as found in *Brown* and other Supreme Court decisions. In this chapter, Lloyd examines the rhetorical trope of the child to conclude that inscribed in the cultural logic of *Brown* is an image of a child that provides hope. According to Lloyd, this image of the child helps to maintain the status quo, for the child of *Brown* does not emerge from the reflections of a marginalized community on its experiences with injustice. Instead, this image of the child is the product of a bourgeoisie, integrationist consciousness of white Supreme Court Justices. This, Lloyd submits, is the false nature of juridical hope, born of a bourgeoisie vision for America. When this false hope is juxtaposed to Bell's much richer notion of hope that is rooted in the despair and oppression of those in marginalized communities, one can see how the former is an illusion that maintains the status quo, while the latter is an authentic expression of a justice-oriented ethos that demands resistance to the status quo, not with any naïve hope of overcoming it, but instead with a wakeful vigilance to keep fighting against all odds.

Chapter 6 titled "Between Hope and a White Body: The Challenge of Racial Realism and Interracial Love," interrogates Racial Realism from within the context of interracial romantic relationships. Desiree Melton argues that although Racial Realism is a legitimate stance to take against systematic racial oppression, it presents difficulties for someone who is in a healthy romantic relationship with a white person. On an institutional level, it is understandable that equality is elusive. Melton claims, however, that equal treatment in a healthy romantic relationship with a white person undermines the claim of racism's permanence. Melton contends that the interpersonal relationship may generate a hopefulness for racial equality on a much broader political scale. In the tradition of storytelling so characteristic of Bell's work in critical race theory, and drawing from Bell's claim in *Ethical Ambition* that his relationship to his first wife was his "most important relationship," Melton tells the story of Deidre and Sean, an interracial couple whose romantic relationship is thoroughly egalitarian, to emphasize that an interracial relationship offers something that the larger society does not offer: a partnership where a Black person is treated equally. Interracial relationships can thus be a source of hope for one who embraces Racial Realism, making it a challenge to continue to hold the racial realist stance.

Part IV, "Racial Realism and Theology," has two essays that discuss the relationship between Racial Realism and Christianity. The first discusses Racial Realism and womanist theology, and the second is a discussion of Bell's use of fiction to articulate Racial Realism, and its relationship to art and Christian theology. In chapter 7, "Rethinking Hope: The Importance of Radical Racial Realism for Womanist Theological Thought," Keri Day discusses a compelling analysis of hope in relationship to womanist theology. Day argues that Bell's understanding of the permanence of racism may actually support rather than problematize the womanist eschatological vision of a world where love and justice reign. Day points out that conceiving of Bell's Racial Realism as hope can diversify the womanist eschatological vision. If we understand Bell's notion of hope as defiance, then oppressed groups of people can derive meaning from resistance to incurably racist structures of injustice. Day concludes that understanding defiance as hope in this way has a transformative effect on the oppressed who resist inasmuch as such persons refuse to allow the racist structures to constitute or define their subjectivity. Thus diversified when read with Bell's Racial Realism, the womanist eschatological vision has room for a defiant hope in the face of injustice rather than exclusively emphasizing the eradication of injustice.

Finally, chapter 8, "Liberalism, Christendom, and Narrative: Paradox and Indirect Communication in Derrick Bell and Søren Kierkegaard," is my analysis of Bell's use of fiction and its resonance with certain aspects of Christian theology. Here, I argue that as a member of what Richard Delgado has called an "outgroup," it is essential for Bell to create a counternarrative that disrupts the narrative of the white "dominant group." But I argue that Bell does much more than just create a counternarrative. Beginning with George Taylor's insights that Racial Realism is fundamentally paradoxical and that Bell's narratives are parables that "manifest" new insight rather than hypotheticals that seek "adequation" to existing norms, I build upon Taylor's work by reading Bell with Søren Kierkegaard. I conclude that the concept of paradox that Taylor argues is at the core of Bell's Racial Realism becomes the catalyst for a radical rethinking and reclamation of the moral and political difficulties of American anti-Black racism through the parabolic-styled medium of what Kierkegaard called "indirect communication." In Kierkegaardian terms, the paradox at the core of Bell's Racial Realism becomes the "passion" of a radical and perpetual resistance to anti-Black racism in America. Even as Kierkegaard used indirect communication to remove what he thought was the deceptive influence of Hegelian theology on Christendom, I argue that Bell's use of narrative can be interpreted as a form of indirect communication to remove what I believe to be the deceptive influence of color-blind legal formalism. For Kierkegaard, indirect communication through pseudonyms reinvigorates a moribund, objective-oriented Christianity, and Bell's use of narrative does something similar for moral and political obligation: it removes liberalism's and formalism's deceptions of racial progress, awakening us from a dogmatic slumber of moral complacency to a robust life of perpetual moral action—a move that represents a sort of teleological suspension of the prevailing racist social and legal ethics of American life and jurisprudence.

Art and the Struggle for Justice

Bell understood the importance of art to African American life. Indeed, as I argue in my chapter on Bell and Kierkegaard, Bell's use of fictional narrative is essential to help disabuse people of liberalism's false idea of racial progress in America. Inspired by Bell, I too have come to understand how vital art—especially Black art—is to the African American pursuit of racial justice. There is something divine about the creative dimension of artistic endeavors; something akin to the Judeo-Christian notion of a God who brings order out of chaos through the spoken word as portrayed in the opening passages of the book of Genesis. The chaos of Black life in America—its ongoing tragedy and relentless disappointment—are certainly part of human experience in general. But American Blacks must deal with the added burden of facing racial violence in myriad forms almost daily, with seemingly no end in sight. Artistic creations like Bell's fictional, revisionist narratives behold such chaos and, at the very least, offer some clarity on the African American predicament of what it means, in the words of Du Bois, "to be a problem."[22] Art thus speaks into the chaos of American anti-Black racism and says, as did God to a void, terrifying and chaotic Earth: "Let there be light."[23]

Recognizing this divine dimension of creativity has led me to perform professionally as an actor. The epigraphs for this introduction are taken from two characters I have portrayed on stage. Part of what makes art so powerful is its capacity to reach people in ways that the formality and rigor of academic discourse simply cannot. So I perform as an actor in an attempt to augment my work as an academic. I do so by indulging my creativity through the portrayal of characters on stage. These characters tell stories that can transform and bring healing to an America that has been torn asunder by the scourge of anti-Black racism. The healing does not signal an end to racism, but rather induces a rejuvenation that enables the struggle against racism to persist. Art empowers us as we contend with injustice.

The two epigraphs of this introduction relate different parts of Bell's thesis of Racial Realism: the first relates to the permanence thesis, and the second to the resistance thesis. In the monologue titled "Superiority Fantasy" in the stage play, *Hands Up*, I portrayed a character—a Black man—whose experiences with anti-Black racism led him to reflect on how whites so often purport to aim for "solutions" to America's race problem, but actually end up making things worse. Hence the character's claim that whites often point to what Bell would call the racial "symbols" of Barack Obama, Michael Jordan, and Oprah Winfrey as evidence of racial progress when the sad reality is that they simply represent rare exceptions to the rule of hyper-aggressive and unconstitutional policing in the form of racial profiling that he experiences so intensely that it is an abiding source of trauma for his Black psyche. The personal successes of the few do not reflect the reality of the many. So the character says that whites are not wearied of racism, but rather are wearied of *talking* about racism, making the exceptions the rule when historical and contemporary realities of Obama, Jordan, and Winfrey demonstrate otherwise. Racism thus not only remains, but is perhaps even strengthened by the belief that individual successes reflect the overall success of the group when they plainly do not.

The second epigraph is taken from August Wilson's stage play *Two Trains Running*. The story is set in 1969, in a diner in Pittsburgh, Pennsylvania (which is coincidentally Bell's hometown). The diner is set to be condemned—perhaps an apt artistic depiction of Black people generally as marked for condemnation—and the owner of the diner, Memphis Lee, wants to ensure that the City of Pittsburgh compensates him justly for his property. The story unfolds in the diner as the characters move about in their daily interactions with one another. One of these characters is Hambone, a mentally disabled Black man who painted a fence for a white butcher shop owner across the street from the diner. Hambone painted the fence because the white butcher shop owner promised to give him a ham upon completion. Per the agreement, Hambone painted the fence. But when he finished, the white butcher shop owner offered him a chicken instead of a ham.

For more than nine years, each day when the butcher comes to open his shop, Hambone demands his ham from him. So persistent is Hambone in his desire for his ham that his only lines in the script are variations of "I want my ham. He gonna give me my ham." Hambone dies without ever receiving what was due to him—just like so many Black people have died without receiving the material benefits of the lofty promises of American political rhetoric. Indeed the Reconstruction Amendments, which were so often the subject of Bell's work, meant little when the United States Supreme Court interpreted them in ways that allowed Black codes, Jim Crow, and lynching to define America deep into the twentieth century. And it seems that where these ended, mass incarceration, voter suppression, and police brutality, rather than abating, have intensified to this point in the twenty-first century. Black people have thus been promised the ham of justice, but despite repeatedly demanding that ham, have only been offered the chicken of racism continuing to run amok.

What makes Hambone such a compelling character is that August Wilson's creative genius situates him on the receiving end of a broken promise. Again, this resembles African American history: a series of broken promises; promises to provide what has been earned (for example, the promise of "Forty acres and a mule," and the failure of the Freedmen's Bureau), just as the promise made to Hambone. And it is with the overwhelming weight and force of history behind him—or perhaps on top of him—that Hambone embodies the traumatized Black psyche and bellows with centuries of frustration: "He gonna give me my ham. He gonna give me my ham. I want my ham. He gonna give me my ham." In the story, Hambone dies without ever receiving his ham. But that does not make Hambone a failure; far from it. To the contrary, Hambone's determination despite his unsuccessful attempts at getting his ham is precisely what makes him a success. Hambone never stopped resisting; he understood that his victory was in the struggle itself. Hambone is thus a success of epic proportions, not because of what he received—for he never received his ham—but because of what he gave. Hambone gave his life to a struggle to fulfill a broken promise. Even as Mrs. Biona McDonald, who Bell met in Mississippi at a civil rights demonstration in 1964, lived "to harass" a legal, political, and social order that denied her justice, Hambone lived "to harass" the white butcher who broke his promise. Hambone was successful the day that he determined he would never quit. It is Hambone's importunity which must be ours. As Bell has encouraged all people of good will to remain vigilant in the struggle against anti-Black racism in America despite its permanence, may we, in the perpetual struggle for justice and in the spirit of Hambone, declare, with zeal and without ceasing, "I want my ham."[24]

Notes

1. Nathan James, "Superiority Fantasy," The New Black Fest's Hands Up: 7 Playwrights, 7 Testaments, ed. Nathan James, Idris Goodwin, and Nathan Yungerberg (London: Samuel French, 2016) 13.
2. August Wilson, *Two Trains Running* (New York: Penguin, 1993), 14.
3. Derrick Bell, *Race, Racism, and American Law* (New York: Aspen Publishers, 2008), xx.
4. Derrick Bell, "Racial Symbols: A Limited Legacy," *Faces at the Bottom of the Well: The Permanence of Racism* (New York: Basic Books, 1992), 19.
5. See *Shelby County, Alabama v. Holder*, 570 U.S. 529 (2013).
6. 83 U.S. 36 (1873).
7. 92 U.S. 542 (1876).
8. 109 U.S. 3 (1883).
9. Eric Foner, *Forever Free: The Story of Emancipation and Reconstruction* (New York: Alfred A. Knopf, 2005), 194.
10. Ibid.
11. T. Thomas Fortune, "The Civil Rights Decision," *T. Thomas Fortune: The Afro-American Agitator*, ed. Shawn Leigh Alexander (Gainesville: University Press of Florida, 2008), 15–16.
12. Derrick Bell, "Black Faith in a Racist Land," *The Derrick Bell Reader*, ed. Richard Delgado and Jean Stefancic (New York: New York University Press, 2005), 129.
13. Ibid. 130.
14. *Shelby County, Alabama v. Holder*, 570 U.S. 529 (2013).
15. Ibid.
16. Mary Frances Berry, *Black Resistance White Law: A History of Constitutional Racism in America* (New York: Penguin Books, 1994), 1.
17. Ibid.
18. Ibid.
19. W.E.B. Du Bois, "The Suppression of the African Slave Trade," *Du Bois: Writings* (New York: Library of America, 1986), 60.
20. Interestingly, in the wake of the *Shelby County* decision and amidst the Reagan administration's crippling criminal justice policies, there are what Bell would call racial "symbols"—meaningless trinkets that ring hollow as compared with political realities for Black people in America that have troubling and far-reaching practical implications. For even as President Reagan signed the legislation declaring Reverend Dr. Martin Luther King Jr.'s birthday a federal holiday in 1986—a moment that many Blacks celebrated—President Reagan's criminal justice policies imposed severe penalties for offenders in the form of mandatory minimum sentencing laws and sentencing guidelines which, as I mention in the

text, ushered in an era that many now call an era of "mass incarceration"—an era in which such Reagan administration–inspired criminal justice policies disproportionately burdened African Americans with the denial of civil rights akin to Jim Crow. See Michelle Alexander, *The New Jim Crow: Mass Incarceration in the Age of Colorblindness* (New York: New Press, 2012). And even as President Biden signed legislation declaring Juneteenth a national holiday in 2021, the John Lewis Voting Rights Restoration Act and the George Floyd Justice in Policing Act, two important bills in the areas of voting rights and police reform, respectively, appear doomed in the Senate, all while neither President Biden nor the country seem to have the political will to make such important federal legislation a reality, George Floyd notwithstanding. Most Blacks, would, I think, if given a choice prefer strong federal protections for voting and against state-sanctioned police violence over Juneteenth being a national holiday. For Bell's discussion of racial symbols, see *Faces at the Bottom of the Well: The Permanence of Racism* (New York: Basic Books, 1992).

21. See *Brnovich v. Democratic National Committee*, 594 U.S. _____ (2021).
22. W.E.B. Du Bois, *The Souls of Black Folk*.
23. *Holy Bible*, Genesis 1:3.
24. I am here reminded of the deep theological affinities between the resistance thesis of Bell's work, Hambone, and the importunate widow of the Gospels. See *Holy Bible*, Luke 18:1–8.

Works Cited

Alexander, Michelle. The New Jim Crow: Mass Incarceration in the Age of Colorblindness. New York: New Press, 2012.

Bell, Derrick. *Race, Racism and American Law*. New York: Aspen Publishers, 2008.

———. "Black Faith in a Racist Land," *The Derrick Bell Reader*, ed. Richard Delgado and Jean Stefancic. New York: New York University Press, 2005.

———. "Racial Symbols: A Limited Legacy," *Faces at the Bottom of the Well: The Permanence of Racism*. New York: Basic Books, 1992.

Berry, Mary Frances. *Black Resistance White Law: A History of Constitutional Racism in* America. New York: Penguin Books, 1994.

Brnovich v. Democratic National Committee, 594 U.S. (2021).

Civil Rights Cases, 109 U.S. 3 (1883).

Du Bois, W.E.B. "The Suppression of the African Slave Trade to the United States of America 1683–1870," *Du Bois: Writings*. New York: Library of America, 1986.

———. "The Souls of Black Folk," *Du Bois:* Writings. New York: Library of America, 1986.

Foner, Eric. *Forever Free: The Story of Emancipation and Reconstruction*. New York: Vintage Books, 2005.

Fortune, T. Thomas. "The Civil Rights Decision," *T. Thomas Fortune: The Afro-American Agitator*, ed. Shawn Leigh Alexander. Gainesville: University Press of Florida, 2008.
Holy Bible, Gen. 1:1–3.
———. Luke 18:1–8.
James, Nathan. "Superiority Fantasy," in *The New Black Fest's Hands Up: 7 Playwrights, 7 Testaments*, ed. Nathan James, Idris Goodwin, and Nathan Yungerberg. London: Samuel French, 2016.
Shelby County, Alabama v. Holder, 570 U.S. 529 (2013).
Slaughterhouse Cases, 83 U.S. 36 (1873).
United States v. Cruikshank, 92 U.S. 542 (1876).
Wilson, August. *Two Trains Running*. New York: Penguin, 1993.

PART I

RACIAL REALISM, RELIGION, AND THE NEGRO PROBLEM

Chapter 1

The Last Decade of Derrick Bell's Thought

GEORGE H. TAYLOR

In the fall of 2006, Derrick Bell returned to his alma mater and my home institution, the School of Law at the University of Pittsburgh, to teach for the semester. On the basis of some writing I had undertaken on his work,[1] Bell had invited me to teach a class with him that fall on the subject of Race, Religion, and Law. As evident from the course's title and true to form for Bell, the class conjoined and addressed two topics often avoided in the classroom: race and religion. Bell was a great advocate of participatory learning, and recounting the many pedagogical highlights of the semester would require a separate writing. Here I want to concentrate on substantive themes in the course. They provide an entry into themes, I will argue, that predominated the last decade or so of Bell's thought. In addition to the course, I will draw principally on his 2002 book, *Ethical Ambition*,[2] his final book, from 2004, *Silent Covenants*,[3] and a number of unpublished speeches from that period.[4] As in the class, the topic of religion became a persistent thread wending across Bell's writing and speeches, a development of interest in itself. But, I shall contend, Bell's attention to religion also extended his insight into a theme constant across his writings: the perdurance of racist beliefs in American society. Characterization of racism as a racist *faith*—a characterization that includes but does not limit faith to religious faith—deepens our understanding of its resilience. Bell's work in his last decade adds to our appreciation that his message was not simply an incisive contribution to the struggles of a prior generation but a missive of continuing vitality for the struggles toward racial justice in the changing landscapes of today and tomorrow. Bell's thought here provides another exemplification of his contributions to critical race theory and critical race methodology.

I proceed in three parts. The first two aim to be at once descriptive and to enrich our awareness of the significance of Bell's work in the last decade of his authorship. The third steps back and takes a more evaluative perspective. Part I examines three themes on religion in Bell's late work: his own religious faith; his query into the way many racists have also claimed to be Christian; and his juxtaposition between religious spirit and institutional structure. Part II demonstrates the applicability of Bell's themes on religion to his analysis of the law's response to racism. Part III appraises how we can honor Bell by building on his work for the future.

I. Three Themes on Religion

Bell's Religious Faith

In his final decade, three themes involving religion arise prominently in Bell's work. The first is his own religious faith. Anticipated in prior work such as *Gospel Choirs*,[5] Bell's reflections on his own faith become most overt in *Ethical Ambition*. In the course of a work on the challenges of an ethical life, Bell includes a chapter on his "evolving faith." Less concerned about doctrinal orthodoxy or theological formulas, Bell's faith provides for him a deep grounding, an anchor in the storm. When asked how he has maintained his commitment to social action promoting racial justice in the midst of the turbulence and resistance of opposing forces, Bell replies:

> I have relied on my faith. Particularly in hard times, my Christian faith provides reassurance that is unseen but no less real. It never fails to give me the fortitude I need when opposing injustice despite the almost certain failure of my action to persuade those in authority to alter their plans or policies. For me it is my most powerful resource.[6]

Bell's faith provides nurturance, the reserves with which to continue. This faith, Bell writes, resonates in the power of the spirituals that he is so drawn to: "Keep your hand on the plow. Hold on."[7] His faith also gives him some confidence that he is pursuing the just path toward the right ends.

Along similar lines Bell frequently quotes the following passage from Patricia Williams:

> Blacks always believed in rights in some larger, mythological sense—as a pantheon of possibility. It is in this sense that blacks believed in rights so much and so hard that we gave them life where there was none before; held onto them, put the hope of them into our wombs, mothered them, not the notion of them; we nurtured rights and gave rights life. And this was not the dry process of reification, from which life is drained and reality fades as the cement of conceptual determinism hardens round, but its opposite. This was the story of the Phoenix; the parthenogenesis of unfertilized hope.[8]

The Phoenix, Williams explains, is "the resurrection of life from ashes four hundred years old."[9] For African Americans, the possibility of full rights under the law has been "a fiercely motivational, almost religious, source of hope."[10]

For present purposes, I take two points from Bell's frequent citation of Williams. First, Bell is not alone among critical race scholars in the recourse to notions of some deep-seated faith or hope. Indeed, I would claim that these kinds of references are a central contribution of critical race theory. In contrast to those who argue that rights are simply a social construction that a society can grant or withdraw,[11] a continuing theme within critical race theory finds something more fundamental: a "truth," a "'really-out-there' object," "a 'real' reality out there."[12] Second, it is instructive that in the passage of Williams that Bell quotes, the hope that Williams emphasizes is not necessarily grounded in religion. As noted, Williams elsewhere describes the hope as "*almost* religious."[13] Although the resource upon which Bell relies derives from his Christian faith, Bell does not insist that this resource can be located within Christian faith alone. I set aside the question whether this resource should or should not be described as best or solely located within Christianity. The point is that Bell—as others within critical race theory—find a deep enduring resource within humanity that can be called upon as a source both of sustenance and of determination of the just. For reasons I shall pursue, I will describe the human sensibility to this resource as a "faith," something potentially broader than but inclusive of Christian faith.

Racist Faith

If the first theme involving religion in Bell's later work is his articulation of the deep positive value of his personal religious faith, the second theme moves in quite an opposite direction. Why, Bell queries, have most racists claimed a Christian faith?[14] Aside from his book *Ethical Ambition*, what permeated Bell's reflections during his last decade was not the value of his own Christian faith or the value that religion brought to the struggles for civil rights,[15] but instead how Christianity was used as a source of inspiration by those hostile to racial equality. Delving into the latter theme was certainly a grounding impetus for the Race, Religion, and Law course that we co-taught. We studied, for example, how Christians drew upon the Old Testament "curse of Ham"[16] as a justification for slavery of Blacks, how the New Testament acquiesced to slavery as an earthly institution,[17] and how the Christian church acquiesced as well, with Catholicism not officially condemning slavery until the 1960s.[18] In the South, before the civil rights movement, "the theology of segregationism was handed down as confirmed dogma."[19]

Historical and theological responses are available to all these linkages between Christianity and racism.[20] Bell's speeches themselves repeatedly advert to the analysis of African American theologian George Kelsey in his book, *Racism and the Christian Understanding of Man*.[21] (It is one of the virtues of Bell's work on religion that he revives attention to two African American theologians, Kelsey and Howard Thurman—whom I shall later discuss—whose work no longer receives sufficient consideration. Both came from a generation prior to Bell; both were theological predecessors and mentors to Dr. King.[22]) Through Kelsey, Bell claims that racism is an idolatrous faith because its focus moves from exaltation of the divine to exaltation of the self. The superiority of the white self and white race becomes the object of devotion.[23] The asserted superiority of this faith interrelates with Bell's invocation of Whiteness as a property right.[24] Whiteness offers privilege, a status that whites seek to protect.[25] In this idolatrous faith, the true spirit of Christianity becomes divorced from its implementation.[26] (This is a topic to which I shall return in discussing the third and final of Bell's themes on religion.) That racism is an idolatrous rather than true Christian faith allows a vantage point of critique. This undermining of racism as a faith is significant because it offers assistance to Bell's elusive goal, to which we shall also return, of changing individuals' inner attitudes.[27]

As throughout his work, Bell recognizes fully that the goal of eliminating racism is an endless challenge. Most racist Christians, for instance, will not find convincing the intellectual theological arguments about the limitations of their Christian understandings. And ultimately, this resistance is core to the importance of Bell's inquiry into the relationship between faith and racism. For Bell, a primary insight of this decade is that he must add to his prior focus on "the economic, political, and cultural dimensions of racism" the *religious* basis for racism as well.[28] This is not merely a historical inquiry, since the religious basis for racism continues also as a contemporary problem.[29] Quoting Kelsey, Bell emphasizes that we have not sufficiently appreciated "the faith characteristic of racist devotion and commitment."[30] When we recognize racism as a faith, we add to our appreciation of its intransigence. As a faith, racism offers substantively a "complete system of meaning, value, and loyalty."[31] It provides stability and reassurance in a threatening world of disparity between haves and have nots.[32] The faith character of racism also illuminates why it is not susceptible to the argument that there should be common economic interests across races, particularly among those of lesser means. The racist faith gives value to something other than mere economic interest,[33] again reinforcing the concept of Whiteness as a property right. Because of its affective power, racism as a faith is resistant to objection and empirical evidence. The "faith nature of . . . racism" may prevent adherents from seeing other views.[34] Given faith as racism, Bell queries: "Need we any further insight to understand why remedies for racial injustice are so hard to come by and how, suppressed in one area, the racially discriminatory practices spring up in others?"[35]

In appraising Bell's theme about why many racists claim a Christian faith, we have seen that one area of inquiry lies in examining the degree to which a racist faith may or may not legitimately derive support for its stance within Christianity. I am less interested in that specific question. Instead, I want to focus on Bell's perceptiveness, building on Kelsey, that the "faith" character of racism is not defined or limited by its sources in Christianity. Like Bell's faith—though to very different ends—a racist faith offers deep roots, deep grounding; it is not easily dislodged or refuted. The racist faith is also a causal origin of racism and in that regard must be added to racism's cultural, psychological, and economic foundations.

The racist faith is not simply an ideological justification for beliefs derived on other, more "material" bases. The racist faith adds a materiality of its own. Individuals and groups do not act simply on the basis of economic interests; they act on the basis of faith interests as well. For racism to be confronted in any adequate way, its "faith" character must be addressed also. As I shall develop with Bell, racism as a faith is a deep cognitive structure. Racism, Bell writes, "is not simply a 'taint' or 'bias,'"[36] something a matter only of a cognitive error in intentionality, something superficial or incidental that is easily correctable and removed. The way in which individuals imagine themselves and U.S. society is not only crucial but also deep-seated.[37] We are far from the Enlightenment project where reason would vanquish and eradicate superstition—a category into which religion was also placed. For good or for ill, the persistence of human faiths—both Bell's stirring faith and racist faiths—remains more enduring and foundational.

The Juxtaposition between Faith and Religious Structure

As anticipated, the third theme attracting Bell's attention to religion in his later thought involves the transposition between the positive, originating spirit of Christianity and its institutionalization, the difference between a faith and the organizational structure developed to perpetuate it. On this subject, Bell persistently draws upon an excerpt from Nikos Kazantzakis's novel, *The Last Temptation of Christ*.[38] Given the importance to Bell's message of his own fictional creations,[39] perhaps it is not surprising that a novel rather than a theological work provides his principal source here, although as we shall see Bell will refer to theology as well. In the Kazantzakis excerpt Bell cites, the setting is a scene following the Last Supper, when Jesus informs his disciples that he knows he must die. While other disciples bemoan Jesus's fate, one disciple, Jacob, reconciles himself to Jesus's end and promises that the disciples will work to ensure that Jesus's words shall not die with him.

> "We'll establish them firmly in new Holy Scriptures, we'll make laws, build our own synagogues and select our own high priests, Scribes and Pharisees."
>
> Jesus is horrified. "You crucify the spirit, Jacob," he shouted. "No, no, I don't want that!"

Jacob tries to reassure him. "This is the only way we can prevent the spirit from turning into air and escaping."

"But it won't be free any more; it won't be spirit!"

"That doesn't matter," Jacob responds. "It will look like spirit. For our work, Rabbi, that's sufficient."[40]

While Bell grants primacy to the legitimacy of Jesus's perspective, he acknowledges some legitimacy in Jacob's perspective as well. On Jacob's side, it is the case that the maintenance and perpetuation of the spirit of Christianity requires an ongoing institutional structure such as the church's.[41] I have examined this claim at greater length elsewhere[42] and will return to it briefly in the next section. But it is plain that Bell locates himself more essentially with Jesus on the side of spirit rather than with Jacob on the side of structure. Structure has tended to supplant spirit or to stifle it with the efflorescence of doctrinal rules and requirements that become ends in themselves. Form replaces substance.[43] For advocates of structure, it is sufficient that structures "look like spirit." Individuals and leaders within the church have granted adherence to the church as an institution but have forgotten "the life and teachings of the man upon whose life the Christian church [was] founded."[44]

In Bell's criticism here, he finds a kindred voice in the work of theologian Howard Thurman. Writing in 1928, Thurman admonished: "We must put a vast faith in the contagion in the Spirit of Jesus rather than into the building of organizations to perpetuate his Spirit."[45] While recognizing the need for institutional organization to protect development of religious spirit, Thurman observed that the spirit "is also destroyed by the very organization that preserved it. Hence the paradox: The power that makes it breaks it."[46] As we examined in our course, the tension between religious spirit and structure was a persistent theme in Thurman's writings. In his 1979 autobiography, published two years before his death, Thurman comments:

> There is an intrinsic contradiction between the freedom of the spirit and the organization through which that freedom manifests itself. . . . The sense of freedom . . . must be structured and contained within a mold. . . . But, when, inevitably, the mold begins to choke the spirit, the mold is broken and the spirit breaks out anew, only to encrust itself in another mold, and so the process continues.[47]

Bell's fidelity to the obligations of his moral and religious spirit—and not to the formalisms of some institutional structure—represents a lasting testament to his person and character. As well known, this fidelity came at great personal cost. Not only did he take a leave of absence from and ultimately lose his tenured position at Harvard Law School in protest of the school's failure to hire a woman of color onto the faculty, but his first wife, Jewel, was dying of cancer at the time that this protest began.[48] Part of Bell's witness in his writings and speeches is to urge and offer support for others in their own ethical investment. This witness is a significant ambition of his book, *Ethical Ambition*—published during his last decade—and his earlier volume, *Confronting Authority*. To get by in the present American society, Bell writes, many think it is enough merely to *appear* to be ethical. "Our posturing will look like spirit and it will appear sufficient." The challenge, though, "for those with ethical ambition is to transform the symbolically sufficient into the substantively real."[49]

Bell's personal integrity—his adherence to his faith, his spirit—is both remarkable and a legacy deserving continued regard. What also needs attention is the role spirit plays for Bell in the task of social change. In his last decade, his vocabulary becomes the following: "The needed revolution is, as Jesus recognized, less about political change than spiritual reformation."[50] In part, this task is about personal responsibility and personal transformation, but it is also the task of how to instantiate change in others. The question, Bell writes, is how to create a spiritual reformation in others that transforms "the vision of a minority into a consensus acknowledged and embraced by the majority."[51] This vocabulary is, of course, not unknown in Bell's earlier works. He had previously written, for example, of the possibility of a "long-overdue revelation" to whites,[52] and his fictional narratives have had the persistent and driving ambition to help people "see."[53] But Bell's focus in his last decade on the vocabulary of faith and spirit incisively sharpens the task at issue. As we have discussed, the terms "faith" and "spirit" should not be understood simply within religious confines but delineate grounding value orientations that inspire and support. To challenge racism requires "spiritual reformation." Consistent with his longstanding arguments, Bell accepts that appreciation of the role played by faith and spirit admits their potential role not only as positive resources but also as sources of resistance to change. We can seek spiritual transformation in others at the same time that we know that "the faith nature of their racism may well prevent them from seeing."[54]

II. Application to Bell's Themes in Law

I now turn to apply Bell's discussion of faith to his arguments in his final decade about the role of law and the possibilities of legal transformation. In some ways this application goes beyond steps undertaken by Bell himself. I hope to show that appreciation of the role of faith deepens his last contentions about legal transformation, contentions that are consistent with and the culmination of a lifetime of arguments on this subject.

The Supreme Court's decision in *Brown v. Board of Education*[55] is one of the most iconic in contemporary U.S. jurisprudence. As is well known, in the case the Court reversed prior precedent upholding the constitutionality of separate but equal state-sponsored schools and held instead that segregated public schools are unconstitutional. Among legal academics, the result became generally hailed not just by liberals but across the political spectrum.[56] In his career as an attorney Bell worked to implement *Brown*, first with the NAACP Legal Defense Fund and then with the federal government.[57] Over time, though, he came to experience reservations about *Brown* that appeared in his initial academic writings and intensified thereafter. A predominant issue for Bell was a very practical one: *Brown* did not work; its mandate did not lead to significant school integration. In one of his first academic writings Bell looked askance at the behavior of civil rights attorneys who continued to push for integration while what their clients wanted was quality schools, integrated or not.[58] Instead, Bell found a 1935 statement of W.E.B. Du Bois to characterize more accurately clients' goals: "The Negro needs neither segregated schools nor mixed schools. What he needs is education."[59] Du Bois's statement became a touchstone for Bell, and it is one to which he has adverted frequently, including at several points in the last decade of his writings.[60]

Bell's objection to the course of strategy taken under *Brown* hearkens back to what we have seen his late writings describe as a division between spirit and institutional structure. Civil rights lawyers became wrapped up in their own goals, not their clients', and totemic *Brown* itself was but an empty totem. Reflecting back on his new perspective, Bell writes: "*Brown* remained Holy Writ, but I now felt we were misreading its message. As happens all too often in religion, disciples lose sight of the basic truths amid all the doctrines that tend to stifle those truths rather than nourish them."[61] Over the years Bell's view became that *Brown* was "a magnificent mirage, the legal equivalent of that city on a hill to which all aspire without any serious thought that it will ever be attained."[62]

What went wrong in *Brown*? Bell's path-breaking thesis of "interest convergence," articulated since at least 1980, argues that racial equality occurs only when that interest converges with white interests.[63] The *Brown* decision and its implementation over time depended not on the morality of racial equality but on the rise and fall of white interest convergence. Interest convergence has influenced three elements of *Brown*'s trajectory. First, when the case was under consideration by the Court, the nation's interest in protecting its image abroad was instrumental in the support for arguments favoring the Court's ultimate holding.[64] Second, the courts engaged in retrenchment over time.[65] Third, communities' negative response to *Brown*'s implementation led to a backlash. Even where the courts offered judicial enforcement, Bell argued in a late speech:

> our hard-won orders—and I handled or supervised hundreds of those cases—led school boards to close black schools, dismiss black teachers and principals, and send black children to white schools (not the best) where they were often met with more hostility than acceptance. Even so, droves of white parents responded to school desegregation by enrolling their children in private schools or moving to suburbs where—they hoped—blacks would not be able to follow.[66]

As Bell perceived early in his writings, laws do not produce substantial results on their own. They are not self-executing but require a political base of continuing support.[67]

One of the great insights of Bell's concept of interest convergence lies in its recognition of the lack of necessary correlation between a judicial decision (or, more generally, passage of any law) and its actual enforcement. This is a point needing much greater appreciation.[68] In one sense, this potential divergence between a law and its implementation may reflect a division between what we may call, with Bell, the originating faith—the originating value impulses—of a law and the law's structure as passed or judicially determined. The normative and substantive values that inspired the law may become detached from the law as implemented. While it is often the assumption that passage of a law is sufficient to determine the course and effectiveness of its implementation, that is not the case. Determination of success does not lie simply with a bill becoming law.

In a second sense, the recognition of divergence between inspiring values and a law's implementation points to the fact that the process of implementation may be captured by a divergent faith—a divergent sense of interests—than that which pushed for its passage. This may be a matter of the law being reinterpreted through legal advocacy and judicial decision or a matter of the law being resisted, ignored, or geographically distanced from in practice. Third, the divergence between originating faith and law undermines a different—liberal—faith in the assumed inevitable, evolutionary path of the law toward equality.[69] In some of his late work, Bell describes this faith as a "fantasy."[70]

Would it have made a difference to the actualization of racial equality if *Brown* had been decided differently? In his late work, Bell addresses this issue directly, but one of his fictional narratives from the early 1990s presages the direction that Bell will ultimately take. This narrative occurs in a mythical future where a President signs into law "The Racial Preference Licensing Act," an Act responding to *Brown*'s failure. As a matter of "racial realism," the Act acknowledges the nonexistence of racial tolerance and instead seeks to create racial justice through a market concept.[71] The Act permits employers and owners of dwellings and public facilities to purchase a license allowing them to discriminate on the basis of race and color. Those with the license would be taxed 3 percent of revenue, and funds from the licenses and taxes would be used to support Black businesses, mortgage loans for Black home buyers, and college and vocational scholarships for Black students.[72] Obviously, the Act permits segregation, and it also seeks to promote racial equality through the license costs and taxes. The model of racial relations advanced is in practice similar to the "separate but equal" standard upheld by the Supreme Court in *Plessy v. Ferguson*,[73] the 1896 decision reversed by *Brown*. Just as equal education should be the goal if the creation of integrated education does not succeed, so more generally the goal of racial equality should be economic fairness regardless of the failure of integration to occur. As Bell's narrative highlights, the Act is a response to *Brown*'s failure. *Brown* failed because "'morals-policing' laws" do not work.[74] In the vocabulary we have been using, Bell's insight is that the law does not change originating faiths, including racist faiths. The development of the law governing racial equality must proceed on other, more realistic grounds.

In his last decade, particularly in his final book, *Silent Covenants*,[75] Bell turns to address more directly how *Brown* should have been decided and offers a revised Court opinion for the 1954 *Brown* Court. Perhaps not surprisingly, but still shockingly, given *Brown*'s reputation, Bell argues for the judicial stance articulated in the *Plessy* decision that *Brown* overruled. Separate but equal should be the constitutional standard.[76] Bell acknowledges the psychological damages segregation does to Black children, yet separate but equal is the most that is possible.[77] Integration will not be achieved and will be resisted.[78] Bell's conclusion is not, however, simply a matter of practical realism. Rather, the *Brown* standard requiring integration at most addresses the requirement of integrated facilities (a requirement that itself will be contested). Once facilities are legally non-separate, many whites would consider that the demand for equality has been satisfied.[79] The *Brown* Court's holding does not address underlying racist beliefs, racist faiths. "Imagining racism as a fixable aberration . . . obfuscates the way in which racism functions as an ideological lens through which Americans perceive themselves, their nation, and their nation's other."[80] By avoiding the issue of deep-seated racist belief, the *Brown* Court would allow racism to continue to flourish under the law. The *Brown* Court's holding would not locate the law as that which redresses racism but rather as "that which participates in its consolidation."[81] Eliminating segregation in certain facilities will not eliminate the underlying belief in white superiority. As Bell writes in a speech earlier in the decade, the *Brown* holding would not affect the "dominant interpretive framework" of racism or the "imaginative lens through which Americans would conceive race going forward."[82] *Brown* would not affect the racist faith.

Bell himself does not believe that any alternative law he could construct would alter racist faith either. He proposes, though, that the law must recognize that fact. Bell wants to move away from *Brown*'s endorsement of integration to *Plessy*'s upholding of separate but equal in order to insist on the second prong: equality. The *Brown* Court should have used the context before it "to test the legal legitimacy of the 'separate but equal' standard, not . . . by overturning *Plessy*, but by ordering for the first time its strict enforcement."[83] Similar to his Racial Preference Licensing Act, Bell acknowledges that racism will continue, but the price is that schools must be made equal. Bell then goes on to elaborate the requisite standards of equalization, school board representation, and judicial oversight.[84] Should any school not comply, the courts would determine at that point whether the proper relief would be the requirement of school integration. The hope is expressed that this gradualist approach would create less white resistance.

In a subsequent chapter in *Silent Covenants*, Bell turns to contemporary educational efforts to provide equal educations for Black and other children of color. He discusses attempts to eliminate significant funding disparities across school districts within several states and other diverse attempts to enhance inner-city education. School-funding efforts have faced significant hurdles, particularly legislative, and the inner-city models have achieved varying levels of success. In neither is equal educational funding achieved.[85] Given Bell's continual recognition of white avoidance of equalization—through flight to the suburbs, enrollment in private school, and so on[86]—this result is not unexpected. Although not directly addressed, Bell's revised *Brown* opinion urging full equality and a gradualist approach does not seem to anticipate success either. The continuance of racist faiths contributes to this failure.

As apparent, as throughout his life, Bell in his last years does not foreswear legal change on behalf of racial equality. Legal change, however, will not occur through morals policing but through seeking more pragmatically to obtain what one really can. As a matter of racial realism, quality education rather than integrated education is the more viable goal.

If Bell does not seek change in people's faiths about race in the legal arena, his work does undertake the task of trying to dislodge and reorient people's faiths about race themselves. His story on the Racial Preference Licensing Act is not intended literally to seek adoption of such a law, but it does seek to jolt the faiths of those—Black or white—who believe in integration.[87] The story, he hopes, may lead some of these individuals to have their "consciousness raised," so that they redirect their goals more realistically.[88] More broadly, Bell's arguments and narratives seek to challenge and reorient all faiths—including racist faiths. The goal is to "make people *see*."[89] Can whites of more modest economic means come to appreciate that they have greater "interest convergence" with Blacks of similar means than with the supposed benefits of white privilege? Bell seeks to disorient in order to reorient, even as he recognizes that this is a Sisyphean task. Once he rolls the stone of racial change up the hill, it will fall back down, and the effort must be undertaken once again.[90]

III. The Road Ahead

As I turn to evaluation from a more descriptive effort to elaborate the depth of Bell's argument in his later thought, I would urge that it is a mistake to evaluate Bell on the measure of how well his work squares with any aspirations for a post-racial society. As we continue to witness since

Bell's death—with perduring insight on his part—the problems of racial division and discrimination continue to proliferate to the dismay of hopes of amelioration. At the same time, I also believe that it is not necessary for his readers to choose for or against Bell on the basis of evaluating his continued claim that racism is permanent.[91]

Instead, we should applaud the works of Bell's last decade for fastening on the lens of faith as a way of comprehending both the resilience of African American social actors such as Bell himself and the recalcitrance to change of racist faiths held in opposition (or, for that matter, of faiths in racial integration). As Bell instantiates, faith can be something very positive, as the witness to a truth whose reality may be presently only a glimmer, a truth that proves to be an enduring resource and ground of inspiration, a truth whose task, as Patricia Williams writes, it is ours to help nurture and bring to life,[92] a truth whose reality we aspire to. In his revision to the *Brown* opinion, Bell lauds the way African Americans have "taken symbolic gains and given them meaning by the sheer force of their *belief* in the freedoms this country guarantees to all," in their "unstinting *faith* in this country's ideals."[93] Yet faith can also, as in the racist faith, generate an extremely destructive worldview, a faith very difficult to dislodge. We must not assume that reason can dislodge such a faith, nor assume either that political, cultural, psychological, or economic change will dislodge this faith.[94] The racist faith is an independent causal origin of racism. The goals of political, cultural, psychological, and economic change are important but insufficient. Bell's last writings are correct that the problem of racism is also one of a racist faith. The task must be to understand that fact and then to respond in two ways. One response must be to pursue change, as difficult as the challenge will endlessly be, at the level of the racist faith, to pursue its adherents' "spiritual reformation."[95] The second response acknowledges that such transformation may not come, and the pursuit of racial justice must adjust to that reality.

I close with two points. The first emphasizes the contributions of Bell's analysis of faith to and its synergies with the current literature on the ways humans reason and categorize. The second addresses practical responses to the challenges presented by racist faiths. First, then, Bell's insight into the abiding and deep-seated nature of contemporary faith offers a significant addition to the growing literature on the nature of human reasoning and categorization. We humans—all of us—are not the rational, dispassionate, utility-maximizing descendants of the Enlightenment model of reason that we posited—and perhaps hoped—we were. As in

Bell's portrayal of faith, these divergences from reason can be positive or negative, but they are divergences. Similar insights are arising in a wide variety of disciplines. Religion is flourishing in the world, not going the way of superstition and disappearing. Ideology continues to operate and manifests itself both negatively as distortion and positively as forms of social identification or integration.[96] Human cognition operates on the basis of conceptual mechanisms whose structure is deeply metaphoric rather than simply propositional.[97] We often think, for example, on the basis of "prototype effects," which reflect the human mind's tendency to promote one type within a category as emblematic of the category.[98] In the West, the prototype has been the white, male, heterosexual, middle class, non-physically challenged individual, and those of another race, gender, and so on have been viewed as divergences from this norm.[99] Also having increasing sway recently are insights from cognitive psychology that we humans often think on the basis of heuristics, shorthand forms of reflection that allow us to categorize and decide quickly—a benefit in our preliterate past as well as today in differentiating friend from threatening enemy—but shorthand that may often be erroneous.[100] In this research, the "representativeness" heuristic is similar to the prototype effect in that we decide on the basis of the similarity of a description to stereotypes.[101] Biologically, we are predisposed to favor our reproductive success, and we act altruistically toward those who are our biological kin, as our genetic material benefits also from their reproductive success.[102] Kinship cues—based on both familiarity and similarity—operate as heuristics that cause us to treat the other as kin and so behave altruistically toward them.[103] The definition of whom we consider familiar and similar and so as kin will vary over time and circumstance, again a finding with import for discrimination. Bell's focus on faith adds measurably to our understanding of the range of human behavior that is not the product of objective reason, intention, or conscious motivation. Discrimination is often predicated upon unconscious factors that are challenging to modify or displace.[104]

My second and final point is a practical one. If, as Bell elucidates, transforming the racist faith is such a Sisyphean task, what strategies remain for us to undertake? As we have discussed, Bell's own racial realism has led him on the one hand to promote equality rather than integration. Here the considered assumption is that due to claims of white privilege there will be a lack of interest convergence between whites and others, and racist faiths will not be overcome. On the other hand, Bell also seeks to pursue the transformation of racist faiths nonetheless. Here Bell proceeds in part on the basis of his own deep faith in what are the right ends, in part on the basis of the principle of acting rightly, whether the ends are achieved or not. Bell's posture mixes the prophetic and the existential. Bell writes, "We're a race of Jeremiahs, prophets calling for the nation to repent."[105] He also speaks approvingly of existentialist Albert Camus's appropriation of the myth of Sisyphus and Camus's realization that while struggle may result in defeat, meaning comes from the struggle.[106] As indicated in the subtitle of Bell's book *Confronting Authority*, he is an "ardent protester."[107]

It is illuminating that Bell describes his protests as typically the act of a "solo protester," one who "acts alone, usually without either seeking or obtaining approval from others who share his or her views."[108] It is true that sometimes Bell is unable to convince others to join him,[109] and it is also true that solo protests can "create a magnetic field" whose influence extends beyond the actions of the protester.[110] Yet largely missing from Bell's accounts are a "community organizing" model that enlarges the movement for change.[111] In his own review of civil rights actions during the 1960s, Bell recognizes that sit-ins, marches, and boycotts led to economic pressure causing interest convergence among affected white store owners that precipitated racial change.[112] Organizing remains a critical task today, including organizing to push for laws and for their enforcement. Organizing can also transform faiths, as the sense of community—and of interests—broadens. Although he does not focus on organizing, Bell appreciates that the movement for racial justice cannot depend on the fortuity of interest convergence recognized after the fact. This movement must also seek to *forge* this fortuity, to spark and nourish the moments that fire history.[113] The attention to organizing intends not a criticism of Bell but an extension. In any effort forward, we must be attentive to Bell's underlying and enduring message, crystallized during his last decade, that the task of racial justice ultimately depends less on logic than on the struggle over deeply held beliefs, deeply held faiths.[114]

Notes

1. George H. Taylor, "Racism as 'The Nation's Crucial Sin': Theology and Derrick Bell," *Michigan Journal of Race & Law* 9 (2004): 269–322; George H, Taylor, "Derrick Bell's Narratives as Parables," *New York University Review of Law & Social Change* 31 (2007): 225–271. The latter Bell had read in draft form.

2. Derrick Bell, *Ethical Ambition: Living a Life of Meaning and Worth* (New York: Bloomsbury, 2002).

3. Derrick Bell, *Silent Covenants: Brown v. Board of Education and the Unfulfilled Hopes for Racial Reform* (New York: Oxford University Press, 2004).

4. I thank Janet Dewart Bell for permission to quote from these unpublished speeches.

5. Derrick Bell, *Gospel Choirs: Psalms of Survival in an Alien Land Called Home* (New York: Basic Books, 1997). This work is less a personal consideration than a tribute to the power of gospel music for all those "searching for God's peace in the midst of a hostile world" (3).

6. Bell, *Ethical Ambition*, 76.

7. Ibid., 92.

8. Derrick Bell, *Faces at the Bottom of the Well: The Permanence of Racism* (New York: Basic Books, 1992), 25 (quoting Patricia J. Williams, "Alchemical Notes: Reconstructing Ideals from Deconstructed Rights," in *A Less Than Perfect Union: Alternative Perspectives on the United States Constitution*, ed. Jules Lobel (New York: Monthly Review Press, 1988), 64. For similar quotations of Williams, see Bell, *Ethical Ambition*, 176; *Gospel Choirs*, 185–186; "Who's Afraid of Critical Race Theory," *University of Illinois Law Review* (1995): 900; Derrick Bell and Preeta Bansal, "The Republican Revival and Racial Politics," *Yale Law Journal* 97 (1988): 1619.

9. Patricia J. Williams, *The Alchemy of Race and Rights: Diary of a Law Professor* (Cambridge, MA: Harvard University Press, 1991): 163 (expanding upon her earlier language).

10. Patricia J. Williams, "Alchemical Notes: Reconstructing Ideals from Deconstructed Rights," *Harvard Civil Rights—Civil Liberties Law Review* 22 (1987): 417.

11. Williams, for example, wrote against this posture as endorsed by advocates within critical legal studies. For a later example, see Mark Tushnet, "The Critique of Rights," *Southern Methodist University Law Review* 47 (1993): 23–34.

12. Angela P. Harris, "Foreword: The Jurisprudence of Reconstruction," *California Law Review* 82 (1994): 751, 753.

13. Williams, "Alchemical Notes," 417 (emphasis added).

14. Derrick Bell, "Howard Thurman and the Christians as Racists Paradox," Howard Thurman Center, Stetson University, Gulfport, Florida, November 15, 2005, 2–3 (on file with author); "Racism's Religious Perspective," Black Law Journal Anniversary Conference, November 18, 2005 (on file with author).

15. See, e.g., David L. Chappell, *A Stone of Hope: Prophetic Religion and the Death of Jim Crow* (Chapel Hill: University of North Carolina Press, 2004).

16. Genesis 9:18–27. In the story, Noah has three sons: Shem, Ham, and Japheth. While Noah is drunk, Ham sees his father naked and tells his two brothers, who cover their father. On learning what Ham had done, Noah curses Ham and condemns his progeny to slavery. Ham becomes linked to Blacks. See David M. Goldenberg, *The Curse of Ham: Race and Slavery in Early Judaism, Christianity, and Islam* (Princeton, NJ: Princeton University Press, 2003), 142–143. In

painstaking detail, Goldenberg's book elaborates the falsity of the appropriation of the Ham story for racist purposes.

17. See, e.g., 1 Corinthians 7:20-21, 24 ("Everyone should remain in the state [life context] in which he was called. Were you a slaved when called? Never mind. . . . So, brethren, in whatever state each was called, there let him remain with God"); Colossians 3:22-24 ("Slaves, obey in everything those who are your earthly masters"); 1 Timothy 6:1-2 ("Let all who are under the yoke of slavery regard their masters as worthy of all honor"); Titus 2:9-10 ("Bid slaves to be submissive to their masters and to give satisfaction in every respect").

18. John T. Noonan Jr., *A Church That Can and Cannot Change: The Development of Catholic Moral Teaching* (South Bend, IN: University of Notre Dame Press, 2005), 119-120. In addition to being a prolific author and noted Catholic commentator, Noonan was a senior judge on the U.S. Court of Appeals for the Ninth Circuit.

19. Paul Harvey, *Freedom's Crossing: Religious Culture and the Shaping of the South from the Civil War Through the Civil Rights Era* (Chapel Hill: University of North Carolina Press, 2005), 229.

20. See, e.g., Galatians 3:23-28 ("Now that faith has come . . . there is neither Jew nor Greek, there is neither slave nor free, there is neither male nor female; for you are all one in Christ Jesus"); Goldenberg, *The Curse of Ham*. (Christian racists would respond that Galatians refers only to the world to come, not our present existence.)

21. George D. Kelsey, *Racism and the Christian Understanding of Man* (New York: Charles Scribner's Sons, 1965).

22. Derrick Bell, "Martin Luther King, Jr. Was He a 20th Century Jesus?," Carnegie Mellon University, 2006 [December 29, 2005 draft], 4 (on Kelsey as King's teacher) (on file with author); Stewart Burns, *To the Mountaintop: Martin Luther King Jr.'s Mission to Save America 1955-1968* (San Francisco: Harper San Francisco, 2004), 452 (on Thurman as a spiritual mentor of King).

23. Derrick Bell, "Racism as Ultimate Deception," The 11th Annual Derrick Bell Lecture, New York University School of Law, November 6, 2006, 4 (on file with author); "Accepting Extinction: Will Christian Doctrine Prove Our Enemy Rather Than Our Salvation?," Braun Memorial Lecture Series, John Marshall Law School, Chicago, October 13. 2006, 5-7 (on file with author); "Martin Luther King, Jr.," 4-5; "Racism's Religious Perspective," 4; "Howard Thurman," 7-8.

24. Derrick Bell, *And We Are Not Saved: The Elusive Quest for Racial Justice* (New York: Basic Books, 1987), 172. Cheryl Harris later developed the concept independently. Cheryl I. Harris, "Whiteness as Property," *Harvard Law Review* 106 (1993): 1713n9 (noting her separate generation of the idea). Bell frequently makes reference to Harris. See Taylor, "Racism as 'The Nation's Crucial Sin,'" 276n46 (documenting this point).

25. Derrick Bell, "Dissenting Opinion," in *What Brown v. Board of Education Should Have Said*, ed. Jack M. Balkin (New York: New York University Press, 2001), 188.

26. Bell, "Howard Thurman," 8.

27. Ibid., 1.

28. Bell, "Racism's Religious Perspective," 2; "Racism as Ultimate Deception," 12 ("racism is the combination of many factors, economic, political, psychological, even religious"). See also David Brion Davis, *Inhuman Bondage: The Rise and Fall of Slavery in the New World* (New York: Oxford University Press, 2006), 78 (arguing that religion was one of the "cultural preconditions for the anti-black racism that dominated the white settlement and development of the Americas, especially from the late seventeenth century onward"); Stephen R. Haynes, *Noah's Curse: The Biblical Justification of American Slavery* (New York: Oxford University Press, 2002), 221 ("Whatever else may be said about the history and dynamics of American racism, its stubborn links with religion in general and scriptural traditions in particular should not be underestimated or approached simplistically.").

29. Bell, "Howard Thurman," 3 ("Why are modern Christians as much a threat to black people and themselves as were the Christian slaveowners and what can be done about this current danger?"); Haynes, *Noah's Curse*, 221 ("It would be naïve indeed to assume that the American mind has become resistant to racist readings of the Bible with the advent of a new millennium.").

30. Bell, "Howard Thurman," 8, quoting Kelsey, *Racism and the Christian Understanding of Man* (page not noted); "Accepting Extinction," 6 (same). See also Bell, "Martin Luther King, Jr.," 5 (observing how "many do not recognize . . . the religious faith-like foundation of so much racist belief and behavior based on those beliefs").

31. Bell, "Racism as Ultimate Deception," 4; "Accepting Extinction," 6; "Racism's Religious Perspective," 4; "Howard Thurman," 7.

32. Bell, "Racism as Ultimate Deception," 13.

33. Derrick Bell, "The Role of Fantasy in Politics and School Desegregation Policy-Setting," Penn State Mitstifer Lecture, University Council for Educational Administration, Kansas City, MI, November 12, 2004 (2nd rev. version, November 18, 2004), 6–7 (on file with author). Bell's vocabulary of "fantasy" in this presentation appears to be changed in subsequent papers to that of "faith."

34. Bell, "Howard Thurman," 6.

35. Bell, "Racism's Religious Perspective," 6; "Accepting Extinction," 7; "Howard Thurman," 8.

36. Bell, "Dissenting Opinion," 190.

37. Bell, "The Role of Fantasy," 6; "Dissenting Opinion," 190.

38. Nikos Kazantzakis, *The Last Temptation of Christ* (New York: Bantam Books, 1961).

39. See Taylor, "Derrick Bell's Narratives."

40. Kazantzakis, *Last Temptation of Christ*, 419. For quotations of this passage, see Bell, *Ethical Ambition*, 83; "Martin Luther King, Jr.," 6; "Racism's Religious Perspective," 6–7; "Howard Thurman," 3. The passage figured significantly in our course as well.

41. Bell, *Ethical Ambition*, 83, 92; "Martin Luther King, Jr.," 7; "Racism's Religious Perspective," 7–8; "Howard Thurman," 3–4.

42. George H. Taylor, "Race, Religion, and Law: The Tension Between Spirit and Its Institutionalization," *University of Maryland Law Journal of Race, Religion, Gender and Class* 6 (2006): 51–67; "The Challenge of Derrick Bell: Civil Rights From Movement to Organization and From Movement to Law," Center on Race and Social Problems, University of Pittsburgh, March 25, 2009.

43. Bell, *Ethical Ambition*, 83, 92; "Martin Luther King, Jr.," 7; "Racism's Religious Perspective," 7–8; "Howard Thurman," 3–4.

44. Bell, "Martin Luther King, Jr.," 5–6.

45. Howard Thurman, "The Task of the Negro Ministry," in *A Strange Freedom: The Best of Howard Thurman on Religious Experience and Public Life*, eds. Walter Earl Fluker and Catherine Tumber (Boston: Beacon Press, 1998), 195. The passage is quoted in Bell, "Racism's Religious Perspective," 7; "Martin Luther King, Jr.," 6; "Howard Thurman," 4.

46. Thurman, "Task of the Negro Ministry," 196, quoted in Bell, "Racism's Religious Perspective," 8; "Martin Luther King, Jr.," 7; "Howard Thurman," 4.

47. Howard Thurman, *With Head and Heart: The Autobiography of Howard Thurman* (San Diego, CA: Harcourt Brace & Co., 1979), 181. To similar ends, Thurman also addresses an issue discussed in the prior subsection: how to articulate and defend the true spirit of Christianity against its adoption by racists. He recalls how during some international travel early in his career he was challenged by an interlocutor from then Ceylon with the following question:

> Your forebears were taken from the west coast of Africa as slaves, by Christians. They were sold in America, a Christian country, to Christians. They were held in slavery for some two hundred years by Christians. They were freed as a result of economic forces rather than Christian idealism. . . . Since that time you have been brutalized, lynched, burned, and denied most civil rights by Christians. (113, 114)

It became part of his lifework to respond to this question, and he did so by distinguishing between the religion of Jesus and Christianity as an institution. For Thurman's sustained response to this question, see Howard Thurman, *Jesus and the Disinherited* (Nashville, TN: Abingdon Press, 1949). This book was significant for Dr. King. See Thurman, *With Head and Heart*, 255.

48. Bell, *Ethical Ambition*, 4; *Confronting Authority: Reflections of an Ardent Protester* (Boston: Beacon Press, 1994), xii.

49. Bell, *Ethical Ambition*, 93; "Howard Thurman," 5. In *Confronting Authority*, Bell urges that "your faith in what you believe is right must be a living, working faith, a faith that draws you away from comfort and security and toward risk, when necessary, through confrontation" (162–163).

50. Bell, "Racism's Religious Perspective," 12; "Howard Thurman," 15.

51. Bell, "Racism's Religious Perspective," 12.

52. Derrick Bell, *Afrolantica Legacies* (Chicago: Third World Press, 1998), 167.

53. Bell, *Faces*, 60. For greater discussion, see Taylor, "Derrick Bell's Narratives."

54. Bell, "Howard Thurman," 13–14.

55. *Brown v. Board of Education*, 347 U.S. 483 (1954).

56. See, e.g., Robert Bork, *The Tempting of America: The Political Seduction of the Law* (New York: Free Press, 1990), 73–74 (calling the decision "one of constitutional law's great triumphs," although going on to disagree with and propose an alternative to the method by which the Court reached its result). The range in the political appropriation of *Brown* will be relevant to Bell's concerns about the decision, a point to which I shall return.

57. Bell, *Silent Covenants*, 3.

58. Derrick A. Bell Jr., "Serving Two Masters: Integration Ideals and Client Interests in School Desegregation Litigation," *Yale Law Journal* 85 (1976): 470–516.

59. Bell, "Serving Two Masters," 515, quoting W.E.B. Du Bois, "Does the Negro need Separate Schools?," *Journal of Negro Education* 4 (1935), 335.

60. Bell, *Silent Covenants*, 23; "Racism as Ultimate Deception," 10; "The Role of Fantasy," 11, 17; "*Brown v. Board*: What Are We Doing with What We Have Learned?," Cleveland-Marshall College of Law, Cleveland, October 9, 2003, 4 (on file with author).

61. Bell, *Silent Covenants*, 4.

62. Ibid., 4.

63. Ibid., 69. For Bell's early development of this thesis, see Derrick A. Bell Jr., "*Brown v. Board of Education* and the Interest-Convergence Dilemma," *Harvard Law Review* 93 (1980): 518–533.

64. Bell, *Silent Covenants*, 59–68.

65. Ibid., 26–27. Bell describes how this retrenchment is a judicial and legislative pattern that exists over the course of U.S. history. See Bell, *Faces*, 53–54; "Bluebeard's Castle: An American Tale," in *Afrolantica Legacies*, 155–168 (allegory).

66. Bell, "The Role of Fantasy," 14.

67. Bell, "Serving Two Masters," 514.

68. For a general inquiry into this issue, see Tushnet, "The Critique of Rights."

69. Bell, *Afrolantica Legacies*, 47.

70. Bell, "The Role of Fantasy," 10 (the "fantasy" of expecting the elimination of racial discrimination through the courts); 11 ("our fantasy that the law would provide equal educational opportunity for our children").

71. Bell, *Faces*, 47.

72. Ibid., 48–49.

73. *Plessy v. Ferguson*, 163 U.S. 537 (1896).
74. Bell, *Faces*, 51.
75. The issue is also the subject of Bell, "Dissenting Opinion."
76. Bell, *Silent Covenants*, 21.
77. Ibid., 23. In this passage, Bell also adverts to the damage segregation does to white children, as they labor under the handicap of the belief that their white privilege is deserved.
78. Bell, *Silent Covenants*, 23.
79. Bell, "The Role of Fantasy," 15.
80. Bell, *Silent Covenants*, 27.
81. Ibid., 27.
82. Bell, "*Brown v. Board*," 15.
83. Bell, *Silent Covenants*, 22. See also Bell, "Dissenting Opinion," 186.
84. Bell, *Silent Covenants*, 24–25.
85. Ibid., 160–179.
86. See text accompanying note 65 in this chapter.
87. Bell, *Faces*, 60.
88. Ibid., 62.
89. Ibid., 60 (quoting the words of his fictional interlocutor, Geneva Crenshaw).
90. See Taylor, "Derrick Bell's Narratives." For Bell's appropriation of the myth of Sisyphus, see Bell, *Confronting Authority*, 161.
91. For elaborations of this thesis, see Taylor, "Racism as 'The Nation's Crucial Sin,'" 272–81.
92. See Williams, "Alchemical Notes," 64.
93. Bell, *Silent Covenants*, 26 (emphases added).
94. For considerations, independent of Bell, of the role of faith in the context of political legitimacy, see George H. Taylor, "Developing Ricoeur's Concept of Political Legitimacy: The Question of Political Faith," in *Paul Ricoeur and the Task of Political Philosophy*, eds. Dan Stiver and Greg Johnson (Lanham, MD: Lexington Books, 2012), 159–182.
95. Bell, "Racism's Religious Perspective," 12; "Howard Thurman," 15.
96. See Paul Ricoeur, *Lectures on Ideology and Utopia*, ed. George H. Taylor (New York: Columbia University Press, 1986).
97. George Lakoff and Mark Johnson, *Philosophy in the Flesh: The Embodied Mind and Its Challenge to Western Thought* (New York: Basic Books, 1999).
98. Ibid., 19. Lakoff and Johnson draw on the classic work in categorization by Eleanor Rosch. See, e.g., Eleanor Rosch and B.B. Lloyd, *Cognition and Categorization* (Hillsdale, NJ: Erlbaum, 1978).
99. For an elaboration, see George H. Taylor, "Approaches to Discrimination by Cognitive Theory," Law and Society Annual Meeting, Pittsburgh, June 2003.

100. Daniel Kahneman, *Thinking, Fast and Slow* (New York: Farrar, Straus and Giroux, 2011). In 2003, Kahneman won the Nobel Prize in Economics for his work on decision making with his late colleague Amos Tversky.

101. Kahneman, *Thinking, Fast and Slow*, 149.

102. David J. Herring, "Evolutionary Theory and Behavioral Biology Research: Implications for Law," in *Applied Evolutionary Psychology*, ed. S. Craig Roberts (Oxford, UK: Oxford University Press, 2012), 241.

103. Ibid., 244.

104. This theme is, of course, prominent, in the discrimination literature. See, e.g., Lu-in Wang, *Discrimination by Default: How Racism Becomes Routine* (New York: New York University Press, 2006); Richard Delgado and Jean Stefancic, "Images of the Outsider in American Law and Culture: Can Free Expression Remedy Systemic Social Ills?," *Cornell Law Review* 77 (1992): 1261 (criticizing as an "empathic fallacy" the belief "that we can enlarge our sympathies through linguistic means alone").

105. Bell, *Faces*, 157. A few lines further on the same page he adds: "About the least dire fate for a prophet is that one preaches, and no one listens; that one risks all to speak the truth, and nobody cares."

106. See Taylor, "Racism as 'The Nation's Crucial Sin,'" 301–305.

107. Bell, *Confronting Authority*.

108. Ibid., 109.

109. Ibid., 108 (describing his failure to convince other Harvard law faculty members to join his protest over the failure of the school to hire a woman of color onto the faculty, although several faculty offered personal support to Bell).

110. Bell, *Confronting Authority*, 130.

111. I witnessed and participated in such community organizing as a boycott organizer in Los Angeles for Cesar Chavez's United Farm Workers.

112. Bell, *Silent Covenants*, 134, 190.

113. Bell, "*Brown v. Board*," 17: "The interest-convergence theory should not remain a seeming fortuity we recognize only after the fact. . . . Recognition of our true status [as a permanent, subordinate class] will serve as gateway to an era where we forge fortuity."

114. Bell, *Silent Covenants*, 93.

Works Cited

Bell, Derrick. "Accepting Extinction: Will Christian Doctrine Prove Our Enemy Rather Than Our Salvation?," Braun Memorial Lecture Series, John Marshall Law School, Chicago, October 13, 2006 (on file with author).

———. *And We Are Not Saved: The Elusive Quest for Racial Justice*. New York:

Basic Books, 1987.

———. "*Brown v. Board*: What Are We Doing With What We Have Learned?," Cleveland-Marshall College of Law, Cleveland, October 9, 2003 (on file with author).

———. "*Brown v. Board of Education* and the Interest-Convergence Dilemma," *Harvard Law Review* 93 (1980): 518–533.

———. "Dissenting Opinion," in *What Brown v. Board of Education Should Have Said*, ed. Jack M. Balkin, 185–199. New York: New York University Press, 2001.

———. *Ethical Ambition: Living a Life of Meaning and Worth*. New York: Bloomsbury, 2002.

———. *Faces at the Bottom of the Well: The Permanence of Racism*. New York: Basic Books, 1992, 25.

———. *Gospel Choirs: Psalms of Survival in an Alien Land Called Home*. New York: Basic Books, 1997.

———. "Howard Thurman and the Christians as Racists Paradox," Howard Thurman Center, Stetson University, Gulfport, Florida, November 15, 2005 (on file with author).

———. "Martin Luther King, Jr. Was He a 20th Century Jesus?," Carnegie Mellon University, 2006 [December 29, 2005 draft].

———. "Racism as Ultimate Deception," The 11th Annual Derrick Bell Lecture, New York University School of Law, November 6, 2006, 4 (on file with author).

———. "Racism's Religious Perspective," Black Law Journal Anniversary Conference, November 18, 2005 (on file with author).

———. "Serving Two Masters: Integration Ideals and Client Interests in School Desegregation Litigation," *Yale Law Journal* 85 (1976): 470–516.

———. *Silent Covenants*: Brown v. Board of Education *and the Unfulfilled Hopes for Racial Reform*. New York: Oxford University Press, 2004.

———. "Who's Afraid of Critical Race Theory?," *University of Illinois Law Review* (1995): 893–910.

Bell, Derrick, and Preeta Bansal. "The Republican Revival and Racial Politics," *Yale Law Journal* 97 (1988): 1609–1621.

Bible.

———. Colossians 3:22–24

———. 1 Corinthians 7:20–21, 24.

———. Galatians 3:23–28.

———. 1 Timothy 6:1–2.

———. Titus 2:9–10.

Bork, Robert. *The Tempting of America: The Political Seduction of the Law*. New York: Free Press, 1990.

Brown v. Board of Education, 347 U.S. 483 (1954).

Burns, Stewart. *To the Mountaintop: Martin Luther King Jr.'s Mission to Save America 1955–1968*. San Francisco: Harper San Francisco, 2004.

Chappell, David A. *A Stone of Hope: Prophetic Religion and the Death of Jim Crow.* Chapel Hill: University of North Carolina Press, 2004.

Davis, David Brion. *Inhuman Bondage: The Rise and Fall of Slavery in the New World.* New York: Oxford University Press, 2006.

Delgado, Richard and Stefancic, Jean. "Images of the Outsider in American Law and Culture: Can Free Expression Remedy Systemic Social Ills?," *Cornell Law Review* 77 (1992): 1258–1291.

Goldenberg, David M. *The Curse of Ham: Race and Slavery in Early Judaism, Christianity, and Islam.* Princeton, NJ: Princeton University Press, 2003.

Harris, Angela P. "Foreword: The Jurisprudence of Reconstruction," *California Law Review* 82 (1994): 741–785.

Harris, Cheryl I. "Whiteness as Property," *Harvard Law Review* 106 (1993): 1707–1791.

Harvey, Paul. *Freedom's Crossing: Religious Culture and the Shaping of the South from the Civil War Through the Civil Rights Era.* Chapel Hill: University of North Carolina Press, 2005.

Haynes, Stephen R. *Noah's Curse: The Biblical Justification of American Slavery.* New York: Oxford University Press, 2002.

Herring, David J. "Evolutionary Theory and Behavioral Biology Research: Implications for Law," in *Applied Evolutionary Psychology*, ed. S. Craig Roberts, 239–256. Oxford, UK: Oxford University Press, 2012.

Kahneman, Daniel. *Thinking, Fast and Slow.* New York: Farrar, Straus and Giroux, 2011.

Kazantzakis, Nikos. *The Last Temptation of Christ.* New York: Bantam Books, 1961.

Kelsey, George D. *Racism and the Christian Understanding of Man.* New York: Charles Scribner's Sons, 1965.

Lakoff, George, and Johnson, Mark. *Philosophy in the Flesh: The Embodied Mind and Its Challenge to Western Thought.* New York: Basic Books, 1999.

Noonan, John T., Jr. *A Church That Can and Cannot Change: The Development of Catholic Moral Teaching.* South Bend, IN: University of Notre Dame Press, 2005.

Plessy v. Ferguson, 163 U.S. 537 (1896).

Ricoeur, Paul. *Lectures on Ideology and Utopia*, edited by George H. Taylor. New York: Columbia University Press, 1986.

Rosch, Eleanor, and Lloyd, B.B. *Cognition and Categorization.* Hillsdale, NJ: Erlbaum, 1978.

Taylor, George H. "Approaches to Discrimination by Cognitive Theory," Law and Society Annual Meeting, Pittsburgh, June 2003.

———. "The Challenge of Derrick Bell: Civil Rights from Movement to Organization and from Movement to Law," Center on Race and Social Problems, University of Pittsburgh, Pittsburgh, Pennsylvania, March 25, 2009.

———. "Derrick Bell's Narratives as Parables," *New York University Review of Law & Social Change* 31 (2007): 225–271.

———. "Developing Ricoeur's Concept of Political Legitimacy: The Question of Political Faith," in *Paul Ricoeur and the Task of Political Philosophy*, ed. Dan Stiver and Greg Johnson, 159–182. Lanham, MD: Lexington Books, 2012.

———. "Race, Religion, and Law: The Tension Between Spirit and Its Institutionalization," *University of Maryland Law Journal of Race, Religion, Gender and Class* 6 (2006): 51–67.

———. "Racism as 'The Nation's Crucial Sin': Theology and Derrick Bell," *Michigan Journal of Race & Law* 9 (2004): 269–322.

Thurman, Howard. *Jesus and the Disinherited*. Nashville, TN: Abingdon Press, 1949.

———. "The Task of the Negro Ministry," in *A Strange Freedom: The Best of Howard Thurman on Religious Experience and Public Life*, ed. Walter Earl Fluker and Catherine Tumber. Boston: Beacon Press, 1998.

———. *With Head and Heart: The Autobiography of Howard Thurman*. San Diego, CA: Harcourt Brace & Co., 1979.

Tushnet, Mark. "The Critique of Rights," *Southern Methodist University Law Review* 47 (1993): 23–34.

Wang, Lu-in *Discrimination by Default: How Racism Becomes Routine*. New York: New York University Press, 2006.

Williams, Patricia J. "Alchemical Notes: Reconstructing Ideals from Deconstructed Rights," *Harvard Civil Rights—Civil Liberties Law Review* 22 (1987): 401–433.

———. *The Alchemy of Race and Rights: Diary of a Law Professor*. Cambridge, MA: Harvard University Press, 1991.

Chapter 2

Derrick Bell and the "Negro Problem"

BILL E. LAWSON

Derrick Bell is well known for his position that racism in the United States is a permanent social and political feature of American life. The goal of this essay is to situate Bell's understanding of the permanence of racism within the historical context of the United States' grappling with what became known as the "Negro Problem." That is, I want to connect Bell's position with America's struggle with one of its most pressing problems: what to do with the Negro?[1] I contend that Bell's position can be read as a response to how he thinks America has tried to resolve the "Negro Problem" and why that attempt has created the conditions for the permanence of racism. Some people will object to my use of the term "Negro," but I contend that the use of the term "Negro Problem" helps to historically situate and to *explicate* the issues of anti-black racism in the United States. The use of the term will also be helpful to understand public policy ramifications for the time period after the Civil War—a period that historian Rayford Logan calls the nadir,[2] those years after Reconstruction that saw the imposition of Jim Crow Laws and practices all across the United States. It was during this historical period that the United States grappled with the "Negro Problem." I contend that Bell's thesis of Racial Realism raises serious problems for our understanding and implementing programs of social equality when it is viewed in light of the historical "Negro Problem" in America. This essay has four sections: the "Negro

Problem," Derrick Bell and the "Long Shadow of *Plessy*," Bell on Myrdal's *Dilemma*, and Bell, Equality, and Struggle. In order to appreciate Bell's position one must first understand and appreciate the "Negro Problem."

I. The "Negro Problem"

The phrase "Negro Problem," according to James Hollandsworth,[3] first appeared in print in a book published in 1864 by Hollis Read, titled *The Negro Problem Solved, or, Africa as She Was, as She Is and as She Shall Be: Her Curse and Her Cure*.[4] Read argues that black people should be sent to Africa to solve the "Negro Problem" in the United States. Hollandsworth notes: "As it turned out, his solution was wildly impracticable, and the 'War Amendments' to the Constitution (Thirteenth, Fourteenth, and Fifteenth), which enfranchised former slaves and ensured their rights as citizens, made the question of what to do with them moot during Reconstruction."[5] It would have been politically and socially problematic to try to deport U.S. citizens to Africa, even citizens who were unwanted.

Still, after the Civil War ended, the U.S. government had, at least, two major social problems: First, what should be the new relationship with the states that had been in rebellion?[6] Second, what should be done with the Negro? The federal government's problem of the relationship with its Southern brothers was resolved with the Hayes-Tilden Compromise of 1877. The presidential election of 1876 gave Democratic candidate Samuel Tilden a popular-vote margin of 250,000 votes, and the preliminary Electoral College vote showed that Tilden would beat Hayes. However, the ballots of four states—Florida, Louisiana, South Carolina, and Oregon—were contested. At stake were twenty electoral votes. Tilden needed only one vote, while Hayes needed all twenty. Because of charges of voter fraud, South Carolina, Florida, and Louisiana submitted two sets of election returns, each with different totals. The second set favored Hayes, and his aides met with moderate Southern Democrats in the congressional electoral commission, convincing them to block the official counting of the first set of votes, with a promise, among other things, to withdraw Union troops from Southern states, allowing Hayes to win. Hayes ordered federal troops out of Louisiana and South Carolina, effectively ending Reconstruction. This compromise peacefully resolved some of the political tensions of the day between the North and South. In essence, the nation's Southern white brothers were welcomed back into the Union. This resolved the problem of national reunification, but it gave the fate of Southern black people back to their former oppressors. While the compromise resolved national political tensions, the relationship between black people and the reconstituted Union was much more contentious.

As it became clear that the North would win the Civil War, what to do with the Negro became a major concern. Historian Rayford Logan writes: "The problem of determining the place that Negroes should occupy in American life was the most difficult of the 'racist' problems that confronted the American government and white people after the Civil War."[7] The problem was intensified by the inclusion of black people as citizens and thus, formally, equal in social and political status to whites. The fact that black people were formally recognized as U.S. citizens did nothing to remove or undo the years of racial animus that had been used to justify the enslavement of black people. Indeed, at the end of the Civil War, a large segment of the white population nationwide believed in the natural inferiority of black people.[8] As such, being inferior, black people neither deserved nor would ever merit citizenship. What should be done with this woeful group? This view of black people, as unfit to be citizens, shaped the "Negro Problem."

Many whites, across the nation, thought the answer was clear. Black people and whites given their physical, emotional, and intellectual differences, with the edge going to whites, would never be able to live together peacefully in the United States. In 1874, H.H. Goodloe wrote an article, "The Negro Problem," that was pessimistic about the future of race relations.[9] Hollandsworth notes:

> According to Goodloe, the problem went beyond the usual struggle between labor and management; it encompassed the most basic feelings of revulsion and rejection. "That antagonism exists between the two races in their relations to each other, and in form and degree different and greater than that usually recognized as between capital and labor is so plainly observable," Goodloe wrote, "that we have only to open our eyes to existing and constantly recurring facts to be convinced [of] its truth."[10]

This assessment of race relations raises at least two questions: what was it about black people, particularly those who had been enslaved, that caused such racial animus, and what should be done with them if they could not be deported? The answers would set the framing of public policy for dealing with issues of race for decades to come. I will address these questions in turn.

What was it about black people that caused so much racial friction? Frederick Douglass noted a number of times, before his death, that there was no "Negro Problem." For Douglass, there was a race problem. In 1871, he realized that without some form of affirmative action, qualified black people would not find employment. In 1888, he questioned the value of the Emancipation Proclamation. In 1890, he addressed the race problem and noted that it was not black people who were the problem, but white attitudes toward the rights of black citizens. In 1894, a year before his death, he again addressed the problem of black people being upright citizens when national, state, and local governments did nothing to protect the rights of black people. For Douglass, it was the attitudes of whites toward black people that caused the race problem. He said whites had a negative attitude toward black people that permeated all racial interactions.

What is the origin of negative white attitudes toward black people, particularly those who were descendants of enslaved Africans? In 1909, Quincy Ewing wrote an article, "The Heart of the Race Problem," to answer the question of what exactly is the "Negro Problem."

> If we listen vainly for the heart-throb of the race problem in the Negro's laziness, and criminality, and brutality, and ignorance, and inefficiency, do we detect it with clearness and certainty in the personal aversion felt by the white people for the black people, aversion which the white people can no more help feeling than the black people can help exciting? Is this the real trouble, the real burden, the real tragedy and sorrow of our white population in those sections of the country where the Negroes are many—that they are compelled to dwell, face-to-face, day by day, with an inferior, degraded population, repulsive to their finer sensibilities, obnoxious to them in countless ways inexplicable? Facts are far from furnishing an affirmative answer.[11]

Ewing argues that claims of laziness, criminality, brutality, ignorance, or inefficiency cannot be the cause of the "Negro Problem." He thinks these unsupported claims about black character cannot explain the attitudes of whites toward black people, that it goes much deeper into the white psyche. He writes—and some will find this disturbing:

> So much for what the race problem is not. Let me without further delay state what it is. The foundation of it, true or false, is the white man's conviction that the Negro as a race, and as an individual, is his inferior: not human in the sense that he is human, not entitled to the exercise of human rights in the sense that he is entitled to the exercise of them. The problem itself, the essence of it, the heart of it, is the white man's determination to make good this conviction, coupled with constant anxiety lest, by some means, he should fail to make it good. The race problem, in other words, is not that the Negro is what he is in relation to the white man, the white man's inferior; but this, rather: How to keep him what he is in relation to the white man; how to prevent his ever achieving or becoming that which would justify the belief on his part, or on the part of other people, that he and the white man stand on common human ground.[12]

Ewing continues that if one views race relations in the South through the inferiority lens, one will see that as long as black people do nothing to upset the white person's sense of superiority, there is no "Negro Problem." For Ewing, whites, it appears, think that black people are not their social or political equals and want to keep the system structure to maintain that social and political distinction. Ewing concludes by noting:

> In the mean time, nothing could be more unwarranted than to suppose that the race problem of one section of this country is peculiar to that section because its white inhabitants are themselves in some sense peculiar because they are peculiarly prejudiced, because they are peculiarly behind the hour which the high clock of civilization has struck. Remove the white inhabitants of the South, give their place to the white people of any other section of the United States, and, beyond a peradventure, the Southern race problem, as I have defined it, would continue to be—revealed, perhaps, in ways more perplexing, more intense and tragic.[13]

Whites across the United States believed in the inferiority of black people, and this belief was not limited to the American South. It was a national phenomenon. This claim that black people were viewed as inferior can be verified if you look at the legal and social practices that were enforced on black people before and after the Hayes-Tilden Compromise. A. Leon Higginbotham argues that there were, at least, ten legal precepts that guided jurisprudence regarding black people. The most enduring precept was the precept of inferiority. Higginbotham points out that:

> the truth was that our nation was founded explicitly, prospered implicitly, and still often lives uneasily on the precept of black inferiority and white superiority. Indeed, that precept helped to legitimize slavery in America and served to justify the segregation of African Americans in this nation long after slavery had been abolished. To this day, the premise of black inferiority and white superiority remains an essential element of the American identity, mesmerized as we still are by race and color.[14]

A quick review of the history of race relations before and during the nadir shows how important the precept of black people's inferiority has been to the understanding of their status as citizens.

Ladelle McWhorter discusses the origins of racism and black inferiority in the United States, particularly the move from race as lineage to race as biology. Wealthy planters realized they could exploit the physical differences between white and black laborers. Changes in the treatment of white workers that benefited their whiteness increase the social distance between white and black workers. By the mid-1700s, laws and social practices had drawn a discordant line between black and white laborers through the use of biological race.

Colonial governments thus deliberately established morphological race as a civil concept that was contrary to tradition and legal precedent. Over the course of the eighteenth century, race, now a form of embodiment, became a form of subjectivity—of citizenship, of social status, and finally of personal identity. By Thomas Jefferson's day, race was no longer a matter of lineage or culture, but was first and foremost a matter of morphology—skin color, hair texture, facial structure, and so on—along with the internal physiology that was thought to accompany such variations, including increased or decreased capacity for rational thought. What had once been a political scheme had become, within sixty years, a kind of common sense. Law and policy in the new United States would thus be based on the assumption that racial subjectivity is real, that members of nonwhite races are incapable of exercising the responsibilities of full citizenship in a free republic, and that lifelong servitude is appropriate for some races and inappropriate for others.[15]

At the end of the Civil War, the belief that black people were racially "other" was a common-sense notion among many or most whites. All of these laws and social practices, of that period, had as their aim to reinforce the view that black people were inferior to whites. Accordingly, Chief Justice Roger Taney had expressed in the *Dred Scott* decision what many whites believed:

> We think they [people of African ancestry] are . . . not included, and were not intended to be included, under the word "citizens" in the Constitution, and can therefore claim none of the rights and privileges which that instrument provides for and secures to citizens of the United States.

The North's victory in the Civil War and the "War Amendments" can be seen as pushback on this position of the inferiority and social status of black people. However, the end of Reconstruction and the reunification of the country came with a vicious shift against the rights and protections of black Americans. While Logan calls the years between 1877 and 1921 the "nadir" I would extend that period to 1954, at a minimum.[16] The period between 1877 and 1954 saw the full-court press against civil rights through a concerted effort to reinforce the inferior status of black people. Note that the nation became more racially segregated during this period after the Hayes-Tilden Compromise with the enforcement of Jim Crow laws, government-sanctioned segregation, sundown towns, lack of political protection, and racial violence against blacks through lynching.[17] Not only was the legal and political system structured to reinforce the concept of inferiority in regard to black people, but a system of social etiquette also was formed. In both the North and South, social practices and customs were in place to foster the perception that black people were not on the same social and political levels as whites. In the North, black people were crowded into areas that became known as ghettos, and jobs and educational opportunities were limited. In the South, interpersonal interactions were circumscribed by race, with public water fountains segregated and labeled "Colored" and "White" being one clear example. The "Colored" fountains always were lower than the "White" fountains. As with slavery, there was a need to reinforce that black people were naturally inferior to justify harsh and racist treatment of them. To this end, as Juliann Sivulka notes in *Stronger than Dirt: A Cultural History of Advertising Personal Hygiene in America, 1875–1940*, science took over:

> Various "scientific" studies reinforced the image of African Americans as less than human. Evolutionary science fitted African American bodies into new classifications of inferiority based on facial angles and physiognomic measurements. Most social scientists during the late nineteenth and early twentieth centuries believed African Americans to be inferior to white Americans; for some, measures of intelligence did not adequately describe the differences. Earlier psychological studies argued that African Americans had stronger emotions, greater volatility, and defective morals. Images of exaggerated racial differences circulated throughout American culture as emblems of this new "scientific" basis for perpetuating racist stereotypes intertwined.[18]

To reinforce the science, black people were portrayed in the movies[19] and on stage as buffoons, mammies, tragic mulattoes, bucks, and coons.[20] The news media, white academic institutions, and many white scholars made the inferiority of black people a major topic of study. All of the supposed evidence was meant to justify treating black people like second-class citizens. What should society do with this supposedly woeful group?

In the 1880s, while the race scientists and white social scientists debated what had become known as the "Negro Problem," I contend that national, state, and local governments put a resolution of the "Negro Problem" into play. The best way to resolve the "Negro Problem" was to isolate the Negro. In the years between 1877 and 1954, national, local, and state governments did everything possible to physically segregate the races. During this period, the nation saw, as noted earlier, the development of sundown towns and neighborhoods, restricted housing covenants, racial zoning, and gerrymandering—all put in place to segregate black people from whites. By the time of the *Brown v. Board* decision in 1954, racial segregation was a de facto law of the land nationwide.

The isolation of black people took place by using the sciences—physical and social—to explain the biological and social differences between the races. One of the more pernicious means of isolating black people was to cast them as criminal by nature. Khalil Gibran Muhammad, at the beginning of his book *The Condemnation of Blackness*, writes:

The link between race and crime is as enduring and influential in the 21st century as it has been in the past. Violent crime rates in the nation's biggest cities are generally understood as a reflection of the presence and behavior of black men, women, and children who live there. The US prison population is larger than at any time in the history of the penitentiary anywhere in the world. Nearly half of the more than 2 million Americans behind bars are African Americans, and an unprecedented number of black men likely will go to prison during the course of their lives. These grim statistics are well known and frequently cited by white and black Americans; indeed, for many, they define black humanity. In all manner of conversations about race—from debates about parenting to education to urban life—black crime statistics are ubiquitous. By the same token, white crime statistics are virtually invisible, except when used to dramatize the excessive criminality of African Americans. Although the statistical language of black criminality often means different things to different people, it is the glue that binds race to crime today, as in the past.[21]

Muhammad notes that racial crime statistics were used to justify public policies connected to the "Negro Problem." To put it another way, between 1890 and 1940, how and why did racial crime statistics become what Ted Porter calls a "strategy of communication"—a subject of dialogue and debate—about blacks' "fitness for modern life?"[22] Negative attributes ascribed to black people were needed to justify the racist treatment of black people.

All of this negative propaganda was done to vilify black people. The constant barrage of negative statistics and news stories had the impact of socially isolating black people from whites. In turn, whites did everything in their power to avoid contact with black people whenever possible. Housing, jobs, schools, graveyards, and churches were segregated to further isolate black people. The principal catalyst was the belief in the inferiority of black people and the reinforcement of that belief. Thus, the nation's goal was to protect whites from contamination by black people, who were being marked as racially "other." Mary Poole, in her book *The Segregated Origins of Social Security: African Americans and the Welfare State*, explains how the language of the times represented the manner in which the socially contingent phenomenon of racial stratification had taken hold in the minds of Americans, both black and white.

As is still true in the United States, the language of race made real/natural what had been invented; "white" and "Negro" were understood to refer to two essentially different types of humans, and as those words were spoken, they created the reality to which they referred. The language of race is problematic, always, because it embodies and therefore reproduces inequality. In the 1930s, "white" was used universally to describe the majority of U.S. citizens. "White" was not strictly a racial category, like "Anglo-Saxon" or "Caucasian"; it specifically identified Americans of European descent who claimed to have no African heritage. The one-drop rule did not apply to other races. A white person could have a Cherokee or Mexican great-grandmother without losing whiteness, but even the most remote ancestral ties to the African continent would disqualify an individual from being classified as "white." Even more than "Negro," "white" was used, as it had been for centuries, to create a false homogeneity out of a diversity of origins and cultures for no other purpose than to artificially enhance the value of certain people and property. In America, people of African descent have continuously struggled to define themselves with a word because words, like "colored" and "Negro," come to absorb the racist stereotypes of a time and place and must be replaced with others. But "white" has never needed to be replaced because the word continues to confer privilege on those it defines.[23]

To be white means that you are a full human being. There is nothing else that needs to be added to that nomenclature. The United States has reinforced the view of the purity and humanity of whites via law and social practices. While most Americans think about the role of whiteness, as a form of humanity status in the South, the North was not without its problems. Sylvia Hood Washington, in her fascinating study *Packing Them In: An Archaeology of Environmental Racism in Chicago, 1865–1954*, examines the manner in which black people were marginalized as "other:"

> The twentieth century's Jim Crow laws, restrictive covenants, racial zoning ordinances, and immigration restriction policies are examples of this type of construction and environmental discipline. These groups identified as "others" were, and still are, forced to live in geographical spaces (communities) within the society that are or are becoming environmentally compromised because of their "otherness." Their communities become dumping grounds where waste and toxic material are disproportionately located; apparently, they are the proper

place for everything deemed to be undesirable (people and waste). These communities become the ultimate sink for the larger body politic. Historically, "normal and healthy" people did not choose to live in the geographical locations of the leper colony. They sought to maximize the distance between themselves and the lepers. Similarly, leper colonies were not given the same care and maintenance provided to non-leper colonies. I believe this phenomenon holds true for both social and political lepers; an environmental history of these groups will validate that assumption.[24]

It is clear that during this period the laws that were enacted helped create and reinforce the concept of race, particularly an inferior black race.[25] Social practices and mores reflected and supported the position of the inferiority of black people. In the South, whites attempted to make the relationship between black and white people as close to that of slavery as it could be. All across the United States, rules of racial etiquette were created or re-coded to segregate and isolate black people.

As bad as it was dealing with state and local racism, the Supreme Court, in its *Plessy v. Ferguson* decision, made it national law that the races could and should be separated, that is, whites could discriminate against black people, and it was not a sign of racial inferiority. Lerone Bennett writes:

> In the infamous case of *Plessy v. Ferguson*, the Court said state laws requiring "separate but equal" accommodations for blacks were a "reasonable" use of state police powers, adding: "The object of the [Fourteenth] Amendment was undoubtedly to enforce the absolute equality of the two races before the law, but in the nature of things, it could not have been intended to abolish distinctions based on color, or to enforce social, as distinguished from political, equality, or a commingling of the two races upon terms unsatisfactory to either."[26]

Whites took the decision in *Plessy* to heart, and separate spaces soon appeared all across the country. As Derrick Bell so poignantly points out:

> Segregation laws were widespread in the dozen or so years before the *Plessy* decision. Now, with the Court's implicit

approval, the first decade of the 20th century witnessed the enactment of a wide variety of segregation statutes. No detail seemed too small as laws required segregation at work, at play, and at home. Public schools were always separate and almost always vastly unequal. Public conveyances, eating and hotel facilities, bathrooms, water fountains, prisons, cemeteries, parks, and sporting and entertainment events were all covered. New Orleans even deemed it in its public interest to enact an ordinance separating Negro and white prostitutes.[27]

The United States had worked to resolve the "Negro Problem." It had segregated and isolated black people. By 1954, many whites and some black people thought the "Negro Problem" had been resolved.[28] The reason it was not a *fait accompli* was the dogged strength and determination of black people not to become the radically racial "other" in the land of their birth. Nonetheless, the state—the United States—had nearly succeeded in isolating and segregating black people. It did, however, entirely succeed in casting a spell of racial inferiority about the status of black people, who were descendants of American chattel slavery, across the United States.[29]

II. Derrick Bell and the "Long Shadow of *Plessy*"

The first chapter in Derrick Bell's *Silent Covenants* is titled "The Long Shadow of *Plessy*." It is the shortest chapter of the book, and because most people think they understand Bell's position, it is possibly the least studied. The above discussion is meant to fill out what Bell very succinctly presents in the chapter. Bell deals with this history in a mere four pages, starting:

> The Supreme Court's 1896 decision in *Plessy v. Ferguson* served to bring the law into a dismal harmony with the nation's view of race in life. The Court decided that segregation in public facilities through "separate but equal" accommodations for black citizens would satisfy the equal protection clause in the Fourteenth Amendment.[30]

This created two worlds in which the races only minimally had social contact. Bell notes that John Hope Franklin reported that the "separation bred suspicion and hatred, fostered rumors and misunderstandings, and created conditions that made any steps toward its reduction extremely difficult."[31] The segregation was so complete that almost every aspect of life was covered by separatist policies.[32] Segregation was not just a Southern policy:

> Public acceptance went beyond the South to encompass hundreds of communities across the nation. It grew by means of practices police were ready to enforce. The purpose of these policies was not simply to exclude or segregate, but to subordinate those who, based on their color and without regard to their accomplishments, were presumed to be inferior to any white person no matter how low or ignorant.[33]

It was preservation of the view that black people were inferior that guided most of the public policies of the period between 1877 and 1954. One sad consequence of this segregation and isolation was the contempt it established in the minds of many whites about the place of and nature of black people. The social condition of black people left them unable to do what was necessary to be successful in this country. Social customs, laws, and the constant barrage of negative media and scientific research, coupled with social segregation and intellectual isolation, stifled any feelings of fellowship that one would expect citizens of a state to feel for each other. Bell expands on this:

> Few whites are able to identify with blacks as a group—the essential prerequisite for feeling empathy with, rather than aversion from, blacks' self-inflicted suffering . . . Unable or unwilling to perceive that "there but for the grace of God, go I," few whites are ready to actively promote civil rights for blacks. Because of an irrational but easily roused fear that any social reform will unjustly benefit blacks, whites fail to support the programs this country desperately needs to address the ever-widening gap between the rich and the poor, both black and white.[34]

By 1897, it was a commonly held conclusion by many white Americans that the race problem had been resolved. In 1903, W.E.B. Du Bois published his classic text *The Souls of Black Folks*, in which he asks the pertinent question: What does it feel like to be a problem? Du Bois understands by this time that appeals to the social sciences would not resolve the "Negro Problem." As James Hackney Jr. notes:

> Transformation of both social policy and spirit would be required to solve the problem. Even in the conclusion of *Souls*, Du Bois acknowledged that our "sociological knowledge" of the race issue is "woefully unorganized" (1969[1903], 275). However, no amount of science would suffice if white America did not recognize the darker other. In Du Bois, we get a sense of deep fatalism.[35]

One hundred years later, Bell is much more pessimistic. Bell thinks that the white reaction to the *Brown* decision indicates the depth of white enmity toward blacks that had been 335 years in the making. The larger white public response to the *Brown* decision seems to illustrate how little the government's resolution of the "Negro Problem" accomplished in terms of white acceptance. With the Supreme Court's mandate to integrate public schools, whites withdrew their children and moved to the suburbs or sent their children to private all-white schools. With their departure went the primary reason for racial-balance remedies.[36] Whites fled the cities, so did jobs, and the tax base of the cities decreased, which caused a drop in public services, leading to poverty and spatial decay. *Brown II* in 1955 did not help either; it reversed the seeming gains from the year before. Whites would do whatever was legally and socially necessary to segregate and isolate themselves from black people.

It is interesting that despite all of this political and social maneuvering to segregate and isolate black people, the idea that with time and changes in black people's behavior, whites would come to accept black people as their social equals remains constant. In this context, racism is a social anomaly, and America is trying to work it out. At this point, *An American Dilemma*, by Gunnar Myrdal, enters into the discussion of the "Negro Problem."

III. Bell on Myrdal's *Dilemma*

It should be noted that we often forget that Myrdal's work on the American race problem was published not even sixty years ago.[37] The title of the book is telling and problematic: *An American Dilemma: The "Negro Problem" and Modern Democracy*.[38] According to Myrdal, the problem was a failure of democratic ideas being applied to the formerly enslaved. Racial equality would come with time. Bell notes that Myrdal's reasoning was flawed.

According to Myrdal, the "Negro Problem" in America represents a moral lag in the development of the nation, and a study of it must record nearly everything which is bad and wrong in America. "However, . . . not since Reconstruction has there been more reason to anticipate fundamental changes in American race relations, changes which will involve a development toward the American ideals."[39]

Seventy years after the end of Reconstruction, the "Negro Problem" was still a problem. Bell thinks that over the history of this country, there has been a racial code among whites, and the glue that holds this coalition together is the belief that black people will always be inferior to whites and that it is the duty of whites to ensure that this woeful status of blacks remains intact.[40]

This "racial bonding" by whites means that black rights and interests are always vulnerable to diminishment if not to outright destruction. The willingness of whites over time to respond to this racial rallying cry explains far more than does the failure of liberal democratic practices (re: black rights) to coincide with liberal democratic theory—blacks' continuing subordinate status. This is, of course, contrary to the philosophy of Gunnar Myrdal's massive midcentury study *The American Dilemma*. Myrdal and two generations of civil rights advocates accepted the idea of racism as merely an odious holdover from slavery, "a terrible and inexplicable anomaly stuck in the middle of our liberal democratic ethos." No one doubted that the standard American policymaking was adequate to the task of abolishing racism. White America, it was assumed, wanted to abolish racism.[41]

Bell, then, references the work of Professor Jennifer Hochschild. Her work *The New American Dilemma* examined what she called Myrdal's "anomaly thesis" and concluded that it cannot explain the persistence of racial discrimination: "Racism is a part of what shapes and energizes the body."[42] Accordingly, Bell continues referencing Hochschild:

> Under this view, "liberal democracy and racism in the United States are historically, even inherently, reinforcing; American society as we know it exists only because of its foundation in racially based slavery, and it thrives only because racial discrimination continues. The apparent anomaly is an actual symbiosis."[43]

Bell then gives his clearest statement on the status of black people:

> The permanence of this "symbiosis" ensures that civil rights gains will be temporary and setbacks inevitable. Consider: In this last decade of the twentieth century, color determines the social and economic status of all African Americans, both those who have been highly successful and their poverty-bound brethren whose lives are grounded in misery and despair. We rise and fall less as a result of our efforts than in response to the needs of a white society that condemns all blacks to quasi-citizenship as surely as it segregated our parents and enslaved their forebears. The fact is that, despite what we designate as progress wrought through struggle over many generations, we remain what we were in the beginning: a dark and foreign presence, always the designated "other." Tolerated in good times, despised when things go wrong, as a people, we are scapegoated and sacrificed as distraction or catalyst for compromise to facilitate resolution of political differences or relieve economic adversity.[44]

The combination of legal and social practices has created a society that is split racially when it comes to relationships between black people and white people in the United States. In the years between 1877 and 1954, the United States became a society in which the masses of black people were segregated and isolated from the masses of whites. In Southern states, where there were more black people, etiquettes of race relations developed that isolated and segregated black people from whites. The resolution of the "Negro Problem" was to segregate and isolate black people. Indeed, when one views the statistics of racial demographics regarding housing and neighborhood integration today, we still find that black people remain the most segregated and isolated group in the United States. Bell would contend that this is so because the ideology of racial inferiority infests practices that are meant to appear race-neutral. I contend that we should read Bell as both assessing how the United States has attempted to solve the "Negro Problem" and how the resolution of that problem depends on the maintenance of the view of black people's inferiority.[45] While the idea of black people's inferiority was always a constant refrain, the last 140 years saw a massive and concerted push to solidify the belief across the nation in the inferiority of black people. Black people know this and pass information along that will attempt to counter beliefs about the inferiority of blacks. One of the mantras of black people is that: "A black person has to be twice as good as a white person for the same position." Whites are not going to think any black person could be as good as any ordinary white person. If it is true that many or most whites think that blacks are inferior, what does it mean to push for social equality? Before black people can be seen as full citizens, they must be seen as fully human. The policies and social practices that have fostered a view of black people as inferior are deeply rooted in the moral fiber of the United States. If it is impossible to change the view of black people from inferiors to social and political equals, without substantial social and political structural change, then racism will be a permanent factor in American life.

The permanence of racism as an inferiority problem means that without deep structural and cognitive changes, the inferior status of blacks will not change. Bell's position is that the civil rights movement, and the new laws it has helped create, will not end racism because these actions do nothing to change the hearts and minds of men. As Martin Luther King Jr. wrote:

> It is not a question either of education or of legislation. Both legislation and education are required. Now people will say, "You can't legislate morals." Well, that may be true. Even though morality may not be legislated, behavior can be regulated. And this is very important. We need religion and education to change attitudes and to change the hearts of men. We need legislation and federal action to control behavior. It may be true that the law cannot make a man love me, but it can keep him from lynching me, and I think that is pretty important also.[46]

Legislation is important, but black people want to be treated as social equals. What exactly that means is unclear. One thing, nevertheless, is clear: to be social and human equals requires mutual regard and respect.

IV. Bell, Equality, and Struggle

Bell's claim about the permanence of racism raises a number of questions. Prominent among these, for the purposes of this chapter, are the questions: What does it mean to be human? What is the nature of social equality? What is the role of struggle in resisting racist oppression?

I want to focus, albeit too briefly, on the role of struggle and the quest for equality. Bell is a strong advocate of black people struggling to maintain their humanity in a racist society. At the same time, it cannot be a struggle for liberal equality. Scholars have found his position here troubling. Bernard Boxill[47] has produced possibly the best analysis of the problematic nature of Bell's position.

Boxill starts with Bell's claim: "Black people will never gain full equality in this country."[48] Essentially, Bell asserts that the legal and social conditions of the United States preclude any chance of black people achieving equality. We, therefore, should neither struggle, nor hope, for equality. Instead, we should struggle to maintain our humanity. The model for this struggle is the behavior of our slave ancestors. Boxill challenges Bell's contention that our slave ancestors did not struggle for equality. Boxill thinks that Bell's position creates a number of problems. First, if Bell claims that our ancestors did not strive for equality, he undermines his argument that equality is impossible. If he insists that equality is impossible because black people tried hard to get it, but failed, then he leaves open the possibility that they maintained their humanity because they hoped and strove for equality. Boxill shows that Bell's position is problematic no matter which angle he chooses.[49]

What should concern us here is the problem that neither Bell nor Boxill gives us any indication of what is meant by struggling for equality. Without some clear understanding of what is meant by equality, we have no real way of assessing Bell's claim. Of course, there will be those who claim that no matter how one defines equality, Bell's position fails. Let us consider that equality meant being seen in the same social and political light as a white person. This claim to equality is also vague. It cannot be that blacks wanted to be mistaken for whites, nor could it mean they wanted to be seen as just human. The move to be considered just human does not work. Blacks during slavery—and if the history I presented above is correct, after slavery—were viewed as not fully functioning human beings. Black people are/were considered permanently morally, socially, and intellectually disabled. They were humans, but not fully functioning humans with the ability to be full legal citizens. As Morgan Marietta notes:

> The issue is the nature of personhood: Who is a full person with all of the associated rights and who is not? Merely being a human as opposed to being a full legal person is not at all the same thing. This is a crucial concept in dealing with the

Constitution and the nature of rights. An important aspect of our legal tradition is that a person must have the capacity to understand and exercise all of their rights. One example of a human who is not a full legal person is someone of limited mental capacity. They have many rights, but not all of them.[50]

Black people have been consistently struggling for full human status, which many thought would mean full legal status.[51] I think that this was the position of Frederick Douglass. Once it was acknowledged that black people were fully human, they would be accorded all of the rights and privileges of citizenship. It is Bell's contention that neither of these things will happen. Here, however, is perhaps what Bell is after: if it is true that whites think that black people are naturally inferior, and that nothing can be done to make them view black people as their social equals, then racism is permanent. Bell thinks nothing can be done to remove the stench of inferiority, even through the granting of more legal rights. As he points out in *Silent Covenants*, the seeming gains on the legal front have not drastically changed how blacks collectively are viewed. In *Faces*, Bell notes:

> the fact of slavery refuses to fade, along with the deeply embedded personal attitudes and public policy assumptions that supported it for so long. Indeed, the racism that made slavery feasible is far from dead in the last decade of twentieth-century America; and the civil rights gains, so hard won, are being steadily eroded. Despite undeniable progress for many, no African Americans are insulated from incidents of racial discrimination. Our careers, even our lives, are threatened because of our color. Even the most successful of us are haunted by the plight of our less fortunate brethren who struggle for existence in what some social scientists call the "underclass." Burdened with life-long poverty and soul-devastating despair, they live beyond the pale of the American Dream. What we designate as "racial progress" is not a solution to that problem. It is a regeneration of the problem in a particularly perverse form.[52]

It is still clear that the success of one black person does not raise the status of the masses of black people. Someone might think that in an individualistic society, that is the way it should be. Each black person should then be concerned with his or her own advancement. However, well-off black people can never be sure that they will not be seen as part of the black masses. It is clear that successful black people understand that until the masses of black people are respected, their positions of status are suspect. If the masses of black people started to behave like it is thought they should behave, would there be a significant change in white attitudes toward blacks? I do not think so, and I think that this is consistent with Bell's view. It should be noted that there is nothing inconsistent with whites being okay with having black faces in high places and still thinking that the masses of black people are inferior, excluding the one before him or her.[53] The permanence of racism can be understood as the impossibility of removing the belief in the inferiority of black people from the intellectual core of the United States. No matter which view of social equality one takes, if it does not take into account the view that black people are seen as morally and socially inferior and attempts to change that view, the struggle for equality on any measure is doomed. King understood that the enforcement of laws could prevent further harsh treatment of black people, even if any new laws did not change how whites viewed black people.

In spite of screams of "over my dead body will any change come," one must not overlook the changes that have come to the South as a result of federal action. There are always those individuals who argue that legislation, court orders, and executive decrees from the federal government are ineffective because they cannot change the heart. They contend that you cannot legislate morals. It may be true that morality cannot be legislated, but behavior can be regulated. The law may not change the heart, but it can restrain the heartless. It will take education and religion to change bad internal attitudes, but legislation and court orders can control the external effects of bad internal attitudes. Federal court decrees have altered transportation patterns and changed educational mores. The habits, if not the hearts, of people have been, and are being, altered every day by federal action. These major social changes have a cumulative force conditioning other segments of life.[54]

We can only hope that these changes do have a cumulative effect on the morals, minds, and hearts of fellow citizens, and that Bell is wrong. However, if it is true that a motivating factor for the racial discrimination of black people who are descendants of slaves in the United States is the deeply held belief that they are naturally inferior and do not deserve the same respect and regard as whites, it is unclear how one can eradicate or transform this belief. As Bell recognized and argued, the legal system was and is complicit in the maintenance of this belief. As A. Leon Higginbotham notes:

> The precept of inferiority did not define any specific right or obligation. Instead, "inferiority" spoke to the state of the mind and the logic of the heart. It posed as an article of faith that African Americans were not quite altogether human. Furthermore, "inferiority" did not owe its existence to the legal process. Although the law came to enforce the precept, it did not create it. From the time the Africans first disembarked here in America, the colonists were prepared to regard them as inferior. When the Thirteenth Amendment abolished slavery and, presumably, all its attendant conditions, it did not eliminate the precept of inferiority. Even much later, when the law abolished state-enforced racial segregation, it still did not eliminate the precept.[55]

This state of affairs raises problematic questions about any future attempts for social equality. How does one group change the beliefs about their inherent negative worth within another group—a situation in which the views of black people have been fostered through processes meant to isolate and segregate them socially, emotionally, legally, politically, and spiritually from the members of the dominant racial group? In the United States, black people have been told that they must work to change the negative views whites have of them. Anna Julia Cooper writes: "a weak and despised people are called upon to vindicate their right to exist in the face of a race of hard, jealous, intolerant, all-subduing instincts."[56] There appears to be something amoral, I mean amiss, when the group that is oppressed in a liberal state has to prove that its members deserve mutual respect and regard. Drawing again from Higginbotham:

> When the majority of white Americans consider the history of this nation, they are apt to conclude that the blood of the Civil War washed clean the sins of slavery and that the marches of the civil rights movement erased the remaining vestiges of segregation and racial oppression. Others not given to excessive historical introspection believe—almost equally sincerely—that they personally have nothing whatever to do with slavery,

segregation, or racial oppression because neither they nor—as far as they know—their ancestors ever enslaved anyone, ever burned a cross in the night in front of anyone's house, or ever denied anyone a seat at the front of a bus. And so, between the self-absolving denial of the latter group and the self-congratulation—which is a deeper form of self-absolution—of the former, it becomes nearly impossible to have an honest discussion about what used to be called the "Negro Problem."[57]

I contend that Bell thought the United States, in trying to resolve the "Negro Problem," had reinforced the view of black people's inferiority. Bell was clear that not all whites think that black people are naturally inferior, but as his *Space Traders* short story illustrates, not enough of them exist to change the basic racist ideology of the system. In this regard, Bell argues that black people have to keep up the struggle to keep the country from completely segregating and isolating black people. If my argument is correct, Bell is looking at the nadir and sees the hardening of hearts against equality of any kind for black people. He is keenly aware that many people, both black and white, see the increasing number of black faces in high places as a sign of racial progress.[58]

It is a sign of progress that Bell thinks has to be measured against the standing of the larger mass of black people who are not able, because of systemic racist institutions, to move into these coveted slots. Is it possible that blacks will ever be seen as full members of the state? Possibility and probability are two different things.

Conclusion

If it is not true that there is a prevailing belief in the inferiority of black people, then the work that goes forward to enlighten those persons who stand in the way of black economic and social advancement is time well spent. However, we must keep this point in mind: this country has done everything to isolate and segregate black people from the dominant society by projecting a view of black people as inferior. The reason that the physical segregation and social isolation of black people has not been a *fait accompli* has been the strength and struggle of black and white people who worked hard to counter the creations of black Bantustans in the

United States. Black and white people have laid their bodies on the line to keep the door from closing on the "Negro Problem." This struggle, however, did not eradicate the view that black people are inferior, and it is the persistence of this view that makes racism in the United States permanent. This is the context in which I think Derrick Bell understood the struggle for black humanity. In part this is his attempt to respond to the country's attempt to resolve the "Negro Problem."

Notes

1. See, generally, W.E.B. Du Bois, *The Souls of Black Folks*.

2. Rayford W. Logan, *The Negro in American Life and Thought: The Nadir, 1877–1901* (New York:: Dial Press, 1954).

3. James G. Hollandsworth, *Portrait of a Scientific Racist: Alfred Holt Stone of Mississippi* (Baton Rouge: Louisiana State University Press, 2008), 6.

4. Hollis Read, *The Negro Problem Solved, or, Africa as She Was, as She Is and as She Shall Be: Her Curse and Her Cure* (New York:: A.A. Constantine, 1864).

5. Hollandsworth, *Portrait of a Scientific Racist*, 6.

6. C. Vann Woodward, *Reunion and Reaction: the Compromise of 1877 and the End of Reconstruction* (Oxford, UK: Oxford University Press, 1991).

7. Rayford W. Logan, *The Betrayal of the Negro, from Rutherford B. Hayes to Woodrow Wilson* (New York:: Collier Books, 1965), 3.

8. George M. Fredrickson, *The Black Image in the White Mind: The Debate on Afro-American Character and Destiny, 1817–1914* (New York:: Harper & Row, 1971).

9. Hollandsworth, *Portrait of a Scientific Racist*, 6.

10. Ibid., 6.

11. Quincy Ewing, "The Heart of the Race Problem," *Atlantic Monthly*, March 1909. www.theatlantic.com/past/docs/issues/09mar/ewing.htm

12. Ibid.

13. Ibid.

14. A. Leon Higginbotham, *Shades of Freedom: Racial Politics and Presumptions of the American Legal Process* (New York: Oxford University Press, 1996), 9.

15. Ladelle McWhorter, Racism and Sexual Oppression in Anglo-America: A Genealogy (Bloomington: Indiana University Press, 2009) 77.

16. Rayford W. Logan, *The Betrayal of the Negro: From Rutherford B. Hayes to Woodrow Wilson* (New York: Collier Books, 1965), xx, 62.

17. Manfred Berg, *Popular Justice: A History of Lynching in America* (Chicago: Ivan R. Dee, 2011).

18. Juliann Sivulka, *Stronger than Dirt: A Cultural History of Advertising Personal Hygiene in America, 1875–1940* (Amherst, MA: Humanity Books, 2001), 257.

19. *The Birth of a Nation*, directed by D.W. Griffith (1915), DVD.

20. Donald Bogle, *Toms, Coons, Mulattoes, Mammies, and Bucks: An Interpretive History of Blacks in American Films*, 4th ed. (New York: Bloomsbury, 2001).

21. Khalil Gibran Muhammad, *The Condemnation of Blackness: Race, Crime, and the Making of Modern Urban America* (Cambridge, MA: Harvard University Press, 2019), 1.

22. Ibid.

23. Mary Poole, *The Segregated Origins of Social Security: African Americans and the Welfare State* (Chapel Hill: North Carolina University Press, 2006) 155–166.

24. Sylvia Hood Washington, *Packing Them In: An Archaeology of Environmental Racism in Chicago, 1865–1954* (Lanham, MD: Lexington Books, 2005), 3.

25. Ian Haney-López, *White by Law: The Legal Construction of Race* (New York:: New York University Press, 1996).

26. Lerone Bennett, *Before the Mayflower: A History of Black America* (New York:: Penguin Books, 1993), 267.

27. Derrick Bell, *Silent Covenants: Brown v. Board of Education and the Unfulfilled Hopes for Racial Reform* (New York:: Oxford University Press, 2004), 12.

28. Derrick Bell, "Review: Meanness as Racial Ideology," *Michigan Law Review* 88.6 (May 1990).

29. Karen E. Fields and Barbara J. Fields, *Racecraft: The Soul of Inequality in American Life* (Brooklyn, NY: New Left, 2012).

30. Bell, *Silent Covenants*, 11.

31. Ibid.

32. Ibid., 12.

33. Ibid.

34. Derrick Bell, *Faces at the Bottom of the Well: The Permanence of Racism* (New York:: Basic Books, 1992), 4.

35. James R. Hackney Jr., "Review: Derrick Bell's Re-Sounding: W.E.B. Du Bois, Modernism, and Critical Race Scholarship," *Law & Social Inquiry*, Winter, 23, no. 1 (1998): 152.

36. Bell, *Silent Covenants*, 7.

37. Gunnar Myrdal, Richard Sterner, and Arnold Marshall Rose, *An American Dilemma* (New York: McGraw-Hill Book Company, 1964).

38. See, e.g., Ralph Ellison, *An American Dilemma: A Review, Teaching American History*, 1944. http://teachingamericanhistory.org/library/document/an-american-dilemma-a-review

39. Bell, *Faces*, 9.

40. Ellison, *An American Dilemma*.

41. Bell, *Faces*, 9.

42. Ibid., 10.

43. Ibid.
44. Ibid.
45. For a provocative and insightful reading of Bell and Myrdal, see Jon Thomas, "Bell's Curve: Why the Arc of American History Bends Toward Racial Inequality" (master's thesis, Georgia State University, 2015).
46. Martin Luther King Jr., *A Testament of Hope: The Essential Writings of Martin Luther King, Jr.*, ed. James M. Washington (San Francisco: Harper & Row, 1986), 213.
47. Bernard Boxill, "Bell on Brown" (reading, APA, Vancouver, BC, April 2009).
48. "Racism Is Here to Stay," *The Derrick Bell Reader*, ed. Richard Delgado and Jean Stefancic (New York: New York University Press, 2005) 85. Later in that essay he also stated that "a yearning for equality is fantasy," 90.
49. Boxill, "Bell on Brown," 3.
50. Morgan Marietta, *A Citizen's Guide to the Constitution and the Supreme Court: Constitutional Conflict in American Politics* (New York: Taylor and Francis, 2014), 243–247.
51. For a discussion of rights and recognition see, e.g., Derrick Darby, *Rights, Race, and Recognition* (Cambridge, UK: Cambridge University Press, 2009) and Bill E. Lawson, "Oppression and Slavery," in *Between Slavery and Freedom: Philosophy and American Slavery* (Bloomington: Indiana University Press, 1992).
52. Bell, *Faces*, 3.
53. Zora Neale Hurston and Alice Walker, "The 'Pet' Negro System," in *I Love Myself When I Am Laughing—and Then Again When I Am Looking Mean and Impressive: A Zora Neale Hurston Reader* (New York:: Feminist Press, 1979), 152–162.
54. Martin Luther King Jr., *A Testament of Hope: The Essential Writings of Martin Luther King, Jr.*, ed. James M. Washington (San Francisco: Harper & Row, 1986), 100–101.
55. Higginbotham, *Shades of Freedom*, 9.
56. Anna J. Cooper, "The Ethics of the Negro Question," in *The Voice of Anna Julia Cooper: Including A Voice from the South and Other Important Essays, Papers, and Letters*, eds. Charles Lemert and Esme Bhan (Lanham, MD: Rowman & Littlefield, 1998), 213–214.
57. Ibid., 8.
58. Leonard Steinhorn and Barbara Diggs-Brown, *By the Color of Our Skin: The Illusion of Integration and the Reality of Race* (New York:: Dutton, 1999).

Works Cited

Bell, Derrick. "Racism Is Here to Stay," *The Derrick Bell Reader*, ed. Richard Delgado and Jean Stefancic. New York: New York University Press, 2005.

———. "Review: Meanness as Racial Ideology," *Michigan Law Review* 88.6 (May 1990).

———. *Faces at the Bottom of the Well: The Permanence of Racism.* New York: Basic Books, 1992.

———. *Silent Covenants:* Brown v. Board of Education *and the Unfulfilled Hopes for Racial Reform.* New York: Oxford University Press, 2004.

Bennett, Lerone. *Before the Mayflower: A History of Black* America. New York: Penguin Books.

Berg, Manfred. *Popular Justice: A History of Lynching in America.* Chicago: Ivan R. Dee, 2011.

Bogle, Donald, and Toms, Coons. *Mulattoes, Mammies, and Bucks: An Interpretive History of Blacks in American Films*, 4th ed. New York: Bloomsbury, 2001.

Cooper, Anna J. "The Ethics of the Negro Question," in *The Voice of Anna Julia Cooper: Including A Voice from the South and Other Important Essays, Papers, and Letters*, ed. Charles Lemert and Esme Bhan. Lanham, MD: Rowman & Littlefield, 1998.

Darby, Derrick. *Rights, Race, and Recognition.* Cambridge, UK: Cambridge University Press, 2009.

Du Bois, W.E.B. "The Souls of Black Folk," in *Du Bois: Writings*. New York: Library of America, 1986. 357–547.

Ellison, Ralph. *An American Dilemma: A Review, Teaching American History*, 1944. http://teachingamericanhistory.org/library/document/an-american-dilemma-a-review

Ewing, Quincy. "The Heart of the Race Problem," *The Atlantic Monthly*, March 1909. www.theatlantic.com/past/docs/issues/09mar/ewing.htm

Fields, Karen E., and Barbara J. Fields. *Racecraft: The Soul of Inequality in American Life.* Brooklyn, NY: New Left, 2012.

Fredrickson, George M. *The Black Image in the White Mind: The Debate on Afro-American Character and Destiny, 1817–1914.* New York: Harper & Row, 1971.

Griffith, D.W. *The Birth of A Nation* [Film]. 1915.

Hackney, James R., Jr. "Review: Derrick Bell's Re-Sounding: W.E.B. Du Bois, Modernism, and Critical Race Scholarship," *Law & Social Inquiry* 23.1 (Winter 1998): 152.

Haney-López, Ian. *White by Law: The Legal Construction of Race.* New York: New York University Press, 1996.

Higginbotham, A. Leon. *Shades of Freedom: Racial Politics and Presumptions of the American Legal Process.* New York: Oxford University Press, 1996.

Hollandsworth, James G. *Portrait of a Scientific Racist: Alfred Holt Stone of Mississippi.* Baton Rouge: Louisiana State University Press, 2008.

Hurston, Zora Neale, and Walker, Alice. "The 'Pet' Negro System," in *I Love Myself When I Am Laughing—and Then Again When I Am Looking Mean and Impressive: A Zora Neale Hurston Reader.* New York: Feminist Press, 1979.

King Jr., Martin Luther. *A Testament of Hope: The Essential Writings of Martin Luther King, Jr.*, edited by James M. Washington. San Francisco: Harper & Row, 1986.

Lawson, Bill E. "Oppression and Slavery," in *Between Slavery and Freedom: Philosophy and American Slavery*. Bloomington: Indiana University Press, 1992.

Logan, Rayford W. *The Betrayal of the Negro, from Rutherford B. Hayes to Woodrow Wilson*. New York: Collier Books, 1965.

———. *The Negro in American Life and Thought: The Nadir, 1877–1901*. New York: Dial Press, 1954.

Marietta, Morgan. *A Citizen's Guide to the Constitution and the Supreme Court: Constitutional Conflict in American Politics*. New York: Taylor and Francis, 2014.

McWhorter, Ladelle. *Racism and Sexual Oppression in Anglo-America: A Genealogy*. Bloomington: Indiana University Press, 2009.

Muhammad, Khalil Gibran. *The Condemnation of Blackness: Race, Crime, and the Making of Modern Urban America*. Cambridge, MA: Harvard University Press, 2019.

Myrdal, Gunnar, Richard Sterner, and Arnold Marshall Rose. *An American Dilemma*. New York: McGraw-Hill Book Company, 1964.

Poole, Mary. *The Segregated Origins of Social Security: African Americans and the Welfare State*. Chapel Hill: North Carolina University Press, 2006.

Read, Hollis. *The Negro Problem Solved, or, Africa as She Was, as She Is and as She Shall Be: Her Curse and Her Cure*. New York: A.A. Constantine, 1864.

Sivulka, Juliann. *Stronger than Dirt: A Cultural History of Advertising Personal Hygiene in America, 1875–1940*. Amherst, MA: Humanity Books, 2001.

Steinhorn, Leonard, and Barbara Diggs-Brown. *By the Color of Our Skin: The Illusion of Integration and the Reality of Race*. New York: Dutton, 1999.

Thomas, Jon. "Bell's Curve: Why the Arc of American History Bends Toward Racial Inequality." Master's thesis, Georgia State University, Atlanta, Georgia, 2015.

Washington, Sylvia Hood. *Packing Them In: An Archaeology of Environmental Racism in Chicago, 1865–1954*. Lanham, MD: Lexington Books, 2005.

Woodward, C. Vann. *Reunion and Reaction: the Compromise of 1877 and the End of Reconstruction*. Oxford, UK: Oxford University Press, 1991.

PART II
RACIAL REALISM AND LEGAL THEORY

Chapter 3

From Psychology to Resistance
Racial Realism and American Legal Realism

Timothy J. Golden

"To have friends coming from distant places—surely that is delightful? But not to be resentful at others' failure to appreciate one—surely that is to be a true gentleman?"

—Confucius, *Analects*, 1.1[1]

"I am a man of substance, of flesh and bone, fiber and liquids—and I might even be said to possess a mind. I am invisible, understand, simply because people refuse to see me."

—Ellison, *Invisible Man*[2]

"If we die, let us die resisting"

—Camus, *Resistance, Rebellion, and Death*[3]

I.

Brian Leiter has authored a comprehensive and authoritative philosophical account of American Legal Realism (ALR). This account is set forth generally throughout his important text *Naturalizing Jurisprudence: Essays on American Legal Realism and Naturalism in Legal Philosophy*, and more specifically in his essay "Rethinking Legal Realism: Toward a Naturalized Jurisprudence" in that same text. In "Rethinking Legal Realism," Leiter wants to reclaim the principal thesis of ALR, which is that, in making decisions, "judges respond primarily to the stimulus of the facts."[4] For Leiter, this "core claim" of realism must be retrieved from what he considers to be unphilosophical and erroneous conceptions of ALR that view it either as a matter of purely unfettered discretion, which he refers to as "judicial volition," or as a matter of fiat, which he refers to as "judicial idiosyncrasy."[5] Neither judicial volition nor judicial idiosyncrasy—both part of what Leiter calls the "Received View" of ALR—provide a philosophically satisfactory account of adjudication. Leiter also points to what he views as the failure of Critical Legal Studies (CLS) to appreciate ALR's core claim. This failure manifests itself in CLS's thesis of legal indeterminacy. According to Leiter, CLS has distorted ALR because of an unwarranted expansion of the classical and narrow realist claim that the law as it relates to cases pending appellate review is indeterminate because no two cases are exactly alike, into the much stronger, and in Leiter's view, the incredible and unjustified claim that the *law itself* is fundamentally indeterminate.[6] For Leiter, this sort of expansion of legal indeterminacy is a serious philosophical error that, while popularizing ALR within the American legal culture, has woefully failed to comprehend just what the Legal Realists were actually trying to do: develop a philosophical account of adjudication through an empirical methodology consistent with the methodology of the natural sciences (hence Leiter's use of the term "naturalized"), which shows that in making decisions, "judges respond primarily to the stimulus of the facts."[7] This is why, in Leiter's view, Quine, often cited along with the later Wittgenstein as a forerunner of a "postmodern jurisprudence," is not a "postmodernist" at all, as he also argues in *Naturalizing Jurisprudence*.[8] According to Leiter, Quine never abandons the natural sciences in favor of relativism, which he thinks postmodernism does.[9] Instead, Quine, through his naturalized epistemology, approaches philosophy as consistent with the task of the natural sciences. This means that Quine sees the task of philosophy as rendering a plausible, but not necessarily "true," description of the world in the strict sense of analytic, a priori "truths" that philosophy sought to clarify through the rigors of pure conceptual analysis under the program of logical positivism. Quine thinks that analytic statements are not "truths" at all in this strict, conceptual sense. They are simply statements that we are less likely to abandon until science reveals their falsity, which is when such concepts and their attendant worldviews must be adjusted accordingly. For Leiter, neither objective truth nor science is expendable on Quine's account.

Interestingly, throughout his critique of CLS—those whom he believes have contributed to the philosophical errors that comprise what he calls the "Received View"—Leiter simply uses the banner "Critical Legal Studies" to critique their view with no regard for the nuances of those within that movement,[10] and despite Derrick Bell's explicit engagement with ALR and its connection to his own thesis of Racial Realism (RR),[11] Bell is conspicuously absent from both Leiter's essay "Rethinking Legal Realism" and also from the remainder of Leiter's *Naturalizing Jurisprudence*.[12] Now, on one hand, Leiter's omission of Bell ought not to be a criticism of Leiter, for it was not his aim in either his essay "Rethinking Legal Realism" or throughout *Naturalizing Jurisprudence* to engage Bell's thesis of RR. Rather, it *was* his aim to render a rigorous philosophical treatment of ALR in an attempt to explain precisely what the Realists hoped to do. But on the other hand, inasmuch as Leiter purports to debunk the views of CLS, he ought to account for the nuance and variety of CLS, rather than dismissing their views *en bloc*, for if he considered Bell's RR, he may not be as quick to dismiss it in that I believe that Bell's RR provides a philosophical account of adjudication. I thus aim to do something in this chapter that Leiter did not do in *Naturalizing Jurisprudence*: present a discussion of Bell's RR and its relation to ALR. Accordingly, this chapter attempts to situate Bell's RR within Leiter's reconstructed account of ALR. Specifically, I want to unpack the jurisprudential implications of Bell's analogical claim that "Racial Realism is to race relations what 'Legal Realism' is to jurisprudential thought"[13] to show not only RR's roots in ALR but also to show how RR has a normative dimension that goes beyond ALR. Bell's RR then, as the chapter's title indicates, moves "from psychology to resistance."

My argument unfolds in three phases. I argue first that RR is about much more than either sociological or historical assertions. Although it is certainly a thesis about race relations, it contemplates a philosophically rigorous critique of abstract, formalist, color-blind notions of "equality" in U.S. constitutional jurisprudence. Bell's RR is thus just as critical of—and as opposed to—Legal Formalism as ALR.

Second, I contend that both Bell's critique of Formalism and his reliance on empirical data to support his thesis about the permanence of racism, which is consistent with scientific method, in addition to Bell's reliance on what Leiter calls a sort of "folk psychology," makes RR, in part at least, a predictive, naturalized theory of adjudication about how courts will decide cases based on race. I thus want to show that, like Quine and the other philosophical naturalists, Bell's RR makes the double move of (1) anti-foundationalism in its critique of formalism, and (2) replacement of formalism's a priori theory of adjudication with a reliance on the data of the social sciences. In the end, Bell, just as the other adjudication naturalists must do, resorts to folk psychology to compensate for the inherent deficiencies of naturalistic theories of adjudication.[14]

And third, I argue that Bell's RR, although rooted in the ALR tradition, represents an advance on ALR, as it is not merely a descriptive psychology of adjudication; it is much more than that. Bell's RR carries with it a demand to resist the injustices of institutionalized racism. This demand is borne of social and political oppression vis-à-vis formalistic, color-blind, Equal Protection jurisprudence from the U.S. Supreme Court that purports to eliminate racial discrimination, but that ultimately re-inscribes white supremacy within a power dynamic that adversely affects Black subjectivity. Drawing from African American social and political philosophy, Bell's RR is tailored to a Black subjectivity that not only encounters the permanence of American anti-Black racism but also must perpetually resist it, as did Mrs. Biona MacDonald.[15] Bell thus moves beyond the descriptive thesis of ALR to the normative, cultralogical thesis of RR. This, I contend, gives RR a normative quality that represents a significant improvement on the moral shortcomings of mere scientific description, which, as Leiter argues, is precisely what puts the "naturalized" in "naturalized jurisprudence."

II.

On the surface, RR has nothing to do with jurisprudence, let alone the philosophically reconstructed, "naturalized" jurisprudence that Leiter advocates. After all, the claim that racism is permanent in America makes RR more closely resemble a sociological or historical claim than a jurisprudential one. And a restatement of the principal thesis of Bell's RR bears this out: "Black people will never attain full equality in this country [America]. Even those herculean efforts we hail as successful will produce no more than temporary 'peaks of progress,' short-lived victories that slide into irrelevance as racial patterns adapt in ways that maintain white dominance."[16] One is thus not immediately reminded of adjudication upon first considering RR. Rather, one may be more likely reminded of something akin to perhaps W.E.B. Du Bois's analysis of racism and its sociological causes and implications, or to an historical reference from Carter G. Woodson to the repeated demands for just treatment of African Americans. Now, although Bell, like Du Bois and Woodson, certainly has much to say about American anti-Black racism that is sociological and historical, the philosophical affinities between RR and ALR lie beneath the surface of Bell's articulation of RR where one can see the link between jurisprudence and race relations in America.[17] This conclusion, however, is not obvious. Indeed, Bell's own words seem to preclude any possible association between RR and jurisprudence, for when he says that "Racial Realism is to race relations what 'Legal Realism' is to jurisprudential thought,"[18] the analogy is apparently clear: RR is applicable to race relations (and not to jurisprudence) and ALR is applicable to jurisprudential thought (and not to race relations). But this rather superficial view of Bell's analogy between RR and ALR makes a critical mistake in that it wrongly separates "jurisprudential thought" from "race relations," when in actuality these two are inextricably linked with one another. Considering the voluminous amount of court decisions and likewise voluminous scholarly authored literature on race and jurisprudence in American legal doctrine, it becomes easier to make the case that race relations is indeed a major subject of judicial and scholarly attention. Indeed, throughout U.S. Supreme Court history, from *Dred Scott*, to *Plessy v. Ferguson*, to *Brown v. Board of Education*, to *Bakke v. Board of Regents of the University of California*, *City of Richmond v. J.A. Croson Co.*, to *Grutter v. Bollinger*, and throughout Bell's corpus where he discusses each of these cases, often in the context of RR, one can see that RR's principal claim about the permanence of racism in America is linked in a significant way to the courts. And since courts are where judges decide cases, RR is as much—if not more—about adjudication as it is about sociology and history.

So if there is a relationship between RR and jurisprudence, what is it? And how does ALR fit within this mix? To answer these questions, I draw from Bell's important 1992 essay, "Racial Realism," and his magnum opus, *Faces at the Bottom of the Well: The Permanence of Racism*, published in the same year. In both of these texts, Bell articulates RR's thesis, and, through a careful examination of the U.S. Supreme Court's Equal Protection jurisprudence, shows its connection to ALR, especially to ALR's critical engagement with Legal Formalism.

Bell's Essay "Racial Realism"

Bell's landmark essay "Racial Realism" shows a strong connection between RR and ALR that demonstrates not only that ALR has profoundly influenced RR, but also that RR has its origin in the ALR tradition that critiques Legal Formalism. Bell begins the essay by pointing out that "Black people need reform of our civil rights strategies as badly as those in law needed a way to consider American jurisprudence prior to the advent of the Legal Realists."[19] Both the "need" to reform civil rights strategies for African Americans and the "need" to "consider American jurisprudence prior to the advent of the Legal Realists" imply some sort of problem that creates the "need" in the first place. What, then, is that need? According to Bell, the need for the Legal Realists is a need to re-examine the judicial process because of an incompatibility between evolving socioeconomic conditions and the strictures of a rigid, formalist approach to adjudication. To make this point, Bell turns to the Legal Realists who argued that formalism was not up to the task of adjudication in an age of transition. The flux of American society and its attendant changes to the legal relationships between private individuals in business relationships demanded an empirical account of adjudication, rather than the formalists' a priori conceptual account. In "Racial Realism," Bell cites a scholar who argues that "the inconsistencies between the practices of a rapidly changing industrial nation and the claims of a mechanical juristic system had grown so acute by the 1920s that in the minds of an increasing number of individuals, the old jurisprudence could no longer justify and explain contemporary practice."[20] Bell also cites Justice Cardozo, who claimed that an increasingly complex industrialized society rendered formalist approaches to judicial decision problematic, as there needed to be "a jurisprudence and philosophy adequate to justify the change," which "the agitations and the promptings of a changing civilization" so strongly demanded.[21] So Formalism was at best problematic and at worst an "old jurisprudence" that "could no longer justify or explain contemporary practice." What makes Formalism so troublesome? To answer this question, we turn to an account of precisely what Formalism is.

According to both Bell and Leiter, the leading formalist was Christopher Columbus Langdell, Dean of the Harvard Law School in the nineteenth century.²² For Langdell, one must first discern the fundamental principles of law in a given area through a study of the precedents in that area of law. These principles, in turn, entail other principles that scholars must articulate with analytic rigor as propositions, which, taken together with the more general and fundamental principles of law, become the system of legal rules that represent what the law is in this or that area.²³ Langdell thus provides an academic juridical science that translates into a normative account of adjudication: judges ought to decide cases based upon a deductive process that leads them to the correct legal principles to be applied in any given case.²⁴ On the formalist account of adjudication, judges simply apply a preexisting body of law either in the form of case precedent or statutes to the facts of the case as those facts are presented to the court. The application of the pertinent rules of law to the facts yields a result. The problem with this approach for the Legal Realist, however, is that, as both Leiter and Bell point out, there is a profound disregard of social and economic conditions. And a true formalist would have to display such indifference because the formalist simply sees the law as a system of deductive a priori rules, applicable in a formulaic manner to achieve a result irrespective of social conditions beyond the closed, a priori deductive system.

Bell and Leiter point to several cases to show how formalism's indifference to social and economic conditions actually works. Bell discusses *Coppage v. Kansas*²⁵ as an example of formalist indifference to social and economic realities in favor of strict conceptual definitions of "liberty." In this case, the Supreme Court declared that legislation invalidating so-called "yellow dog contracts" was unconstitutional based on notions of liberty in the Due Process clause of the Fourteenth Amendment. Yellow dog contracts prohibited employees from joining labor unions and demanded that if one was a member of a labor union, resignation from union membership was a condition of one's employment. When the Kansas legislature enacted prohibitions to eliminate yellow dog contracts, the employers successfully argued in the Supreme Court that the state's enactment of such legislation violated the liberty of the parties to come to contractual terms of employment as they saw fit. Bell points out: "Although the court did not deny the presence of unequal bargaining power, it reasoned that the employees merely encountered economic coercion. Because the formal common law definition of duress that would have excused nonperformance of the contracts did not include economic coercion, the workers were deemed to have freely exercised their choice. The Court would not allow the state to invade the liberty rights of contracting parties."[26] In *Coppage*, then, through a strict analytic reading of the established common law doctrine, considered in the Langdellian sense to be the established body of law as it relates to duress, and combined with an analytical reading of the "Liberty" clause of the Fourteenth Amendment stripped from its sociological and historical moorings, the Court acted consistent with formalist doctrine.

Leiter points to *United States v. E. C. Knight Co.*, a case that held, based on a hypertechnical formalist interpretation of the term "interstate" from the Commerce clause of the Constitution, that Congress lacked regulatory authority over a sugar manufacturer on the grounds that since "manufacturing" occurs within one state, it is, by definition, not implied in the term "interstate."[27] As Leiter points out, the astonishing result of this decision is that a sugar manufacturer, responsible for the production of 90 percent of the sugar in the United States, and whose decisions "would affect the sugar market nationwide was of no concern to a formalistically minded court applying 'plain meanings' and clear-cut rules."[28] A more contemporary example of formalist legal argumentation is the U.S. Supreme Court's recent decision *King v. Burwell*,[29] in which the petitioners argued that a plain reading of the Affordable Care Act (ACA) meant that, since the statute used the term "State" with respect to the entity that establishes an exchange, only "states," and not the federal government could establish exchanges for their citizens to participate in the benefits of the ACA. If the Court would have adopted this argument, it would have resulted in millions of Americans being without health care in those jurisdictions in which the state government did not participate in the ACA and the federal government established exchanges to administer the ACA in those states. In rejecting this reasoning, Chief Justice John Roberts ruled that "Congress passed the Affordable Care Act to improve health insurance markets, not to destroy them. If at all possible, we must interpret the Act in a way that is consistent with the former, and avoids the latter."[30] The Court appears to have taken a less formalist stance here.

Bell and Leiter have similar conceptions of formalism: it is an account of adjudication that purports to deduce law from a priori principles and concepts that ignores social and economic realities in favor of a mechanistic application of the law to the facts. The Realists, for both Bell and Leiter, are critical of this approach and favor an empirical, scientific approach to adjudication that is more attentive to social and economic circumstances. Bell's RR offers this criticism of formalism in his essay "Racial

Realism," where he discusses *Bakke v. Board of Regents of the University of California*.³¹

Bell holds up the *Bakke* decision as an example of how "despite law school indoctrination and the 'rule of law'—abstract principles lead to legal results that harm Blacks and perpetuate their inferior status. Racism provides a basis for a judge to select one available premise rather than another when incompatible claims arise."³² In *Bakke*, the Court relied on abstract notions of "equality" under the Fourteenth Amendment in a manner similar to how the Court relied on an abstract meaning of "liberty" under the Fourteenth Amendment in *Coppage v. Kansas*, and the abstract meaning of "manufacturing" as related to "interstate" in *United States v. E. C. Knight Co.* The *Bakke* Court, instead of being attentive to the social and economic realities that lead to serious disparities in access to educational opportunities for Blacks, interpreted "equal" protection to mean that a white litigant could successfully challenge an affirmative action program as violative of equal protection even though the program was intended to remedy the effects of past discrimination. Of the formalist nature of the *Bakke* decision, Bell writes:

> Relying heavily on the formalistic language of the Fourteenth Amendment, and utterly ignoring social questions about which race in fact has power and advantages and which race has been denied entry for centuries into academia, the Court held that an affirmative action policy may not unseat white candidates on the basis of their race. By introducing an artificial and inappropriate parity in its reasoning, the Court effectively made a choice to ignore historical patterns, to ignore contemporary statistics, and to ignore flexible reasoning.³³

In contrast, Bell points to a Realist approach to deciding *Bakke*:

> Following a Realist approach, the Court would have observed the social landscape and noticed the skewed representation of minority medical school students. It would have reflected on the possible reasons for these demographics, including inadequate school systems in urban ghettos, lack of minority professionals to serve as role models, and the use of standardized tests evaluated by "white" standards. Taking these factors

into consideration, the Court may very well have decided *Bakke* differently.[34]

The contrast between formalism and realism in both ALR and Bell's RR is strong: the former ignores historical, social, and economic considerations, while the latter does not. Moreover—and this is the crucial insight for Bell's RR—the abstractions of formalism are appropriated to maintain rather than dismantle the various institutionalized forms of white domination. Beyond the surface, then, Bell's RR is much more about jurisprudence than one might think, which is what leads Bell to say of *Bakke* that it "serves as an example of how formalists may use abstract concepts, such as equality, to mask policy choices and value judgments. Abstraction, in the place of flexible judicial reasoning, removes a heavy burden from a judge's task. At the same time, her opinion appears to render the 'right' result."[35] In light of this, Bell claims that "cases such as *Bakke* should inspire many civil rights lawyers to reexamine the potential of equality jurisprudence to improve the lives of African-Americans."[36]

FACES AT THE BOTTOM OF THE WELL

The same year that "Racial Realism" was published, Bell published his landmark text *Faces at the Bottom of the Well: The Permanence of Racism* (*Faces*). Bell expounds on his thesis of RR throughout *Faces*, but in the chapter entitled "Divining a Racial Realism Theory," he provides an extended discussion of formalism and its shortcomings as compared with ALR and RR. Here again, one sees the jurisprudential nature of RR, as Bell discusses it with his fictional interlocutor, Erika Wechsler.[37] After discussing ALR,[38] Bell writes that "the realist attack on short-sighted and stubborn judicial formalism is quite like the realistic assessment we're making of formal civil rights policy."[39] For Bell, "the legal rules regarding racial discrimination have become not only reified (that is, ascribing material existence and power to what are really just ideas)—as the modern inheritor of realism, critical legal studies would say—but deified."[40] This deification means that "the worship of equality rules as having absolute power benefits whites by preserving a benevolent but fictional self-image, and such worship benefits blacks by preserving hope."[41] In response to Erika Wechsler's question about whether there is "a parallel" between the formalist commitments to "supposedly apolitical principles" and "the modern captivation with colorblind neutrality," Bell responds enthusiastically in the affirmative:

Of course! I exclaimed, agreeing with her analysis. And, as we have seen, even the laws or court decisions that abolish one form of discrimination may well allow for its appearance in another form, subtle though no less damaging. Thus, the *Brown* decision invalidated "separate but equal," replacing it—as civil rights advocates urged—with "equal opportunity." But given the continued motivations for racism, the society has managed to discriminate against blacks as effectively under the remedy as under the prior law—more effectively really, because discrimination today is covert, harder to prove, its ill effects easier to blame on its black victims.[42]

The thrust of Bell's RR as a critique of formalism is strong: RR is—as is ALR—critical of formalist approaches to adjudication except that RR accounts for instances of racial subordination in a way that ALR does not. Whereas the latter is more focused on socioeconomic issues (which are at times deeply connected to issues of race), the former is a much more explicit and robust engagement with formalism for reasons directly related to formalism's role in maintaining structural inequities of institutions that facilitate white domination.

Thus it is that Bell's RR brings with it a critique of the abstractions of formalist jurisprudence in favor of ALR's attentiveness to social conditions. For Bell, the principal social condition most strongly emphasized is the role that race plays in adjudication on the supposed formalist account. I now turn to the second affinity between Bell's RR and ALR: an empirical, scientific, and thus naturalized methodology, which includes reliance on Bell's own version of what Leiter calls a "folk psychology."

III.

What precisely is it that makes any jurisprudence a "naturalized" one? For Leiter, "naturalism in philosophy is always first a methodological view to the effect that philosophical theorizing should be continuous with empirical inquiry in the sciences."[43] Even as Quine argues that there is no "first philosophy," a philosophical naturalist will likewise reject the notion that there is "a philosophical solution to problems that proceeds a priori, that is, prior to any experience."[44] As Leiter puts it, Quine's rejection of a first philosophy is much like ALR's rejection of the formalist notion of a priori legal rules that are mechanically applied to a set of facts to reach a singularly "correct" result in adjudication. To further show this similarity, consider that, for Leiter, Quine's naturalized epistemology, which he styles as "Replacement Naturalism," makes two moves: first, it attacks Cartesian foundationalism as it is recast in logical positivism's epistemic program.[45] Here, the foundationalist wants to legitimate philosophy as justifying knowledge claims based on the notion that the immediacy of sense data renders empirically based beliefs—those of natural science—apodictically certain because of a direct correlation between evidence and theory. Quine rejects this notion through his "meaning-holism" (the notion that concepts derive their meaning from their role in a larger theoretical whole rather than through a direct correlation of evidence to theory) and through his theory of under-determination, where he claims that evidence under-determines theory insofar as there are multiple theories consistent with evidential phenomena.[46] After Quine attacks foundationalism, he then makes the second move, which is a "replacement" of foundationalism with psychology; or to put it another way, Quine replaces philosophical justification with scientific description by "naturalizing" epistemology so that its task is consistent with that of a scientific one, which is to give a description of the world.

On Leiter's view, the ALR analogue to Quine is straightforward: even as Quine attacks foundationalism and moves from justification to description, ALR attacks formalism, moving away from its notion that legal reasons provide an a priori justification for a particular decision and toward an empirically based theory of adjudication. The upshot of this move is a naturalized jurisprudence where ALR replaces a formalist justification of adjudication with a realist description of adjudication consistent with the natural sciences, as on Quine's account of naturalized epistemology.[47] Although Leiter points out some potential problems with this account of naturalized jurisprudence, he vigorously defends this view.[48] But even on this account of ALR as operating with the methodology of the natural sciences, Leiter still questions the legitimacy of the realist account. He writes that the realists "may not give us paradigms of good empirical studies; but perhaps we should not look to them for that. The Realists give us the philosophical motivation and cues for how we should proceed, even if they do not carry off the project themselves."[49] How, then, can we justify a realist account of adjudication? One does this through what Leiter calls a "folk" social scientific theory of adjudication.[50] This theory is rooted in "informal psychological, political and cultural knowledge about judges and courts."[51] For Leiter, folk theories of adjudication meet the criteria for the methodological continuity with the natural and social sciences that are necessary to designate them as "naturalized," as they are predicated upon empirical observation, in search of causal explanations for court decisions, and they look for law-like patterns of decision making.[52] Of the folk theories of adjudication, Leiter concludes that "lawyers possess workable, if informal, folk theories of judicial decision" that "vindicate and instantiate Realism's naturalistic program."[53]

From its empiricism to its folk theory of adjudication, Bell's RR bears each of the hallmarks of the reconstructed ALR program as Leiter has outlined it. First, Bell makes both of the analogical Quinean moves: with his critique of formalism in the Supreme Court's Equal Protection jurisprudence, he points out that there is no singularly "correct" reason that justifies the decision that the Court reaches. Instead, he argues for an under-determination of legal reasons for Supreme Court adjudication, and points to a pernicious formalist notion of color-blind equality as one such reason that the Court has chosen to disregard the empirical data regarding disparities in areas such as employment, education, and housing that disadvantage African Americans. Arguing in this manner, Bell has rejected the foundationalism of the formalists. Bell then makes the replacement move of naturalism through a heavy reliance of RR on the empiricism of the social sciences. That Bell relies on the empirical approach taken in the social sciences is undeniable, for he makes an explicit appeal to empiricism in both "Racial Realism" and in *Faces*. In "Racial Realism," Bell points out that empiricism is of the utmost importance to RR, first in a footnote, and then throughout the text of the essay. In the footnote, Bell writes: "Empiricism is a crucial aspect of Racial Realism. By taking into consideration the abysmal statistics regarding the social status of black Americans, their oppression is validated."[54] Bell expounds upon this point later in the essay, where he writes:

> Today, blacks experiencing rejection for a job, a home, a promotion, anguish over whether race or individual failing prompted their exclusion. Either conclusion breeds frustration and eventually despair. We call ourselves African-Americans, but despite centuries of struggle, none of us—no matter our prestige or position—is more than a few steps away from a racially motivated exclusion, restriction or affront. There is little reason to be shocked at my prediction that blacks will

not be accepted as equals, a status which has eluded us as a group for more than 300 years. The current condition of most blacks provides support for this decision. It is surely possible to use statistics to distort, and I do wish for revelations showing that any of the dreadful data illustrating the plight of so many black people is false or misleading. But there is little effort to discredit the shocking disparities contained in these reports. Even so, the reports have little effect on policy makers or on society in general. Statistics and studies reflect racial conditions that transformed the "We Have a Dream" mentality of the 1960s into the trial by racial ordeal so many blacks are suffering in the 1990s.[55]

Notice Bell's language in this passage. First, he references the efforts of Blacks to gain access to basic human goods such as employment and housing, and both are areas in which the "statistics and studies" that he also refers to in the passage show that things have significantly worsened for Blacks over the thirty-year period from the 1960s to the 1990s. To bolster his point, in a footnote to this part of the essay, Bell refers to statistical data in three areas to show significant disparities unfavorable for African Americans.[56] First, he discusses the mortality rates in Harlem, which indicate that in central Harlem, where 96 percent of the residents were African American with 41 percent living below the poverty level, the mortality rate was more than twice that of whites and 50 percent higher than African Americans generally.[57] According to this empirical study that Bell cites, "Black men in Harlem are less likely to reach the age of 65 than men in Bangladesh."[58] In the same footnote, Bell then turns to unemployment data, which show that Black unemployment is 2.5 percent higher than that of white males, with similar data for black women and Black teenagers.[59] He also points to disparities in income levels between whites and Blacks, which are likely understated as the study did not account for "lower participation, part-time workers, or discouraged workers."[60] The study concludes that the economic disparity between African Americans and whites "appears to be a permanent feature of the American economy."[61] Bell relies on many of these same statistics in *Faces*.[62] Bell is so committed to the use of the hard sciences that he points out that it is only through an overwhelming amount of statistical data on the woeful socioeconomic and health conditions of African Americans that a sense of empathy can be generated among whites that is significant enough to lead to genuine reform. The point here is not to argue that whites armed with statistical data will somehow be able to change structural racism—indeed, Bell himself argues elsewhere that not only will this not happen, but also that such efforts will likely, despite the "best efforts" of whites, "serve to reinforce existing power structures."[63] Instead, my aim here is to show that Bell's reliance on such data situates him squarely within the scientific, descriptive realm of ALR.

What then are the implications of Bell's pervasive use of statistical data throughout his corpus for a naturalized theory of adjudication? The implications are that if the dismal statistical data from the natural and social sciences are actually taken seriously, then cases such as *Bakke* and *Brown* would have been decided differently. One sees this in Bell's later work, *Silent Covenants*, where he employs a naturalized approach in re-imagining the *Brown* decision.[64] Bell delivers an "opinion" of the Supreme Court based upon the Court's emphasis on affirming *Plessy* based on making conditions "equal," rather than focusing on the "separate" and demanding integration. He writes, "The 'separate' in the 'separate but equal' has been rigorously enforced. The 'equal' has served as a total refutation of equality. Within the limits of judicial authority, the Court recognizes these cases as an opportunity to test the legal legitimacy of the 'separate but equal' standard not . . . by overturning *Plessy* . . . but by ordering its strict enforcement."[65] Bell points out that if the Court had given real consideration to the deplorable conditions in segregated black schools and had actually tried to hold *Plessy* to its "equality" demand, the results of *Brown* would have been much more effective than they had been. In order to make this ruling, however, the overwhelming psychological and sociological data would have had to be taken much more seriously than they were. Indeed, "Counsel for the Negro children have gone to great lengths to prove what must be obvious to every person who gives the matter even cursory attention: With some notable exceptions, schools provided for Negroes in segregated systems are unequal in facilities—often obscenely so."[66] Forced integration would not change this state of affairs. For when the court mandated integration, according to Bell, it simply replaced the problem of inequality with the problem of outright violence against Blacks, which would perpetuate rather than eliminate the inequality that the Constitution demands. In his re-imagined opinion of the *Brown* decision, Bell, writing for the Court that would uphold *Plessy*, writes:

> Again, it would seem appropriate to declare wrong what is clearly wrong. Given the history of segregation and the substantial reliance placed on our decisions as to its constitutionality, though, a finding by this Court in these cases that state supported racial segregation is an obsolete artifact of a bygone age, one that no longer conforms to the Constitution, will set the stage not for compliance, but for levels of defiance that will prove the antithesis of the equal educational opportunity the petitioners seek.[67]

One need only recall the sight of federal troops accompanying school children into white schools to be reminded that such an environment is not conducive to learning. Instead, the inequitable lack of physical resources is replaced with Black children experiencing the terror stemming from the threat of physical violence against them. This is in no way conducive to the sort of educational opportunities that African Americans were seeking. To the contrary, it was profoundly counterproductive. The Supreme Court, of course, did not uphold *Plessy* and enforce its equal prong. The overwhelming statistical data regarding inequities in educational opportunity were unpersuasive, and instead the Court chose another path. So the data alone are insufficient to explain how Bell can be committed to the core claim of ALR, which is that in deciding cases, judges respond to the stimulus of the facts, and yet the judges seem to ignore the facts. Bell's point here is clear enough: reliance on statistical data alone leads neither to a good empirical study of adjudication, because judges appear unresponsive to the stimulus of the facts in the form of the statistical data regarding the plight of African Americans, nor to meaningful reform. How can one explain this? This problem leads us to Bell's use of what Leiter calls folk psychology, to which I now turn.

We can see from Bell's discussion of *Brown* in *Silent Covenants* that empirical studies are supposed to give a satisfactory account of adjudication. That is, the facts of a case, when presented to judges, will stimulate the judges to rule accordingly. And what is this but the core claim of Realism? The fundamental presupposition of Realism's core claim is that the empirical data will bring knowledge and that the knowledge will stimulate the judges to rule consistent with the data, thus leading to a predictable theory of adjudication. But, as *Brown* and *Bakke* both show us, this is not always the case. Bell makes this point in the broader context of social reform in *Faces* in a chapter titled "Racism's Secret Bonding" that

I argue implies an application to adjudication. There, in another of Bell's fictional accounts, whites are bombarded with "statistical data about the number of Africans who had been captured, brought to these shores, and enslaved during the years of the slave trade."[68] There also "rained down statistics on Black unemployment and the consistently large disparities (averaging two and one half times) between jobless figures for Blacks and whites . . . infant death rates, educational prison terms for the same crime, the death sentence, and housing and health care costs and availability."[69] Accompanying the data storms were "the feelings of frustration, despair, and rage that blacks experience when discrimination bars them from jobs they would otherwise obtain. These data-related feelings were unnerving even to unemployed whites."[70] The point of Bell's fictional dialogue is that an overwhelming amount of statistical data will bring knowledge, and knowledge will bring empathy, and empathy will lead to meaningful reform. Bell puts the strategy of his story in the logical form of a hypothetical syllogism: "education leads to enlightenment. Enlightenment opens the way to empathy. Empathy foreshadows reform. In other words . . . whites—once given a true understanding of the evils of racial discrimination, once able to feel how it harms blacks—would find it easy, or easier, to give up racism."[71] By the end of the story, the data storms had generated such empathy among whites for the plight of African Americans that there were meaningful legislative reforms, because for the first time whites had a genuine sense of "feeling what discrimination is really like,"[72] such that "many white people were eager to comply with the new laws."[73] Some of the whites bombarded with data in Bell's story are undoubtedly judges who are called upon to decide cases involving race, and who obviously have ignored the data for a long time, as in the *Bakke* case that Bell discusses in "Racial Realism." In the story, whites are moved to reform, and presumably the white judges, also affected by the data storms, are likewise affected. But in reality this has not happened. Data have thus failed to deliver a reliable account of adjudication. This puts Bell's RR in a similar position to ALR. Of what value then is RR as a theory of adjudication?[74]

The answer to this question lies in Bell's use of an informal folk psychology in his RR. According to Leiter, informal folk theories help lawyers predict how cases will be decided: "lawyers work with some degree of informal psychological, political and cultural knowledge about judges and courts that constitutes what we might call a 'folk' social scientific theory of adjudication. The success of this folk theory . . . constitutes the core of a naturalized jurisprudence."⁷⁵ There are, for Leiter, three reasons why a folk psychology is consistent with a naturalist methodology. First, folk psychology is rooted in empirical observation of adjudication. Second, it seeks causal explanations for judicial decisions. And third, folk theories seek law-like patterns in court rulings.⁷⁶ Bell's RR exhibits each of these three characteristics of folk psychology; it is, first and foremost, predicated upon an empirical observation of Supreme Court decisions, as Bell delves deeply into cases such as *Brown*, *Bakke*, *Grutter v. Bollinger*, and *Coppage v. Kansas* throughout his work. Also, Bell seeks causal explanations for these decisions (e.g., in the form of his theory of interest convergence, which purports to explain why the Court decides cases based on race the way that it does, as in *Brown*), and his theory of interest convergence exhibits, on his view, a sort of law-like quality emerging as a pattern of adjudication, indicating that the Courts will adjudicate cases in a way that benefits African Americans so long as the decision also advances the interests of whites. Interestingly, Bell, in his discussion of Justice Clarence Thomas, seeks to give some insight into why Justice Thomas would be so hostile to African Americans.⁷⁷ In doing so, Bell is applying a folk psychology to adjudication—a folk psychology that Jerome Frank thought impossible, but that Leiter thinks is desirable, and may actually be worthwhile.⁷⁸

IV.

Thus far, I have argued that there are similarities between RR and ALR. Here, I turn to a significant difference. I now argue that RR has a normative dimension that moves it from a descriptive theory of adjudication into the realm of subjectivity and moral praxis. Bell's RR is a legal theory that consists of two parts: (1) the claim that racism is a permanent feature of American life that American law reinforces, and (2) the claim that despite this permanence there remains a moral obligation to resist racism. My aim is to elaborate on each of these parts of RR, showing how African American thought, specifically the work of Ralph Bunche,⁷⁹ not only informs Bell's understanding of racism's permanence but also enables Bell to make a unique contribution to Critical Legal Studies—the body of legal scholarship that Leiter dismisses *en bloc* without regard for its theoretical nuance and its ethnic and jurisprudential diversity.

First, I address the permanence part of RR. I draw from the work of Kenneth Nunn and Tommy J. Curry to show how Bell's RR not only emerges from Bell's understanding of Black subjectivity but also deals with oppressive power relations that liberalism's theory of abstract rights and color-blindness obscure. These features make RR a "naturalized" account of adjudication in a much deeper and richer sense than ALR. For unlike ALR, Bell's RR is deeply connected to racial identity and its role in the formation of the legal subject. And it is the legal subject understood as Black that Bell would argue too often finds itself on the wrong end of a court decision that reinforces white supremacy in the name of color-blind concepts such as "rights" or "equality." For Bell, it is this sort of legal reasoning that makes racism a permanent feature of American social and political life. And Bell's work is, as Curry would put it, "cultralogically" informed with African American social and political thought, immunizing it from what Curry views as the destructive influence of Eurocentric philosophy.

I then discuss the resistance thesis of RR to show how RR arises out of a tradition of Black struggle, and how it is thus much more than simply a descriptive theory of adjudication. To do so, I rely on two of Bell's important texts: his 1992 essay "Racial Realism" and his short story "The Handmaid's Tale," from *Afrolantica Legacies*. I now turn to RR as a theory about Black subjectivity and its role in articulating the permanence of racism.

Racial Realism: Black Subjectivity, Power, and the Permanence of Racism

More often than not, abstraction and hyper-theorization are harmful to Black people.[80] Abstract methodologies erase Black identity, forget black history, and reinforce the structural dimensions of white supremacy. Whether it be political theory, social theory, or theology, theoretical movements away from concrete, lived experience typically cause an erasure of Black identity and Black life such that not only is Black life ignored but also that white supremacy is reinforced. As I have argued elsewhere, in Christian theology, abstraction removes even the most revolutionary religious figures who have strong experiential affinities with Black people from their historical, social, and political contexts, and in doing so, such revolutionary figures become sanitized icons of the white imagination that maintain rather than overcome the status quo.[81] In this same vein, Charles Mills has argued that John Rawls's political theory is inclined to maintain oppression because hypothetical experiments like the original position fail to address the historical realities of American chattel slavery and its legacy of injustice.[82]

Legal theory is no different. Abstractions abound in legal theory—so much so that Jack M. Balkin has argued that "we must transform the subject of jurisprudence into a jurisprudence of the subject."[83] This move is significant in that it makes the law more about people rather than abstract ideas. Formalism, with its emphasis on law as an a priori form independent of human activity, fails to account for how law—specifically American law—has been used to target and oppress Black people.[84] One need look no further than the infamous Black Codes of the post-Reconstruction era that initiated Jim Crow to see that law, far from being an enterprise independent of human interests, is ultimately a function of how people are constituted as subjects, and how those subjects think the law ought to be. So the normative dimension of law, natural law theory notwithstanding, is an endeavor of a sociologically and ideologically informed subjectivity, and the real insight of Critical Legal Studies is that the courtroom is not the site of "justice" as an abstract concept, but rather is a battleground for competing political ideologies. The insight of Critical Legal Studies is that law is politics.

But as Tommy J. Curry argues, Balkin's move—and the move of the idealist school of Critical Race Theory—away from abstraction gives an insufficient account of the legal subject. Curry writes:

> Balkin fails to give an explanation of what happens when groups, societies, and institutions, moved by their subjective belief and individual actions, have determined a course of law, society, and thought, not as competing individuals but as racialized groups. Only recently has Balkin clarified his stance and developed a theory of transcendental deconstruction that presupposes "the existence of transcendental human values articulated in culture but never adequately captured by culture"; but, again, this account rests on the assumption that all people share the same ontological perspectives as a consequence of their innate rationality and that this rational humanism serves as the basis for social and legal construction. Clearly, CRT needs a fundamental overhaul to eliminate the pretension of this "one size fits all" transcendentalism.

For Curry, Balkin's view provides an insufficient account of the legal subject because it fails to account for the experiences of racialized groups before the law and how those groups understand law and legal systems. Instead of understanding subjectivity at the deeper level of racial identity, Balkin makes an appeal to what Curry calls a "theory of transcendental deconstruction" that is rooted in Eurocentric ontological assumptions about human cognition, i.e., a Kantian-styled sort of universal human reason. So although Balkin gestures in the right direction, purporting to give an account of the "jurisprudence of the subject," according to Curry, Balkin leaves us with an account of subjectivity that short-circuits the racial identity of the Black legal subject *as a racialized subject*. And in doing so, Balkin fails to account for how Black people experience racial oppression in American law, and, because of his reliance on a Eurocentric conception of human reason that is itself hegemonically oriented in virtue of its origin in European culture, Balkin's view will inevitably reinforce racial oppression rather than eliminate it.

Enter Curry's notion of "cultralogics" as exemplified in the work of Bell. Responding to Kenneth Nunn's call for "African-descended" people "to successfully resist Euro-centricity,"[85] Curry argues for an Afrocentric, culturally informed hermeneutic, advocating for Critical Race Theory to return to its realist roots and thus "silence" the idealist school of Critical Race Theory. For Curry, the idealist school of Critical Race Theory derives from Eurocentric conceptions of transcendental human reason that ultimately reduce Black subjectivity to a mere "polemics of discontent."[86] But Curry argues that Black subjectivity is much richer than that. This is why Eurocentric notions of human reason are so problematic: when such notions are applied in the context of Critical Race Theory, Critical Race Theory ends up reinforcing that which it is supposed to dismantle. And, if that were not bad enough, the richness of Black subjectivity, present in African American social and political thought (e.g., Ida B. Wells, Ralph Bunche, Martin Delany, Paul Robeson, W.E.B. Du Bois, etc.) is neglected altogether. It is precisely this sort of erasure of Black subjectivity and neglect of Black thought that is problematic for Curry because, according to Nunn, law itself is constituted according to white cultural norms, and among those norms is a hegemonic disposition toward Black people, whose experiences with oppression demand a culturally informed legal hermeneutic rich with the social and political thought of "African descended" people rather than white European philosophers. Curry thus offers cultralogics as an answer to this call, and points to Bell as the quintessential cultralogical critical race theorist who can ultimately silence the idealist school of critical race theory.

Curry's work is pertinent here because the first part of Bell's RR concerning the permanence of racism is a view of a culturally informed Black legal subject in Bell himself, who, with self-determination, not only makes the diagnosis of racism's permanence due to the inadequacy of the American legal system but also prescribes an ethic of defiant resistance consistent with the traditions of African American social and political thought that, unlike the idealist approach in Critical Race Theory, does not reinforce white hegemony, but rather will consistently resist it. Curry's cultralogical turn in jurisprudence thus emphasizes the profound influences of Ralph Bunche, Paul Robeson and W.E.B. Du Bois on Bell's work, which is situated squarely within a longstanding tradition of African American social and political thought; a tradition that the idealist school of Critical Race Theory overlooks altogether.

RACIAL REALISM AND RESISTANCE TO RACISM

The normativity of Bell's RR represents a significant advance on ALR's naturalized theory of adjudication because a fundamental characteristic of descriptive theories is their lack of normativity. And if one wants to do more than provide naturalized description—as in the case of Bell—then more is required. So although Quine's naturalized epistemology and Leiter's reconstructed ALR (with its reliance on folk psychology) take us to the place of a plausible theory of adjudication, they do not get as far as moral theory because their aim is description. But Bell goes further, giving us not only a naturalized account of adjudication but also a moral imperative to resist. Seemingly at odds with his claim about the permanence of racism, Bell's demand to resist oppression causes one to reorient one's thinking away from the success of the resistance and toward the notion that one's deliverance from oppression is in one's struggle against it. This is seen in several places throughout Bell's work, including his essay, "Racial Realism,"[87] *Faces*,[88] and *Afrolantica Legacies*.[89]

"RACIAL REALISM" AND *FACES*

Bell recounts the story of being in Harmony, Mississippi, in 1964, organizing a group of citizens in an effort to ensure compliance with a school desegregation order. While working on this hot evening, Bell describes an encounter he had with Mrs. Biona MacDonald, a local committed civil rights worker who displayed remarkable courage to remain involved in the civil rights struggle despite being intimidated in the form of her son's job loss, the bank's attempt to foreclose on her mortgage, and having shots fired through her living room window.[90] Marveled by her display of courage in the face of this intimidation, Bell asked where she got the strength to continue the fight. Her response was telling: "Derrick . . . I am an old woman. I lives to harass white folks."[91] Bell's response to Mrs. MacDonald's display of courage shows the normative dimension of Bell's RR:

> Mrs. MacDonald did not say she risked everything because she hoped or expected to win out over the whites who, as she well knew, held all the economic and political power, and the guns as well. Rather, she recognized that—powerless as she was—she had intended to use courage and determination as weapons "to harass white folks." Her fight, in itself, gave her strength and empowerment in a society that relentlessly attempted to wear her down. Mrs. MacDonald did not even hint that her harassment would topple whites' well-entrenched power. Rather, her goal was defiance and its harassing effect was more potent precisely because she placed herself in confrontation with her oppressors with full knowledge of the power and willingness to use it.
>
> Mrs. MacDonald avoided discouragement and defeat because at the point that she determined to resist her oppression, she was triumphant. Nothing the all-powerful whites could do would diminish her triumph. Mrs. MacDonald understood twenty-five years ago the theory that I am espousing in the 1990s for black leaders and civil rights lawyers to adopt. If you remember her story, you will understand my message.[92]

Bell's lesson from Mrs. MacDonald is clear: her victory was in her resistance. Despite the scare tactics and power of oppression from whites, Mrs. MacDonald's courage never waned. She understood that if her purpose was to "harass white folks," this implied that the struggle would never end. But it also implied that she would have to keep fighting. And this is Bell's message to the civil rights community today: re-conceptualize civil rights success in terms of the vigor and resolve of your struggle, rather than evidence of linear progress, which for Bell is fleeting because accompanying that progress will be a retrogression, as in the cases of *Bakke* and *Brown*. Mrs. MacDonald's recognition that her victory was in her struggle is significant because she rejected "any philosophy that insists on measuring life's success on the achieving of specific goals—overlooking the process of living. More affirmatively and as a matter of faith," she believed that "despite the lack of linear progress, there is satisfaction in the struggle itself."[93]

Justice Marshall and The Handmaid's Tale

One of Bell's later texts shows how Mrs. MacDonald's spirit of resistance is found in the late Supreme Court Justice Thurgood Marshall. In Bell's book *Afrolantica Legacies*, he reads Justice Marshall's lifelong struggle for African American civil rights with a character named Offred from Margaret Atwood's novel *The Handmaid's Tale*. In Atwood's novel, a woman whose name was changed to Offred was once a wife and mother living an ordinary life. She then became part of an oppressive regime that changed her name. Her oppression was comprehensive in that not only was her former identity taken from her, but the new authoritarian regime exercised absolute control over her life. In the midst of this oppression, Offred attempted to retain her humanity by recording her experiences on audiotapes. These tapes were discovered but scholars could not analyze their content because portions of the tapes were inaudible. The scientists thus dismissed the value of the tapes. But Bell retorts: "the true significance of the tapes was in their existence, not in what they contained. The scientists' misdirected inquiries sharpen rather than obscure our appreciation of the indomitable spirit of the woman who lived the Handmaid's Tale."[94] The point here is that like Mrs. MacDonald, who understood that her victory was not in overcoming the struggle, but in the struggle itself, Offred should be lauded not necessarily for what she achieved, but for what she attempted: the preservation of her humanity through heroically attempting to document her experiences under the rule of an oppressive regime. And the same can be said of Justice Marshall and other civil rights giants: they overcame by the struggle, not by the victory. Says Bell of Justice Marshall and Offred: "We hail Justice Marshall and the heroine of Margaret Atwood's novel, not because they won, but because they persevered."[95] Perhaps no statement exemplifies the spirit of Justice Thurgood Marshall's perseverance more than his words in a speech that he gave on August 10, 1988, when he received the "Jurist of the 20th Century Award" from the National Bar Association. In his acceptance speech for this prestigious award, Justice Marshall said the following of the struggles of Black people against racism in America:

> We're not gaining ground, my friends. We might be losing. But one thing I'm sure of, this is no time to stop. And I say, and I don't know whether or how I could say more, all of us have a job. And one thing, we can't do it as an individual and we can't do it as small groups. We've got to have the one thing in mind. And I'm going to close with what I've been saying for fifty to sixty years. I don't care about the Constitution alone or the Declaration of Independence, or all of the books together. It's not that important. What is important is a goal toward which you're moving. A goal that is the basis of true democracy, which is over and above the law. And it's something that won't happen, but you must pray for it and work for it. And that goal is very simple. That goal is that if a child, a Negro child is born to a Black mother in a state like Mississippi or any other state like that. Born to the dumbest, poorest sharecropper, is, by merely drawing its first breath in a democracy, there and without anymore is born with the exact same rights as a similar child born to a white parent of the wealthiest person in the United States. No it's not true. Of course it's not true. It never will be true. But I challenge anybody to take the position that that is not the goal we should be shooting for. And stop talking about how far we've come and start talking about how close we are.[96]

Justice Marshall, in these words, captures the normative spirit of Bell's RR. It is the spirit of resistance that refuses to stop resisting although the goal is impossible to reach. Justice Marshall tells us first and foremost that the goal of racial equality is unattainable, but that we must work toward it. And he also tells us that our struggle is not about how far we have come, but rather about how close we are to that unattainable goal. So again, Justice Marshall and Offred deserve our homage because, like Mrs. Biona McDonald, they recognize the value in the struggle despite the impossibility of the goal.

V.

Bell's RR and ALR have more in common than one might first be able to see. Their difference, however, is just as significant as their affinities. On one hand, both present a powerful critique of the epistemic foundationalism at the core of the formalist endeavor. Rejecting the a priori nature of Langdellian formalism because of its use to maintain the abiding structural forms of white hegemony, Bell turns to the hard sciences and argues that an attentiveness to socioeconomic data leads to a more just result. Rather than abstract notions like equality, Bell argues with the other legal realists that the statistical data of the social sciences are among the reasons that, as the Realists claim, judges will "respond primarily to the stimulus of the facts." Making both moves of the "Replacement Naturalist" of a Quinean sort, RR is very much a naturalized jurisprudence. But it is much more than just a descriptive theory of adjudication; it is a normative theory of Black resistance to anti-Black racism. In recognizing the permanence of racism, RR demands a struggle against it that is equally as permanent as anti-Black racism itself.

Notes

1. Confucius, *Analects*, trans. Raymond Dawson (New York: Oxford University Press, 2008), 3. This epigraph is apropos for this chapter in that, on the surface, Leiter's reconstruction of American Legal Realism (ALR) as a descriptive philosophical thesis about adjudication, and Bell's Racial Realism (RR) as a philosophical thesis about the permanence of racism in America, are, to use Confucius's words, "from distant places." But this chapter is an attempt to show a closer proximity between RR and Leiter's reconstruction of ALR than one might see on the surface; that Bell comes to visit Leiter as a "friend" from a "distant" place, but a place only superficially distant, as I contend that Bell's RR and Leiter's account of ALR have more in common than one might ordinarily think. It is also true that Derrick Bell is not referenced in Leiter's account of ALR as a "naturalized" jurisprudence. Again, in fairness to Leiter, I write this chapter not as a criticism of him, but rather to seek rapprochement between ALR and RR, except that I argue that Bell's normativity is preferable to ALR's descriptive account of adjudication. My real target here is the moral shortcomings of Quine's critique of logical positivism as applied to adjudication, which, according to Leiter, is the methodology that "naturalizes" ALR's jurisprudence. I thus try, in the words of Confucius, "not to be resentful" because of any failure to appreciate Bell's deep connection to ALR, and thus be a true "gentleman."

2. Ralph Ellison, *Invisible Man* (New York: Vintage Books, 1980), 3.

3. Albert Camus, *Resistance, Rebellion, and Death* (New York: Random House, 1988).

4. See Brian Leiter, *Naturalizing Jurisprudence: Essays on American Legal Realism and Naturalism in Legal Philosophy* (London, UK: Oxford University Press, 2007), 16.

5. Ibid.

6. Ibid., 19–20.

7. Ibid., 21.

8. See Leiter's chapter "Why Quine is not a Postmodernist," in *Naturalizing Jurisprudence*, 137–151.

9. Ibid., 141–143.

10. Leiter and Jules Coleman do, however, address CLS in their essay "Determinacy, Objectivity and Authority," *University of Pennsylvania Law Review* 142 (1993): 549–637. But even in this essay their emphasis is a broad critique of CLS views on determinacy and objectivity generally, and Bell is merely mentioned in a footnote on the first page of the essay as an example of a CLS thinker who questions the objectivity of law, with no regard for Bell's RR and its relationship to ALR. See page 549.

11. See Derrick Bell's essay "Racial Realism," *Connecticut Law Review* 24.2 (1992): 363–379. I draw from this essay heavily throughout this chapter, as it represents, along with Bell's *Faces at the Bottom of the Well*, Bell's most comprehensive articulation of RR.

12. Leiter references Critical Race Theory in passing, referring to it as one of "many other trendy movements that legal academia absorbed more peacefully" than CLS. See *Naturalizing Jurisprudence*, 99. But there is no analysis of either Bell's brand of Critical Race Theory or of his RR and its connection to ALR to be found anywhere in *Naturalizing Jurisprudence*.

13. Bell, "Racial Realism," 364.

14. For a discussion of these deficiencies, see Leiter, "Rethinking Legal Realism: Toward a Naturalized Jurisprudence," in *Naturalizing Jurisprudence*, 54–57.

15. Bell, "Racial Realism," 378–379.

16. *Faces*, 12.

17. In *Faces*, Bell articulates four major themes of RR: (1) the historical principle, which is that there has been no linear progress in civil rights, and that "American racial history has demonstrated both steady subordination of Blacks in one way or another and, if examined closely, a pattern of cyclical progress and cyclical regression," (2) an economic theme, which demands that meaningful attention be paid to the socioeconomic condition of African Americans, (3) the theme of fulfillment, or "salvation through struggle," which calls for a reorientation of success away from "the achieving of specific goals," and toward the understanding that "there is satisfaction in the struggle itself," and (4) the theme of adopting a realistic stance toward the status and future of African Americans

in order to disrupt the cycle of oppression. See Bell, *Faces*, 98–99. I engage the first three of these themes throughout this chapter: the historical, in that I argue that, for Bell, the lack of linear progress contemplates a philosophically rigorous critique of Legal Formalism (as does ALR); the economic theme, which I argue implies the "naturalized" dimension of Bell's RR in Bell's reliance on the data of the social sciences (and also consistent with the methodology of ALR); and the theme of fulfillment, or "salvation through struggle," which I believe represents Bell's moral improvement on ALR.

18. Ibid.
19. Bell, "Racial Realism," 363–364.
20. Ibid., 364.
21. Ibid.
22. See Leiter, *Naturalizing Jurisprudence*, 87, and Bell, "Racial Realism," 365.
23. Leiter, *Naturalizing Jurisprudence*, 87, and his discussion of Anthony Kronman.
24. Leiter, *Naturalizing Jurisprudence*, 88.
25. *Coppage v. Kansas*, 236 U.S. 1 (1915).
26. Bell, "Racial Realism," 366n7. The Wagner Act of 1935 later outlawed yellow dog contracts. In 1937, the U.S. Supreme Court decided *National Labor Relations Board v. Jones & Laughlin Steel Corp.*, 301 U.S. 1 (1937), which upheld the Wagner Act and brought an end to yellow dog contracts.
27. Leiter, *Naturalizing Jurisprudence*, 88–89.
28. Ibid., 89.
29. *King v. Burwell*, 576 U.S. 473 (2015).
30. Ibid. at 21.
31. Bell, "Racial Realism," 369–370.
32. Ibid., 369.
33. Ibid.
34. Ibid.
35. Ibid.
36. Ibid.
37. Bell, *Faces*, 91. That Bell resorts to fiction here ought not to be troublesome for at least two reasons. First, although Bell fabricates interlocutors to make his points, *he has not fabricated the data*. And, second, Bell's fictional literary style is consistent with a long philosophical tradition that runs from the ancient period in Plato, through the modern period in Descartes and Hume, and into contemporary fictional yet profoundly philosophical presentations such as the one Leiter himself resorts to in *Naturalizing Jurisprudence*. See "The Methodology Problem in Jurisprudence," 168–170. See also René Descartes, *Meditations on First Philosophy*, 3rd ed., trans. Donald A. Cress (Indianapolis, IN: Hackett Publishing, 1993) (especially meditations one and two), and David Hume, *Dialogues Concerning Natural Religion* (Indianapolis, IN: Hackett Publishing) 1998. For a fuller

discussion of Bell's use of fiction and its continuity with the broader philosophical use of fiction, see chapter 8 in this book, "Liberalism, Christendom and Narrative: Paradox and Indirect Communication in Derrick Bell and Søren Kierkegaard."

38. Bell here discusses ALR as something of a political movement rather than a naturalistic, scientific approach to judicial decision making, as Leiter does. See page 100, where Bell speaks of ALR as part of "the political Progressive movement, concerned with social welfare legislation and administrative regulation." But this does not diminish continuity between RR and ALR that I am arguing for in this chapter, for insofar as Bell's RR implies a critique of Legal Formalism, and it relies on empirical statistical data and a "folk psychology," RR bears the traits of a naturalized philosophical theory of adjudication.

39. Bell, *Faces*, 101.
40. Ibid.
41. Ibid.
42. Ibid., 104.
43. Leiter, "Rethinking Legal Realism," 34.
44. Ibid.
45. Ibid., 36.
46. Ibid.
47. Ibid., 39–40.
48. Ibid., 40–46. In the end, Leiter argues that although there may be room for a "non-naturalized jurisprudence," this does not affect his claim about ALR, which is that ALR is a philosophical thesis specifically about adjudication in a narrow sense rather than a philosophical thesis that is generally about jurisprudence in a broad sense. He points out that Quine's naturalized epistemology is "especially radical" in its attempt to put philosophers out of business by surrendering epistemology to the natural sciences. Yet and still, many naturalistic philosophers believe that there is philosophical work to be done in the area of conceptual analysis. Similarly, although the Realists are arguing for a naturalized jurisprudence, Leiter still believes that there is "conventionally philosophical work to be done in the broader field of jurisprudence" (46). Leiter himself, however, calls this notion into question (46n142).

49. Ibid., 55.
50. Ibid.
51. Ibid.
52. Ibid., 56.
53. Ibid.
54. Bell, "Racial Realism," 365.
55. Ibid., 374–375.
56. Ibid., 374.
57. Ibid.
58. Ibid.

59. Ibid., 374–375.
60. Ibid., 375.
61. Ibid.
62. Bell, *Faces*, 3–4.
63. Bell, "Wanted: A White Leader Able to Free Whites of Racism," *University of California Davis Law Review* (Spring 2000): 536–557, 543.
64. Derrick Bell, *Silent Covenants: Brown v. Board of Education and the Unfulfilled Hopes for Racial Reform* (New York: Oxford University Press, 2004), 20–28.
65. Ibid., 22.
66. Ibid.
67. Ibid., 23.
68. Ibid., 147–148.
69. Ibid., 149.
70. Ibid., 149.
71. Ibid., 150.
72. Ibid.
73. Ibid.
74. Since no Realist can predict adjudication with certainty—this is impossible since every naturalized philosophical viewpoint, whether in epistemology or jurisprudence, is scientific and thus inductive—Bell resorts to folk psychology to make his case regarding adjudications based on race.
75. Leiter, *Naturalizing Jurisprudence*, 55.
76. Ibid., 56.
77. Bell "Racial Realism," 372.
78. Leiter, *Naturalizing Jurisprudence*, 56–57.
79. Ralph Bunche, "A Critical Analysis of the Programs and Tactics of Minority Groups," *The Journal of Negro Education* 4.3 (1935): 308–320.
80. For a thorough discussion of this point, see my monograph *Frederick Douglass and the Philosophy of Religion: An Interpretation of Narrative, Art, and the Political* (Lanham, MD: Lexington Books, 2022). There, I interrogate abstraction in the philosophy of religion, akin to Charles W. Mills' critique of Rawlsian abstraction in political philosophy and James H. Cone's critique of the abstractions of white theologians in Christian theology. What I aim to show in *Frederick Douglass and the Philosophy of Religion* is that in the philosophy of religion, the reformed epistemology of analytic theism, through abstraction, renders Christian theology impotent against injustice as compared with the narrative methodology of Douglass, whose theology transforms the "word" of abstraction into the "flesh" of moral and political praxis. In contrast, the reformed epistemology of analytic theism, its epistemic anti-foundationalism notwithstanding, transforms the flesh of the Christian Gospel—its abiding moral commitments, its suffering, and its sacrificial love—into an abstract "word." In a Christian theological context, abstraction thus excludes the history and the real social, political, and moral concerns of

Black people, and thus impedes rather than facilitates and emphasis on matters of racial justice. And, as I have been arguing in this chapter, abstraction is likewise an impediment to racial justice in jurisprudence.

81. Tim Golden, "From *Logos* to *Sarx*: Black Philosophy and the Philosophy of Religion," *The Black Scholar: Journal of Black Studies and Research* 43 (2013): 94–100.

82. Charles Mills, "Rawls on Race/Race in Rawls," *Southern Journal of Philosophy* 47 (2009): 161–184.

83. J.M. Balkin, "Understanding Legal Understanding: The Legal Subject and the Problem of Legal Coherence," *Yale Law Journal* 103 (1993): 105.

84. Lewis Gordon writes of American chattel slavery and Frederick Douglass's experience that "Douglass's chains can never be legitimated except through false consciousness and the most crass form of legal positivism wherein the laws simply are "right" by virtue of being laws of the state." See "Frederick Douglass as an Existentialist" in *Existentia Africana: Understanding Africana Existential Thought* (New York: Routledge, 2000), 44–45. Wrestling with the "most crass" forms of legal positivism, as Gordon has put it, has indeed been an abiding form of oppression directed at Black people.

85. Kenneth B. Nunn, "Law as a Eurocentric Enterprise," *Law and Inequality* 15 (1997): 323, 370.

86. Tommy J. Curry, "Shut Your Mouth When You're Talking to Me: Silencing the Idealist Turn in Critical Race Theory through a Cultralogic Turn in Jurisprudence," *Georgetown Journal of Law and Modern Critical Race Perspectives* 3 (2011): 4.

87. See "Racial Realism," 378–379.

88. See Bell, *Faces*, 98.

89. See Derrick Bell, "Justice Marshall and the Handmaid's Tale," in *Afrolantica Legacies* (Chicago: Third World Press, 1998), 123–136.

90. "Racial Realism," 378.

91. Ibid.

92. Ibid., 378–379.

93. Bell, *Faces*, 98.

94. Bell, *Afrolantica Legacies*, 125.

95. Ibid., 135.

96. Thurgood Marshall. "Justice Marshall Receives National Bar Association Award" August 10, 1988. https://www.c-span.org/video/?3962-1/justice-marshall-receives-national-bar-association-award/.

Works Cited

Balkin J.M., "Understanding Legal Understanding: The Legal Subject and the Problem of Legal Coherence," *Yale Law Journal* 103 (1993): 105–76.

Bell, Derrick. *Faces at the Bottom of the Well: The Permanence of Racism.* New York: Basic Books, 1992.

———. "Justice Marshall and the Handmaid's Tale," in *Afrolantica Legacies.* Chicago: Third World Press, 1998. 123–136.

———. "Racial Realism," *Connecticut Law Review* 24.2 (1992): 363–379.

———. "Wanted: A White Leader Able to Free Whites of Racism," *University of California Davis Law Review* (Spring 2000): 536–557.

———. *Silent Covenants:* Brown v. Board of Education *and the Unfulfilled Hopes for Racial Reform.* New York: Oxford University Press, 2004.

Bunche, Ralph. "A Critical Analysis of the Programs and Tactics of Minority Groups," *The Journal of Negro Education* 4.3 (1935): 308–320.

Camus, Albert. *Resistance, Rebellion, and Death.* New York: Random House, 1988.

Confucius, *Analects.* Translated by Raymond Dawson. New York: Oxford University Press, 2008.

Coppage v. Kansas, 236 U.S. 1 (1915).

Curry, Tommy J. "Shut Your Mouth When You're Talking to Me: Silencing the Idealist Turn in Critical Race Theory through a Cultralogic Turn in Jurisprudence," *Georgetown Journal of Law and Modern Critical Race Perspectives* 3 (2011): 1–38.

Descartes, René. *Meditations on First Philosophy,* 3rd ed. Translated by Donald A. Cress. Indianapolis, IN: Hackett Publishing, 1993.

Ellison, Ralph. *Invisible Man.* New York: Vintage Books, 1980.

Golden, Timothy J., *Frederick Douglass and the Philosophy of Religion: An Interpretation of Narrative, Art, and the Political.* Lanham, MD: Lexington Books, 2022.

———. "From *Logos* to *Sarx*: Black Philosophy and the Philosophy of Religion," *The Black Scholar: Journal of Black Studies and Research* 43 (2013): 94–100.

Gordon, Lewis R. "Frederick Douglass as an Existentialist," in *Existentia Africana: Understanding Africana Existential Thought.* New York: Routledge, 2000. 44–45.

Leiter, Brian, and Jules Coleman. "Determinacy, Objectivity and Authority," *University of Pennsylvania Law Review* 142 (1993): 549–637.

Leiter, Brian. *Naturalizing Jurisprudence: Essays on American Legal Realism and Naturalism in Legal Philosophy.* London, UK: Oxford University Press, 2007.

———. "The Methodology Problem in Jurisprudence," in *Naturalizing Jurisprudence: Essays on American Legal Realism and Naturalism in Legal Philosophy.* London: Oxford University Press, 2007. 168–170.

———. "Why Quine is not a Postmodernist," in *Naturalizing Jurisprudence: Essays on American Legal Realism and Naturalism in Legal Philosophy.* London: Oxford University Press, 2007. 137–151.

Marshall, Thurgood. "Justice Marshall Receives National Bar Association Award" August 10, 1988. https://www.c-span.org/video/?3962-1/justice-marshall-receives-national-bar-association-award/.

Mills, Charles. "Rawls on Race/Race in Rawls," *Southern Journal of Philosophy* 47 (2009): 161–184.
National Labor Relations Board v. Jones & Laughlin Steel Corp., 301 U.S. 1 (1937).
Nunn, Kenneth B. "Law as a Eurocentric Enterprise," *Law and Inequality* 15 (1997): 323–71.

Chapter 4

A Rock and a Hard Place

Interest Convergence for the Racial-Religious Minority

Audra Savage

> We are a Christian people, and the morality of the country is deeply ingrafted upon Christianity, and not upon the doctrines or worship of . . . impostors.
>
> —Chancellor Kent, *People v. Ruggles*[1]

Galen Black went to the Sweathouse Lodge in Cascadia, Oregon, to attend his first Native American Church teepee ceremony in September 1983. He walked into the Lodge as a new believer of the Native American church, interested in deepening his faith and to participate in the sacraments. He walked out as a champion of religious freedom, albeit unknowingly. For it was Mr. Black's use of peyote during the sacraments that day that would lead to his termination of employment at a drug and alcohol rehabilitation center. It would then lead to a Supreme Court case challenging the denial of his religious rights protected by the First Amendment to the U.S. Constitution.[2] Unfortunately for Mr. Black, and his friend Al Smith, the U.S. Supreme Court did not rule in their favor. While acknowledging the sincerity of their beliefs and the limited right to exercise those beliefs, the Court decided that the State of Oregon had a more compelling interest in controlling illegal substances within its borders. This interest of the state was weighty enough, significant enough, to topple the rights of the individual to their religious freedom.[3]

The public outcry against the Court's decision was loud, vehement, and swift.[4] Many could not believe the Court would subject the free exercise rights of individuals to state control. Others decried the decision as inconsistent with established doctrine regarding free exercise rights, especially when those rights conflict with state unemployment schemes.[5] They could not understand the Court's sharp turn from years of decisions championing the individual's right to practice the religion of their choosing without having to sacrifice any other right. For those who had been following the Supreme Court's adjudication of Native American religious rights, however, it was hardly surprising. While it is true that the Supreme Court was seemingly in favor of guaranteeing an individual's right to religious freedom—at least until the *Smith* decision—it is also true that the U.S. Supreme Court has never ruled in favor of certain religious minorities who pressed a free exercise claim. Most notably, the Court has denied religious rights to groups who were not only religious minorities, but also racial minorities. This group includes Native Americans, Jews, and Muslims.

To be a minority is to be feared, pitied, and scapegoated by those who are more privileged in society. This is true regardless of the classification in which the minority finds themselves. Oppression and discrimination from the ruling class can be based not only on religion, but on race, ethnicity, gender, sexual orientation, nationality, or age. This oppression is often rooted in history and based on generations of bias, animosity, and stereotypes toward a group of people. For Derrick Bell, the oppression of people in America based on race is rooted from the very beginning in the nation's founding. The legacy of slavery has tainted the early promises of equality and liberty for all, and the country has yet to recover from its original sin. As such, the challenges faced by members of a racial minority can be numerous and overwhelming. How much more so, then, are the challenges of individuals who are double minorities—those whose fate in life is to not only be nonwhite in America, but to fall into another grouping open to discrimination and bias.

Such is the case of the racial-religious minority. This is a group of people who are not only racially distinct, but also practice a religion outside of Christianity—the religion practiced, or at least professed, by the majority of Americans. The racial-religious minority is distinct from the traditional category of "religious minority," which can be defined in multiple ways. The religious minority can be a group of individuals who practice a religion or denomination not practiced or recognized by a large swath of the population, such as Jehovah's Witnesses. Alternatively, a religious minority can be defined as the religion practiced by a minority group, such as the black Christian church or Roman Catholicism practiced by Latino Americans. Unlike the religious minority, the challenge of the racial-religious minority is locating the basis for oppression. Are the denial of rights based on race or on the religion practiced? Is it a mixture of the two, and if so, which constitutional claims does one pursue?

Derrick Bell urged society to view the law through the prism of power and subordination and to question whether legal outcomes are truly a just result, or an attempt to maintain the dominance of the majority group over black bodies and black potential. One perspective in studying the interplay of race and the law is the role of religion in the power-subordination dynamic. As one commentator has suggested, the role of religion in critical race theory has not been studied enough or considered in the literature.[6] In 2017, as America adjusted to a new president who was banning Muslims while threatening to give preferential treatment to Christians, the nation was confronted with its history of prejudice based on race and religion. Now would seem the time to take a closer look at the jurisprudence of First Amendment religion cases through the eyes of Derrick Bell and use one of his theories to analyze court cases involving racial-religious minorities.

I. Racist Foundation

The mythology of America's founding suggests that the men who gathered in Philadelphia in the summer of 1787 were champions of freedom, equality, and liberty for all of humanity. Debate among the delegates centered primarily on the axis of large states versus smaller ones, but they were able to find creative and thoughtful compromises in order to finish the work of drafting a document to govern a new nation. They had a temporary lapse in judgment when drafting the article declaring slaves to be three-fifths of a person for purposes of determining representation and taxation, but otherwise they produced a document that heralded in a new world order and created a country that would be the shining light of freedom for all of eternity.

While it is true the creation of the Constitution is a stunning achievement and America is a blueprint of democracy worthy to be copied by many countries for centuries, it is an overstatement to suggest that the Three-Fifths Compromise was an aberration in an otherwise sound document guaranteeing individual rights. The fact is, the debate between delegates at the Constitutional Convention was mostly between states interested in protecting the "peculiar institution" of slavery and states that wanted to abolish it, or at least limit the power of Southern states employing it. The Three-Fifths Compromise is but one of many provisions in the Constitution evidencing the compromises between the Northern and Southern states over slavery. Indeed, the Constitution is infused with enough clauses directly or indirectly supporting slavery that it is hard not to conclude that the foundation of our country was set upon guaranteeing the unjust and unequal treatment of people of color.

THE CONSTITUTION OF SLAVERY[7]

There are three key provisions of the Constitution directly protecting, if not encouraging, the institution of slavery. The aforementioned Three-Fifths Compromise (Article I, Section 2, clause 3) allowed Southern states to gain more political muscle by adding slaves to the population of each state, thereby gaining more representatives in the House of Representatives than would be the case if only whites were counted.[8] Blacks were used to increase the influence of landowners of the states in the national congress but were not worthy enough to receive rights of citizenship or even be given the acknowledgment of humanity.

Article I, Section 9, clause 1 prevents Congress from ending the slave trade before 1808, though it does not require Congress to ban the slave trade after that date. This provision is notable not only because the Founders agreed to let states continue the inhumane business of trafficking in human misery, but also because it was a major exception to the general power granted to Congress to regulate commerce. The debates over this provision centered less on the morality of slavery or trading humans for money, and more on the political maneuverings of Georgia and South Carolina to counter Virginia and North Carolina's monopoly in slaves.[9] Georgia and South Carolina were aided in their efforts by New England states who may have believed the slave trade horrific, but needed allies in protecting commerce in general, and wanted the ability of the new nation to regulate commerce, in particular. In essence, the states that had abolished, or were in the process of abolishing, slavery and the slave trade found it politically expedient to argue against their own principles in order to create the nation and grow the economy.

Finally, the Fugitive Slave Clause required states to return runaway slaves to their owners on claim and prevented states from emancipating the slaves. This was a major win for the Southern states as there had never been an affirmative duty of non-slave-owning states to return runaway slaves before this provision. Now, all states were obligated to incur the cost of time and money in apprehending slaves and returning them to their owners, despite any personal misgivings surrounding slavery on the part of lawmakers, law enforcement officials, or judges.[10]

There were other provisions of the Constitution indirectly supporting the institution of slavery. Article I, Section 9, clause 4 allowed for slaves to be counted three-fifths the rate of whites if a capitation tax were ever levied. Article V prohibited any amendment to the slave importation or capitation tax clauses before 1808. The domestic insurrections clause (Article I, Section 8, clause 15) allowed Congress to call the militia to "suppress insurrections," which ostensibly included slave rebellions.[11] Certain provisions (Article I, Section 9, clause 5 and Article I, Section 10, clause 2) prohibited the federal government from excising taxes on goods imported or exported by any state. This prevented an indirect tax on goods produced from the fruits of slave labor, notably tobacco, rice, and cotton. Further, the Electoral College was created in part to ensure the Southern states had voting rights equal to the North. As such, the same three-fifths formula used elsewhere in the Constitution was used in Article II, Section 1, clause 2 establishing the Electoral College. It gave whites in slave states disproportionate influence in the election of the president. Other clauses protecting slavery included the clause on admission of new states (Article IV, Section 3, clause 1), which was drafted in anticipation of adding new slave states to the Union, and the clause on ratifying the Constitution, which was drafted to ensure the slaveholding states would have a perpetual veto over any constitutional changes.[12]

Taken together, these clauses show that the debate and subsequent compromises during the Constitutional Convention centered on the political and economic justifications for slavery, and not the moral ones. Indeed, the Constitution never uses the word "slavery," nor "slave," so as to make the document more agreeable to delegates from Northern states.[13] Or as the delegate from North Carolina, James Iredell, said at the ratifying convention, "the word *slave* is not mentioned owing to the [northern delegates'] particular scruples on the subject of slavery."[14] This suggests that Northern states had moral misgivings against slavery. Whatever the "scruples" might have been, however, the Northern states were comfortable allowing the institution of slavery not only to continue, but to have its continuation protected from the very beginning of the nation's founding. Even if they believed the institution would soon come to an end (and there is no evidence to suggest they held such belief[15]), they were complicit in creating a legal system that valued individuals not based on their inherent worth as human beings, but on the advantages and benefits these individuals can offer those with more power. This established a dangerous template that was to be followed for the course of this country's history.

The Historical Limitations of the First Amendment

The racism established in the Constitution by the Founders carried into American law and society. It was a pervasive force affecting all subjects of the law, including the First Amendment. The First Amendment guarantees that Congress shall not make any laws respecting the free exercise of religion.[16] Although it does not contain explicit statements about race, the context in which this amendment was created suggests racial limitations.

Once the drafters of the Constitution finished their work at the Convention in Philadelphia, they then had the arduous task of getting it ratified by their state conventions. This process would take up to two years, with the Constitution becoming effective in 1789. The politicians at the ratifying conventions immediately noticed one aspect of this new document to create a united set of states—a lack of explicit protection for religious freedom.[17] Members of the various state ratifying conventions were concerned that there was no statement explicitly protecting certain freedoms and liberties, most notably the freedom of religion.[18] Individual states began the task of drafting their version of a bill of rights to add these guarantees into the Constitution. In fact, the creation of amendments guaranteeing basic freedoms was a condition upon which many states approved the Constitution and voted for its adoption.[19] The states gave the First Congress one year to create this bill of rights, using the various drafts from the states.

The concerns among drafters of the First Amendment centered on the extent to which the liberty of conscience is protected, the limits on government action concerning religion, and whether there would be equality among religions. "Religions" were understood to mean Christian denominations. So, in essence, the debate was the extent to which Episcopalians would enjoy the same rights as Baptists, and so forth. Some of the Founders had deference to other monotheistic religions, like Islam and Judaism, in their rhetoric; in reality, however, it was generally understood the protection of religion extended only to those practiced by the white landowners—Protestant Christianity.[20]

The religions of the indigenous people and the slaves were never considered in any discussions or debates surrounding the freedom of religion, generally, or the drafting of the First Amendment, in particular. The importance of Christianity was so strong, in fact, that early in the period when slavery was first introduced in America, a slave could be manumitted if they converted to Christianity.[21] Once a slave was baptized, they gained their freedom. This practice lasted only a few decades because landowners needed a more stable workforce and larger numbers of workers.[22] They could no longer afford to let slaves go free; however, the expectation that slaves would relinquish their native religion and convert to Christianity continued and became part of the culture of slavery. Similarly, the religion of Native Americans was treated with disdain and seen as an obstacle to overcome in converting the indigenous population to Christianity. Indeed, an early Supreme Court case granted the right of a Catholic school to receive federal funds in order to educate (and undoubtedly convert) Native American children.[23]

The idea that some religions are more legitimate and therefore worthy of constitutional and legal protection was established at the very beginning of our nation. It is no surprise, as the nation's founding also established that some individuals are more valuable than others. It is no wonder, then, that the guarantees of the First Amendment have always rung hollow for people of color who practiced a different religion.

II. Prejudice in First Amendment Jurisprudence

Overview of Free Exercise Clause Jurisprudence

Despite the many discussions among the Founders about the need for religious freedom and the debates over the drafting of the First Amendment, this amendment was seldom used for the first 150 years of the nation as a recourse for those seeking protection of free exercise rights.[24] Most free exercise rights, when even pressed, were done at the state level, as all states had the concept of free exercise in their state constitutions or charters before the Constitution was drafted. This changed in 1940 with the Supreme Court's decision in *Cantwell v. Connecticut*.[25] The Court in *Cantwell* incorporated the First Amendment into the Fourteenth Amendment, thereby expressly applying the responsibility of granting free exercise rights to the government of the states. States were accustomed to honoring religious freedom guarantees; now, for the first time, individuals had a constitutional right guaranteed by the federal government against action by the state.

There was an explosion of free exercise cases after *Cantwell* and the standard of review for reviewing these cases evolved over time. From the first free exercise case, *Reynolds v. U.S.*,[26] until *Cantwell*, the Supreme Court employed a rational basis review, the lowest form of scrutiny. The government is given leeway to enact laws that are reasonable and within its authority to make. The Court checks to ensure there is no outright tyranny by the government. If it is satisfied, the government wins, as it did every time in the first sixty years of free exercise jurisprudence.[27] The Court used a more rigorous form of review in *Cantwell*. The government had to show its interest in adopting a particular law is important and significant, and not merely legitimate. This heightened scrutiny cordoned off areas of religion not to be regulated by the government unless the government could show its law was not discriminatory, nor prohibited religious beliefs.[28] Beginning in 1963, a strict scrutiny form of review was used by the Court for the first time. In *Sherbert v. Verner*,[29] the Court articulated that the government must have a compelling interest in enacting a law that has the effect of curbing the free exercise of religion and that the government has used the most narrow means to achieve its interest without curbing free exercise.[30] Ten cases were adjudicated using this standard of review, and it was generally thought to be the settled standard. Then came the *Smith* decision.[31] The Court rejected the evolution of review for free exercise cases and rejected outright strict scrutiny in favor of regressing back to a lower-level scrutiny test. It required individuals to comply with a "valid and neutral law of general applicability" regardless of its effect on the individual's ability to adhere to religious tenets. This form of review is somewhat more protective than the low level used in *Reynolds*, as it requires a law that is not neutral or not generally applicable to show it meets a compelling government interest and is narrowly tailored to achieve that interest. However, the free exercise clause was weakened considerably by the *Smith* decision.[32]

In light of the seismic shift in free exercise jurisprudence brought by *Smith*, the public demanded greater protections guaranteed by the First Amendment. As a result, Congress enacted the Religious Freedom Restoration Act (RFRA) in 1993. RFRA reinstated the strict scrutiny level of review typified in the *Sherbert* case and its progeny. After a series of cases, the Court has clarified RFRA's application to federal laws only—it does not apply to state or local laws.[33] As far as the free exercise clause of the First Amendment is concerned, however, the standard of review is still the low-level scrutiny established in *Smith*.

Given the trajectory of the standard of review for cases involving free exercise, it would seem the *Smith* decision dealt a significant blow to the individual's ability to seek redress for a violation of the constitutional right to free exercise. This ability, however, has been illusory for the racial-religious minority since the beginning of free exercise jurisprudence.

Free Exercise Jurisprudence for the Racial-Religious Minority

A review of free exercise jurisprudence since incorporation shows there are three groups of people pressing First Amendment claims who could be considered a racial-religious minority: Native Americans, Jews, and Muslims. Individuals in this group possess the traits, and the ensuing discrimination, common to both a racial classification and a religious one. There may be individual members in each of these groups who do not possess the racial trait (e.g., a person of Anglo-Saxon decent who converts to any of these religions, or a person with physical traits more common to white or black Americans but sharing a Native American ancestry), and thereby would not be a racial-religious minority in a strict sense. However, as a whole, people in these groups have not fared well at the Supreme Court.

NATIVE AMERICANS

The history of the government's treatment of Native Americans, generally, and their religion, specifically, is troublesome. Despite the plethora of laws and statutes protecting indigenous peoples and their exercise of religion, the rights of Native Americans continue to be violated. In several cases, the Native American plaintiffs could assert claims not only under the First Amendment to the Constitution, but also under the American

Indian Religious Freedom Act (AIRFA).[34] In spite of the ability to press claims using two different areas of law, the Supreme Court ruled against the religionists in derogation of their rights under federal protection.[35]

In *Bowen v. Roy*[36] the Court dictated the manner in which Native American parents could raise their children. A father objected to the requirement to have a social security number for his daughter, as he felt the number would rob the child's spirit according to his religious belief. He sought an exemption from the requirement until the daughter turned sixteen years old, the age of spiritual maturity. The Court denied this exemption, saying that the government was not required to "conduct its own internal affairs in ways that comport with the religious beliefs of particular citizens."[37] This was fourteen years after the same Court allowed Amish parents to remove their children from school in contravention of compulsory school attendance laws[38]—laws applicable to other parents. In that opinion of the court, the same Chief Justice who authored the *Bowen* decision expressed appreciation for the older, traditional religious practices of the Amish and said the compulsory attendance law "carries with it a very real threat of undermining the Amish community and religious practice as they exist today." Apparently this solicitude toward older, long-practiced religions applied only to white Christian groups and did not extend to Native American religious practices—practices that existed before the founding of the nation.

The Court continued its lack of concern for protecting Native American religious practices two years later when it allowed the destruction of sacred burial sites in *Lyng v. Northwest Indian Cemetery Protective Association*.[39] The Court ruled in favor of the U.S. Forest Service's decision to build a road directly through a sacred burial ground used for centuries by three Native American tribes. These sites are key areas of communal worship, no less important than a church or mosque. There were alternative plans available for the road that would have kept the sanctity of the burial site, but they were more costly to the Forest Service.[40] Essentially, the Court allowed the government to be more prudent about money than a group's right to the free exercise of religion.

The Supreme Court allowed the state to punish members of a Native American church for engaging in a certain spiritual sacrament because that sacrament included peyote, a Schedule I controlled narcotic in Oregon. In *Smith*, the plaintiffs requested unemployment compensation from the state of Oregon after they were fired from the drug rehabilitation facility. The state denied the request arguing that Messrs. Smith and Black violated the state's narcotics statute by ingesting peyote during the spiritual ritual. The Court agreed with the state. There was no exemption granted, nor any legal recognition of the importance of this religious practice to the person and their culture. It is especially egregious in light of Supreme Court cases prior to *Smith* where the plaintiffs were successful in pressing free exercise rights against the denial of unemployment compensation by state governments. In four cases—*Sherbert* (mentioned in section II(A)); *Thomas v. Review Board*; *Hobbie v. Unemployment Appeals Commission of Florida*; and *Frazee v. Illinois Department of Employment Security*[41]—the Court was concerned with the burden placed on religion by the state when it requires the religious practitioner to modify their behavior in order to receive state benefits.[42] The beliefs at issue in the four cases varied, but they did have one thing in common—all four plaintiffs were Christian.[43]

Smith was decided one year after the last of these cases and yet had a vastly different outcome. One reason the Court gave for this difference is the fact that the plaintiffs were requesting an exemption from a general criminal law and the state has an overwhelming interest in maintaining law and order.[44] This reason rings hollow, however, as governments have been proven capable of granting exemptions to criminal laws for religious reasons, such as when Catholic priests were allowed to continue using wine for communion during the prohibition of alcohol.[45] In fact, the state of Oregon soon passed a law allowing the use of peyote for religious purposes after *Smith* was decided,[46] proving that it is indeed possible for state governments to provide exemptions to criminal laws for religious reasons.

JEWS

Jewish believers have not fared any better than their Native American counterparts. Two Jewish merchants lost cases challenging the government's imposition of Sunday as a Sabbath, prohibiting any labor or commerce on Sunday not considered necessary or essential.[47] According to Jewish religious law, the Sabbath occurs on Saturday and it prevents adherents from working or doing any labor on that day. The merchants claimed that these "Sunday blue laws" established religion, burdened the exercise of their own religion, and impeded their ability to earn a living in a manner best suited for them. The Court was not sympathetic to these claims, noting that the laws regulated the plaintiff's store hours and not their religious practices. The Court gave no accommodation to the liberty of conscience or worship. This is particularly troubling because the regulations involved in the *Gallagher* case had numerous exceptions for other types of businesses (e.g., retail sale of tobacco, frozen desserts, and live bait) on Sundays, while denying the same opportunity to a close-knit Jewish community. Adding insult to injury, just two years later, the Supreme Court granted an exemption in the *Sherbert* case, allowing a Christian worker to receive unemployment benefits for refusing to work on the Saturday Sabbath in accordance with her religious beliefs. Sherbert was allowed to earn a living in a manner denied to Jews—fellow Saturday Sabbatarians.

Twenty-five years after *Braunfeld* and *Gallagher*, a Jewish Air Force psychologist challenged military regulations prohibiting the wearing of his yarmulke.[48] For three years, Rabbi Goldman wore his yarmulke on base as part of his military uniform, that is, until he testified in military court. He was challenged for wearing the yarmulke in violation of the military dress code. The Supreme Court upheld his conviction because free exercise rights are "severely diminished" on a military base. The Court argued that the "requirements for military discipline and uniformity outweighed any countervailing religious interests,"[49] despite the fact that the military granted exemptions to the dress code for other religious garb, including crucifixes.

It is interesting to note that the Court decisions regarding Jewish believers were later nullified by legislatures. State and local governments eventually did away with Sunday blue laws, allowing Jewish merchants to conduct business on Sunday. And following the *Goldman* decision, the U.S. Congress amended the military dress code to allow yarmulkes.[50] This may be little comfort to Jewish practitioners at the time. They had to rely on politicians to protect their free exercise rights as a racial-religious minority instead of the Court.

MUSLIMS

There has been only one Supreme Court with a Muslim plaintiff requesting protection of First Amendment free exercise rights. In *O'Lone v. Estate of Shabazz*,[51] Muslim inmates challenged a change in prison policy resulting in the loss of their ability to attend Jumu'ah, their Friday collective worship service. The Court ruled in favor of the prison, saying the prison had reasonable penological objectives in depriving the inmates of access to worship services and these objectives outweighed their free exercise rights. The need to maintain security is a heightened concern in the prison context and, therefore, on the surface it seems reasonable for the Court to uphold the government's discretion in setting prison policy. When contrasted against other cases with plaintiffs in prison claiming violations of rights, however, it would seem this deference to prison policy is questionable. In the four other cases decided by the Court, the plaintiffs were successful in obtaining protection for religious rights, or at least granted leave to pursue their claims in court.[52] The religions at issue in these cases were religious minorities, as in *O'Lone*—Islam, Buddhism, and a group of nonmainstream religions (Satanist, Wicca, Asatru religions, and the Church of Jesus Christ Christian). What is unique about these cases is that they were brought under various statutory provisions and not under a First Amendment free exercise claim. Again it seems it is more beneficial for a racial-religious minority to seek redress from a legislature other than from the Supreme Court.

OTHER RELIGIOUS MINORITIES

The above discussion should not be read to suggest that other religious minorities were always successful and protected in their desire to maintain free exercise rights. Indeed, there are two groups who have a long and difficult history at the Supreme Court: Mormons and Jehovah's Witnesses. In fact, the very first application of the free exercise clause at the Supreme Court was a case involving a Mormon challenging laws against polygamy on the ground of free exercise rights.[53] For several years, Mormons would continue to pursue free exercise exemptions against anti-polygamy laws, but to no avail. Jehovah's Witnesses also have the privilege of having a first at the Supreme Court. As mentioned earlier, *Cantwell v. Connecticut* was the first time the Court incorporated the free exercise clause of the First Amendment into the Fourteenth Amendment. That case involved the violation by Jehovah's Witnesses of a local ordinance requiring a license to distribute religious materials. Although they won this first battle, members of the Jehovah's Witness church would have mixed success at the Supreme Court.

It is interesting to note the nature of the opposition Mormons face regarding polygamy. The Church of Jesus Christ of Latter-day Saints had several tenets that were antithetical to late nineteenth- to early twentieth-century Americans. There was strong, and often violent, opposition to Mormonism. Polygamy was one of the reasons. It was seen as a barbaric practice not belonging in "civilized" cultures. It was seen as appropriate for "inferior" peoples, such as Muslims (Africans) or Asians, but not for people of the West.[54] Although white, Mormons suffered from the same oppressive and discriminatory thinking as the racial-religious minority—the idea that certain practices and beliefs of racial groups and religions are appropriate for society, while others are not. This was the thinking of the Founders that was established in the Constitution and one that continued into the adjudication of free exercise rights.

III. Interest Convergence for the Racial-Religious Minority

Given the generally unsuccessful attempts by Native Americans, Jews, and Muslims to protect their free exercise rights, the fact that there is a case where a racial-religious minority group successfully fought for their religious rights is notable. In *Church of the Lukumi Babalu Aye, Inc. v. City of Hialeah*,[55] practitioners of the Santeria religion overturned a local city ordinance that sought to extinguish their rights to practice a central doctrine to their religion, to wit, animal sacrifice. This decision was three years after the demoralizing *Smith* decision and followed 150 years of Supreme Court jurisprudence that ignored the rights of the racial-religious minority. Before one celebrates this achievement and suggests that racial-religious minorities in particular and religious minorities in general will now enjoy more protection of their rights, it is important to analyze the case through the prism of Bell's interest-convergence theory. This theory scrutinizes cases through the sobering reality of racial realism.

Bell's Interest-Convergence Theory

Derrick Bell turned traditional thinking about civil rights on its head when he posited the interest-convergence theory, a theory born from a critical re-examination of the watershed decision of *Brown v. Board of Education*.[56] Generally thought to be one of the most consequential decisions of the Supreme Court, and therefore society at large, Bell suggested that the justices decided the case less on moral and legal reasons for guaranteeing equality for blacks, but more on advancing the interests of whites. He stated that the "interest of blacks in achieving racial equality will be accommodated only when it converges with the interests of whites. However, the Fourteenth Amendment, standing alone, will not authorize a judicial remedy providing effective racial equality for blacks where the remedy sought threatens the superior societal status of middle and upper class whites."[57]

He further suggested that courts will provide remedies to counter the racial inequality faced by blacks only when such remedies "secure, advance, or at least not harm societal interests deemed important by middle and upper class whites."[58] For support of this principle, Bell considers the history of race relations and segregation in the country prior to the *Brown* decision. Blacks attacked the validity of school segregation for 100 years, but they were not successful until *Brown*. This was not the first time the Court was confronted with the immorality of racial inequality and segregation, so Bell questioned what could account for the Court finally overturning the odious practice of segregating school children.

The answer lay not only in law and morality, but also in politics, economics, and foreign policy. The decision to end segregation would lend needed credibility to America's fight against Communism by showing the people of the emerging third world that America was true to its promise of equality. Also, it reassured blacks facing increased violence and discrimination after returning home from World War II that the country did indeed support the values they had fought and died for overseas. There was a fear that the anger and disillusionment of blacks could make Communism more attractive to them. Finally, ending segregation would help the South transition from a rural society to a more industrialized economy.[59]

Bell does not suggest these were the only reasons for whites to support desegregation. Indeed, many whites had fought and died for racial equality for decades based on moral reasons. However, the self-interested reasons would persuade the courts to finally enact racial reform after 100 years of allowing segregation to continue.

Essentially, then, there are several aspects of Bell's theory of interest convergence that can be gleaned. First, there is a long history of unsuccessfully advocating for rights of the minority group until the Court finally protects the group's rights. Second, there are reasons beyond morality that drive the decision. It is not enough for the Court to decide a certain way because it is the right thing to do. There must be concrete, pragmatic reasons. Third, the reasons must advance, or at least not hinder, the standing and interests of the majority group.

Although Bell developed the interest-convergence theory in the context of racial equality for blacks, it is an important theory applicable to other minority groups. Given that the *Hialeah* case is the first successful case for the racial-religious minority, it is appropriate to apply the theory to that case.

Overview of the Hialeah Case

The Santeria religion is centuries old and was practiced by slaves from Africa in Cuba. It is an amalgamation of practices from the Yoruba people of western Africa with Roman Catholicism. Since its inception, there has been hostility from Catholics in Cuba toward practitioners of Santeria, no doubt owing to the fact that the religion was one originated and practiced by black slaves. In fact, it was an underground religion and rarely practiced in the open. Pastor Ernesto Pichardo decided to change this for his community of worshippers in southern Florida. He obtained a permit for a new worship center in Hialeah, Florida, consisting of a church, school, cultural center, and museum. Shortly thereafter, the city council adopted several local ordinances preventing the unsanctioned slaughter of animals. As animal sacrifice is a central tenet of the Santeria faith, the ordinances had the effect of prohibiting the religionists from exercising their religion. The church challenged the local ordinances in court, claiming the laws violated its members' First Amendment right to free exercise.

The Supreme Court found in favor of the Santerians.[60] Using the recently revised level of review as promulgated in *Smith*, the Court found the laws were neither neutral in scope nor general in application. Failing that, the Court then considered whether the government's interest in the laws was compelling and whether the laws were drawn narrowly to achieve that interest. The town failed on both fronts. One of the key features of the laws leading the Court to strike them down were the numerous exceptions to the laws. The ordinances allowed unregulated slaughter of animals by businesses, hunters, and other religious groups (e.g., Jewish kosher slaughter). Another factor in the Court's decision was the blatant animosity toward Santeria expressed by city council members and townspeople at the town hall meetings discussing the ordinances. Taken together, the Court found the ordinances to intentionally single out one particular religion for the purposes of discrimination and prohibition.[61]

Interest Convergence in Hialeah

Fifty years of Supreme Court jurisprudence showed the insensitivity, if not downright hostility, toward free exercise rights for the racial-religious minority. The *Hialeah* case changed that perspective. While it is an achievement, it is indeed a curious aberration. It is useful to apply Bell's theory of interest convergence to this case to analyze the contours of this decision.

The first aspect of the interest-convergence theory is evidenced by the earlier discussion of free exercise rights for Native Americans, Jews, and Mormons. Without a doubt, there has been a long history of discrimination and unsuccessful constitutional challenges against racial-religious minorities, mimicking the long history of discrimination faced by black Americans. Like these earlier cases, Santerians challenged laws that directly and negatively impacted the practice of their religion. They were prevented from sacrificing animals, no less an important ritual than ingesting peyote or purposefully taking a day of Sabbath rest on Saturday. Perhaps the Court would argue *Hialeah* was different because the ordinance at issue contained so many exceptions that it was clear the law had a discriminatory purpose against the Santeria faith. The same could be said in earlier cases, however. For instance, there were exceptions against the Sunday blue laws at issue in *Gallagher*, allowing the sale of tobacco, frozen desserts, and live bait, and yet no exemption could be granted for the Jewish merchants. Further, there were exceptions to the regulations governing military dress at issue in *Goldman*, allowing religious garb such as crucifixes, and yet no exemption could be granted for the Jewish Air Force psychologist. It would appear that other factors were possibly at play in the Court's decision.

While morality may have played a part in the Court's decision, there were other, more pragmatic reasons for the Court's reasons consistent with the second aspect of Bell's theory. First, *Hialeah* followed in the wake of the fallout from the Court's *Smith* decision. The furor over that decision cannot be overstated. It was not limited to just the small circle of religious freedom scholars and jurists but involved constitutional scholars, politicians, and news media. In fact, the U.S. Congress moved quickly, and a bill to restore religious freedom (and the strict scrutiny level of review established in *Sherbert*) was introduced within a year after the *Smith* decision in 1991. There was bipartisan support for the bill as it was debated and revised. The new act, the Religious Freedom Restoration Act (RFRA),[62] was signed by the president and became law a few short months after the Court released its opinion for the case. Fundamentally, RFRA was a legislative overruling of the Supreme Court's decision. In light of this, it is not hard to imagine that the Court wanted to show it needed no such overruling as it was still capable of protecting religious rights in general and religious rights for minority groups in particular under the new standard introduced in *Smith*. The justices would have known about RFRA, as the Court agreed to review the case after RFRA had been introduced in Congress. The oral arguments, Court deliberation, and final decision were all taking place while RFRA was being debated and revised a few blocks away on Capitol Hill. *Hialeah* allowed the Court to save face while another branch was moving to act against it.

In addition to national politics, the Court decided *Hialeah* in the midst of consequential global affairs. The Court considered the case just months after the end of the Cold War. President George H.W. Bush and Russian President Boris Yeltsin signed a declaration on February 1, 1992, formally ending the ideological battle between the two superpowers. Global conflicts would continue, but they would no longer be cast as democracy and capitalism against Communism. It is ironic that in the wake of this declaration of a new world order the Court was deliberating on a case regarding constitutional rights of people practicing a religion originating from a Communist country (Cuba). It is not hard to imagine that this played a part in the Court's decision to protect the Santeria religionists, who were openly practicing their religion after decades of repression and being driven underground. It would be a reminder that America's commitment to freedom and equality defeated Communism. This reminder was needed at the time as the country was increasing its involvement in the conflicts in Somalia and Bosnia-Herzegovina.

A final aspect of the interest-convergence theory is the effect on the interests of the majority group. The *Hialeah* decision did not hinder the Christian majority. In striking down the ordinances, the Court did not impair the importance or dominance of Christianity or subvert the political or economic interests of the majority, as would be the case in the decisions affecting other racial-religious minorities. In the cases involving Native Americans, granting them exemptions from the laws could be seen as weakening the social security system or the government's "tough on crime" stance, or could interfere with the government's most cost-effective plan for federal land. For the cases involving Jews and Muslims, exemptions could have interfered with the majority's recognition and reverence for Christ's resurrection by acknowledging a different day of rest or undermined the government's interest in a specific type of uniformity in the military or in the prison system. However, in the *Hialeah* case, overturning the ordinances did not affect preexisting laws or interfere with businesses or the economy. It had a tangential impact on members of the city who may have opposed animal sacrifice on religious grounds, among others, or Cuban Catholics who had a cultural antipathy toward Santeria; however, it did not affect their ability to practice Christianity or question the dominance of Christianity in the community or in the law.

Given the above, it would appear that the Santeria challengers to local ordinances had the fortune of choosing the right moment in time. For history suggested that if not for the convergence of these circumstances and interests, the outcome would likely have been different. It is difficult to determine if this case was truly an anomaly or if it represented a watershed change for Supreme Court jurisprudence for the racial-religious minority. Since *Hialeah*, there have been very few cases involving religious minorities of any stripe pressing free exercise claims because of the proliferation of statutes regarding religious rights that occurred after RFRA was enacted. Religionists have sought protection under state constitutions and laws, and not under the First Amendment. The reasons for this shift to relying on a statutory scheme for religious protection are obvious and understandable. However, it is not a desired outcome. Minorities leave themselves vulnerable when relying on the political will of the majority for protection and amplification of their rights. At any moment, the interests of the majority could change, and along with it, the will to protect minority rights. This will has not historically been a concern of the majority, which is not surprising given the nation's original Constitution and laws. Using the perspective of Derrick Bell's work, one can better appreciate the fragility of rights for the racial-religious minority. One hopes that this fragility will dissipate as the country continues to value the protection of religious freedom—for all religious groups.

Notes

1. *People v. Ruggles*, 8 Johns. 290, 294, 295 (1811).

2. *Employment Div. Dept. of Human Resources of Ore. v. Smith*, 494 U.S. 872 (1990).

3. Ibid.

4. For example, there are an estimated 385 law review articles referencing the *Smith* decision published within the first two years of the decision (according to a review of Westlaw on February 26, 2017).

5. See *Sherbert v. Verner*, 374 U.S. 398 (1963); *Thomas v. Review Board of the Indiana Employment Security Division*, 450 U.S. 707 (1981); *Hobbie v. Unemployment Appeals Commission of Florida*, 480 U.S. 136 (1987); and *Frazee v. Illinois Department of Employment Security*, 489 U.S. 829 (1989). See section II(B), "Free Exercise Jurisprudence for the Racial-Religious Minority."

6. Brandon Paradise, "How Critical Race Theory Marginalizes the African American Christian Tradition," *Michigan Journal of Race and Law* 20 (Fall 2014): 117–211.

7. Savage, Audra L. "The Religion of Race: The Supreme Court as Priests of Racial Politics," *Utah Law Review* 2021 (2021): 569, 576–79, 589.

8. Paul Finkelman, *Slavery and the Founders: Race and Liberty in the Age of Jefferson* (New York: Routledge, 2015), 7–18.

9. Ibid., 19–29.

10. See Robert M. Cover, *Justice Accused: Antislavery and the Judicial Process* (New Haven, CT: Yale University Press, 1975).

11. Slave states argued against language suggesting "domestic violence" out of fear of the federal government coming into their states to regulate slavery. However, once the clause was narrowed to protect against insurrections, this was acceptable because they saw it as a protection against slave revolts—one of their biggest fears. See Finkelman, *Slavery and the Founders*, 30.

12. Ibid., 3–7.

13. Ibid., 3.

14. Ibid.

15. Derrick Bell, "White Superiority in America: Its Legal Legacy, Its Economic Costs," *Villanova Law Review* 33.5 (1988): 767, 768.

16. U.S. Const. amend. I.

17. There were two clauses related to religion in the Constitution—the prohibition on religious tests for office in Article VI and the allowance of affirmations in lieu of oaths in Article I, Section 3, clause 6; Article II, Section 1, clause 8; and Article VI. However, neither of these clauses related to religious freedom guarantees.

18. John Witte Jr. and Joel A. Nichols, *Religion and the American Constitutional Experiment*, 3rd ed. (New York: Oxford University Press, 2011), 79.

19. Michael W. McConnell, "The Origins and Historical Understanding of Free Exercise of Religion," *Harvard Law Review* 103 (May 1990): 1409, 1476.

20. Witte and Nichols, *Religion and the American Constitutional Experiment*, 102, 119. Neither Catholicism nor Eastern Orthodox Christianity were seen as equal to Protestantism. Discrimination occurred against these groups as well.

21. William M. Wiecek, "The Statutory Law of Slavery and Race in the Thirteen Mainland Colonies of British America," *The William & Mary Quarterly* 34.2 (April 1977): 258, 263–264.

22. Ibid.

23. *Quick Bear v. Leupp*, 210 U.S. 50 (1907).

24. Most First Amendment claims before 1940 were brought by Mormons as a defense against prosecution for violating anti-polygamy statutes. See section II(C), "Other Religious Minorities."

25. *Cantwell v. Connecticut*, 310 U.S. 296 (1940).

26. *Reynolds v. U.S.*, 98 U.S. 145 (1879).

27. Witte and Nichols, *Religion and the American Constitutional Experiment*, 136–137.

28. Ibid.
29. *Sherbert*, 374 U.S. 398 (1963).
30. Witte and Nichols, *Religion and the American Constitutional Experiment*, 136–137.
31. *Smith*, 494 U.S. 872 (1990).
32. Witte and Nichols, *Religion and the American Constitutional Experiment*, 136–137.
33. See *City of Boerne v. Flores*, 521 U.S. 507 (1997) and *Gonzales v. O Centro Espirita Beneficiente Uniao Do Vegetal*, 546 U.S. 418 (2006).
34. American Indian Religious Freedom Act (AIRFA), 42 U.S.C. § 1996 et seq. (Supp. IV 1980).
35. Witte and Nichols, *Religion and the American Constitutional Experiment*, 162.
36. *Bowen v. Roy*, 476 U.S. 693 (1986).
37. Ibid. at 699.
38. *Wisconsin v. Yoder*, 406 U.S. 205 (1972).
39. *Lyng v. Northwest Indian Cemetery Protective Association*, 485 U.S. 439 (1988).
40. Witte and Nichols, *Religion and the American Constitutional Experiment*, 157.
41. *Thomas*, 450 U.S. 707 (1981); *Hobbie*, 480 U.S. 136 (1987); and *Frazee*, 489 U.S. 829 (1989).
42. This was expressed by Chief Justice Burger in *Thomas*, the same Chief Justice who decided in favor of the Amish parents but against the Native American parents.
43. The plaintiffs were two Seventh-day Adventists, one Jehovah's Witness and one Christian with an idiosyncratic belief in the Sabbath rest of watching football on Sunday.
44. *Smith*, 494 U.S. 872 (1990).
45. National Prohibition Act ("Volstead Act"), 41 Stat. 305, 308–39 (1919), repealed by U.S. Const. amend. 21 (1933).
46. "Oregon Peyote Law Leaves 1983 Defendant Unvindicated," *New York Times*, July 9, 1991, www.nytimes.com/1991/07/09/us/oregon-peyote-law-leaves-1983-defendant-unvindicated.html.
47. *Braunfeld v. Brown*, 366 U.S. 599 (1961) and *Gallagher v. Crown Kosher Super Market of Massachusetts*, 366 U.S. 617 (1961).
48. *Goldman v. Weinberger*, 475 U.S. 503 (1986).
49. Ibid.
50. 10 U.S.C. § 774 (2009).
51. *O'Lone v. Estate of Shabazz*, 482 U.S. 342 (1987).
52. See *Cooper v. Pate*, 378 U.S. 546 (1964); *Cruz v. Beto*, 405 U.S. 319 (1972); *Cutter v. Wilkinson*, 544 U.S. 709 (2005); and *Holt v. Hobbs*, 574 U.S. 352 (2015).

53. *Reynolds*, 98 U.S. 145 (1879).

54. "Polygamy has always been odious among the northern and western nations of Europe, and, until the establishment of the Mormon Church, was almost exclusively a feature of the life of Asiatic and of African people." *Reynolds*, 98 U.S. at 164.

55. *Church of the Lukumi Babalu Aye v. City of Hialeah*, 508 U.S. 520 (1993).

56. *Brown v. Board of Education*, 347 U.S. 483 (1954).

57. Derrick A. Bell, Jr, "Brown v. Board of Education and the Interest-Convergence Dilemma," *Harvard Law Review* 93 (1980): 518, 523.

58. Ibid.

59. Ibid., 523–525.

60. *Church of the Lukumi Babalu Aye*, 508 U.S. 520 (1993).

61. The concurrences of several justices noted the use of the new standard of review following *Smith* and expressed concern that the new standard varied wildly from decades of jurisprudence. One justice went so far to say *Smith* was wrongly decided. *Church of the Lukumi Babalu Aye*, 508 U.S. at 577–580 (J. Blackmun, concurring).

62. Religious Freedom Restoration Act of 1993 (RFRA), 107 Stat. 1488, 42 U.S.C. § 2000bb et seq.

Works Cited

"Oregon Peyote Law Leaves 1983 Defendant Unvindicated," *New York Times*, July 9, 1991. www.nytimes.com/1991/07/09/us/oregon-peyote-law-leaves-1983-defendant-unvindicated.html.

American Indian Religious Freedom Act (AIRFA), 42 U.S.C. § 1996 et seq. (Supp. IV 1980).

Bell, Derrick. "*Brown v. Board of Education* and the Interest-Convergence Dilemma," *Harvard Law Review* 93 (1980): 518, 523.

———. "White Superiority in America: Its Legal Legacy, Its Economic Costs," *Villanova Law Review* 33.5 (1988): 767, 768.

Bowen v. Roy, 476 U.S. 693 (1986).

Braunfeld v. Brown, 366 U.S. 599 (1961).

Brown v. Board of Education, 347 U.S. 483 (1954).

Cantwell v. Connecticut, 310 U.S. 296 (1940).

Church of the Lukumi Babalu Aye v. City of Hialeah, 508 U.S. 520 (1993).

City of Boerne v. Flores, 521 U.S. 507 (1997).

Cooper v. Pate, 378 U.S. 546 (1964).

Cover, Robert M. *Justice Accused: Antislavery and the Judicial Process*. New Haven, CT: Yale University Press, 1975.

Cruz v. Beto, 405 U.S. 319 (1972).

Cutter v. Wilkinson, 544 U.S. 709 (2005).
Employment Div. Dept. of Human Resources of Oregon v. Smith, 494 U.S. 872 (1990).
Finkelman, Paul. *Slavery and the Founders: Race and Liberty in the Age of Jefferson.* New York: Routledge, 2015.
Frazee v. Illinois Department of Employment Security, 489 U.S. 829 (1989).
Gallagher v. Crown Kosher Super Market of Massachusetts, 366 U.S. 617 (1961).
Goldman v. Weinberger, 475 U.S. 503 (1986).
Gonzales v. O Centro Espirita Beneficiente Uniao Do Vegetal, 546 U.S. 418 (2006).
Hobbie v. Unemployment Appeals Commission of Florida, 480 U.S. 136 (1987).
Holt v. Hobbs, 574 U.S. 352 (2015).
Lyng v. Northwest Indian Cemetery Protective Association, 485 U.S. 439 (1988).
McConnell, Michael W. "The Origins and Historical Understanding of Free Exercise of Religion," *Harvard Law Review* 103 (May 1990): 1409, 1476.
National Prohibition Act ("Volstead Act"), 41 Stat. 305, 308–339 (1919), repealed by U.S. Const. amend. 21 (1933).
O'Lone v. Estate of Shabazz, 482 U.S. 342 (1987).
Paradise, Brandon. "How Critical Race Theory Marginalizes the African American Christian Tradition," *Michigan Journal of Race and Law* 20 (Fall 2014): 117–211
People v. Ruggles, 8 Johns. 290, 294, 295 (1811).
Quick Bear v. Leupp, 210 U.S. 50 (1907).
Religious Freedom Restoration Act of 1993 (RFRA), 107 Stat. 1488, 42 U.S.C. § 2000bb et seq.
Reynolds v. U.S., 98 U.S. 145 (1879).
Savage, Audra L. "The Religion of Race: The Supreme Court as Priests of Racial Politics," *Utah Law Review* 2021 (2021): 569, 576–79, 589.
Sherbert v. Verner, 374 U.S. 398 (1963).
Thomas v. Review Board of the Indiana Employment Security Division, 450 U.S. 707 (1981).
Wiecek, William M. "The Statutory Law of Slavery and Race in the Thirteen Mainland Colonies of British America," *The William & Mary Quarterly* 34.2 (April 1977): 258, 263–264.
Wisconsin v. Yoder, 406 U.S. 205 (1972).
Witte, John, Jr., and Joel A. Nichols. *Religion and the American Constitutional Experiment*, 3rd ed. New York: Oxford University Press, 2011.

PART III

RACIAL REALISM AND HOPE

Chapter 5

The Authority of Hope

Hopeful Illusions in
Brown v. Board of Education and Beyond

VINCENT LLOYD

Derrick Bell's path-breaking scholarship and activism are at once pessimistic and optimistic. He limns the intractable racial injustices of American life and law while describing his own commitment to struggle as more than fatalistic rebellion. Often employing religious idioms and citations, Bell narrates "psalms of survival" that appeal to African American religious traditions and their characteristic virtue: hope.[1] Bell's profound and provocative writings, like slave spirituals, join together bitter despair and a better world to come. This is a necessarily subtle connection. Despair purges false hopes—worldly hopes—and it is only after grappling with the depths of this despair that genuine hope is possible.[2] In other words, hope is theological not only because it is described in religious texts but, more importantly, because it rejects worldly objects yet persists in the practices and effects that characterize hope. The epilogue to Bell's *Faces at the Bottom of the Well* is titled "Beyond Despair." To move beyond despair, Bell argues, we must reject the anodyne optimism found in narratives of American progress, narratives that ignore the marginalized. We must instead turn to the marginalized: "Knowing there was no escape, no way out, the slaves nonetheless continued to engage themselves. To carve out a humanity. To defy the murder of selfhood." Here, Bell tells us, we find "hope rather than despair."[3]

What relevance does Bell's account of hope have for the law in particular? It could be that Bell is describing how individuals who work with the law, including lawyers, judges, politicians, and academics, ought to be disposed. This certainly makes sense if Bell has in mind the figure of the civil rights lawyer or progressive-minded judge who sees anti-Black racism taking new and more virulent forms. But Bell does not find hope in law. He finds hope outside of law, in the soul of marginalized communities—and perhaps in literature. Indeed, Bell tries to show how *Brown v. Board of Education* results in pessimism.[4] According to Bell, American law is not progressively developing in the direction of racial justice. Instead, when decisions appear to be made in that direction, they are actually the result of what Bell calls interest convergence—temporary shared interests among political actors rather than a real commitment to some genuine moral principle or ideal. Moreover, for Bell, a Supreme Court decision may advance merely the image of justice instead of its substance—what Bell calls a racial "symbol." On Bell's account, a racial symbol is an image manufactured as a marketing tool of advocacy organizations at the expense of specific individuals suffering specific injustices. In short, Bell shows how careful attention to law dismantles false hopes. And it is in the embrace of the stories and songs of a marginalized community, specifically African Americans, that something like hope—deep and soulful rather than hollow and ultimately false—may be found.

Yet hope does appear in law, and it does seem to motivate lawyers and judges. Do these hopes problematize Bell's racial realism? Does the existence of this kind of juridical hope mean that Bell is wrong in his critique of law as a source of hope? In this chapter I answer these questions in the negative by defending Bell's claim that juridical hopes are false hopes, that is, that they are actually just morally corrupt, worldly desires. Such hopes therefore do not problematize Bell's racial realism. Bell's skepticism of American law on the issue of racial justice is thus, in my view, justified.

My defense of Bell's claim about the false hopes of American law and racial justice develops in two phases. First, in the next section, I interrogate juridical hope in order to show that it is precisely the type of narrative that genuine theological hope rejects. Whereas the former is rooted either in a judge's sense of personal morality or political expediency, the latter is rooted in a deeply theological—indeed an almost eschatological—vision of the future that eschews politically expedient, status quo-maintaining narratives, as does the work of Bell. Here we encounter the problem of landmark Supreme Court decisions, for it appears that such decisions are hopeful in the theological sense. But they are not. Far from it. What appear to be genuinely moral hopes in Supreme Court jurisprudence are actually rhetorical tropes that mask arbitrary personal preference and political expediency. This is how one explains the jurisprudential move from *Plessy* to *Brown*: what is expressed in the *Brown* decision is not a genuinely moral hope that can eradicate racism, but rather a rhetorical trope of the child as an emblem of the future that ultimately justifies racism. This leads to the second phase of my argument.

To underscore the significance of the child as a judicial rhetorical strategy and the overall moral insufficiency of juridical hope, I turn to an analysis of *Skinner v. Oklahoma*, *Lawrence v. Texas*, and *Roe v. Wade*. In *Skinner*, the child figure is once again front and center. But it is not just that children are a rhetorical strategy that makes juridical hope so problematic. It is the arbitrariness of it all. For when children are not the trope of choice, there are others that the Court will use to reach its desired conclusion, such as romantic relationships. We see this at work in *Lawrence v. Texas*, where the Supreme Court wants to justify the move from *Bowers v. Hardwick*. And in *Roe v. Wade*, we see a failure of juridical hope as opposed to the "successful" hope of *Brown*, *Skinner*, and *Lawrence*: society has yet to generally endorse abortion the way that it has endorsed racial integration (*Brown*), personal integrity in the form of rejecting state-imposed sterilization (*Skinner*), and anti-sodomy laws (*Lawrence*). Such are the vagaries of false judicial hope: not only do rhetorical tropes mask personal preference and political expediency, but it also seems that any trope will do, and that because of the arbitrary and rather weak moral core of judicial hope, it leads to results that are either a societal hit (*Brown*) or miss (*Roe*). For Bell, such hope is no hope at all.

I then conclude where I began: with the assertion—now argued—that Bell's notion of theological hope is much stronger than hope of the juridical sort. We can thus prefer Bell's racial realism over juridical hope, for Bell's racial realism is not only highly skeptical of Supreme Court adjudication as a reliable measure of racial progress, but also demands continued resistance in the face of the impossible. In contrast, juridical hope both conceals problems and demands moral complacency. Bell demands much more of us than that.

I. Hope and Law

Judges, particularly in landmark decisions, appear to rely on the sort of theological hope that Bell describes. This is not cheery hope, hopefulness as a mere emotion. Rather, certain landmark rulings do not seem explicable in terms of precedent or social facts; they appear to open us up to new possibilities, to the unexpected—seemingly evidence of a deep hope, what I will call theological hope. Yet Bell assures us that this is a misreading: legal and social facts are, at the end of the day, decisive. How, then, to explain the simulacrum of theological hope in a text such as Earl Warren's majority opinion in *Brown v. Board*? I argue that there is an overinvestment in the future, and specifically in future generations, that motivates this hope. Such an overinvestment is the result of the social conditions Bell diagnosed so astutely: white supremacy maintained through a cultural logic that invests ultimate value in (white) children, in the relationship between parent and child. The hope Bell commends, Black hope, which is to say genuinely theological hope, he locates in forms of community not structured by the nexus of patriarchy and white supremacy.

There has recently be an increase in scholarship about law and the emotions, two domains easily considered antithetical when law is understood as essentially about reason, and reason thought to be the opposite of emotion.[5] Kathryn Abrams and Hila Keren have written specifically about how law can cultivate hope, including not only the hope evoked by advocating for the marginalized but also the hope evoked by laws creating institutions, such as the Head Start program for disadvantaged children and prison reentry programs.[6] Although my interest is rather different, I would note that the account of hope developed by Abrams and Keren does not grow out of despair (although they do distinguish hope from optimism). I worry that hope, when it does not arise out of despair and when it is not cultivated in marginalized communities—as Bell demands that it must—often names desires and dispositions that further the interests of the wealthy and powerful. I worry that the hope that government programs give to disadvantaged children or the formerly incarcerated is really a desire to become middle class together with the habits necessary to pursue that desire. Hope in such cases is individual and incremental. It is a secular hope, accepting the wisdom of the world rather than challenging the wisdom of the world from the perspective of the marginalized.

But theological hope is different. It is directed toward the future, particularly toward objects in the future that are desired but not certain to be obtained, or worse, that evidential considerations suggest are unattainable. When hope is theological, in the rather loose sense I am using the term, hope rejects the false sense of security arising from narratives that overlook the experience of the downtrodden and oppressed; this sort of genuine hope is not anesthetized into believing a political theodicy. Instead, this hope is directed at a future dramatically different from the present, even unrecognizable from the perspective of the present, yet again, with no certainty as to how such a future could ever come to be. In the twentieth century, Jewish thinkers such as Walter Benjamin and Ernst Bloch and Christian thinkers such as Johann Baptist Metz and Jürgen Moltmann elaborated accounts of hope based on the paradigm of the Messiah arriving unexpectedly and upending the ways of the world. This is a sort of Messianic, eschatological hope. On this account of hope, there is no knowable path from here to there, from our world now to the hoped-for world to come. All that we can do is prepare ourselves and wait. The more marginal one is, the easier it is to hope, for the marginal are less invested in maintaining the ways of the world—really the ways of the rulers of the world. They—we—are more open to the totally new. The status quo is not legitimated. The Messiah overthrows and replaces it.

Bell's notion of hope both fits within and extends far beyond this Judeo-Christian theological tradition. As George Taylor has pointed out, there is a paradox at the core of Bell's thesis of racial realism: racism is permanent and it also demands our resistance. This paradox forms the basis for Bell's inclusion in and advance on the Judeo-Christian tradition. For insofar as Bell rejects juridical narratives that do not originate from the experiences of oppressed communities, racial realism is within the Judeo-Christian tradition. But Bell also concedes the permanence of racism, which puts him at odds with the Judeo-Christian notion of a genuine eschatological moment where the status quo is utterly overthrown and replaced. How can this be?

Bell gives us several examples to show how his thesis of racial realism works in action. Some discussion of these examples will illustrate both Bell's continuity and discontinuity with the larger Judeo-Christian theological tradition. In his 1992 landmark essay, "Racial Realism," in the *Connecticut Law Review*, Bell concludes his discussion of racial realism with an anecdote about an elderly African American woman named Mrs.

MacDonald who, according to Bell, claimed to live to "harass white folks." Bell explains:

> Mrs. MacDonald did not say she risked everything because she hoped or expected to win out over the whites who, as she well knew, held all the economic and political power, and the guns as well. Rather, she recognized that—powerless as she was—she had and intended to use courage and determination as weapons "to harass white folks." Her fight, in itself, gave her strength and empowerment in a society that relentlessly attempted to wear her down. Mrs. MacDonald did not even hint that her harassment would topple whites' well-entrenched power. Rather, her goal was defiance and its harassing effect was more potent precisely because she placed herself in confrontation with her oppressors with full knowledge of their power and willingness to use it.
>
> Mrs. MacDonald avoided discouragement and defeat because at the point that she determined to resist her oppression, she was triumphant. Nothing the all-powerful whites could do to her would diminish her triumph. Mrs. MacDonald understood twenty-five years ago the theory that I am espousing in the 1990s for black leaders and civil rights lawyers to adopt. If you remember her story, you will understand my message.[7]

The departure from the Judeo-Christian theological notion of hope should be clear: there will be no victory in America for the oppressed on Bell's account. Mrs. MacDonald gains victory through her struggle, not through any literal, objective overthrow of an oppressive state. Moreover, the locus of the source of the transformation has shifted from an external God who will bring justice to a courageous individual who demands justice. So it is that the transformation is not a transformation of the external world in a Messianic, eschatological sense of a Divine overthrow of an unjust government and reestablishment of a just government, but rather is a transformation of the individual in an existential/moral sense. On this existential/moral account, the individual is victorious precisely because of recognizing that she cannot win, but instead that she must freely choose to continue to fight. And the similarity should also be clear: Mrs. MacDonald "lives to harass white folks" precisely because the prevailing narrative that maintains the status quo must be rejected. The rejection of the status quo-reinforcing narrative is found in Mrs. MacDonald's relentless resistance.

Another example is the discussion in the epilogue of Bell's landmark text, *Faces at the Bottom of the Well: The Permanence of Racism*, which is titled "Beyond Despair." There, Bell writes of the slaves that "Knowing there was no escape, no way out, the slaves nonetheless continued to engage themselves. To carve out a humanity. To defy the murder of selfhood. Their lives were brutally shackled, certainly—but not without meaning despite being imprisoned."[8] Again, Bell locates victory not in a Messianic overthrow of an unjust political system, but rather in a people's existential and moral resistance to that system. So like the traditional theological narrative, Bell rejects the status quo. But unlike that narrative—and perhaps even an advance on it—the site of transformation is not Divine transcendence, but rather courageous, existential immanence. For Bell, there is no deferral until an eschatological day of judgment. The "Day of Judgment," that is, the time for action, and the site of victory is resistance in the here and now.

Described in this way, theological hope would seem deeply counter to law; it would seem outright disrespectful of law and perhaps even anarchic.[9] Indeed, we have seen how Bell understands this difference. But might theological hope be at work in paradigm-shifting decisions of supreme courts? At first, juridical hope appears to buy into a pre-critical, junior high school level understanding of the judicial process: that judges decide based on their feelings. Surely we know that decisions are based on precedent—if one is a legal formalist—or, if one is more inclined toward a realist or critical theory of adjudication, are based on either factual considerations or some material interest masked as precedent. Neither of these leaves any room for hope. And an account of natural law that would claim judicial decisions ought to be informed by moral principles leaves no room for hope either. Although philosophers debate the details, our intuition is that hope has little role in judicial reasoning; if anything, it distorts judicial reasoning.

For example, imagine the nine justices of the U.S. Supreme Court confront with a practice that they all feel, personally, is despicable. Imagine that this practice is well established in statutory law and in a series of Court rulings. Imagine further that public opinion is divided on this practice. It seems possible that, in upholding the practice, the Court could have its credibility drastically undermined and could foment division in the nation. It also seems possible that, in ruling against the practice, the

Court could effect a change in public opinion and could, in the long term, strengthen its moral authority. The probability of each of these two outcomes is impossible to calculate. If the Court chooses to rule against the practice, it might seem as if the best explanation is hope. This would not be ordinary, anodyne hope, but hope for a totally different world, a world in which the practice in question is broadly considered a moral horror. There is no clear path from the present world to that future world. In a sense, the justices must despair at the tragic circumstances that face them: compromise their own moral values or compromise the rule of law, based on (at least the veneer of) authoritative precedent.

This scenario is effectively what the Court faced in *Brown v. Board of Education*, as will be discussed in detail below.[10] For now, it is important to distinguish the necessary from the contingent features of this scenario that I suggest defines judicial hope. Necessarily, there is a desired state of affairs in the future and uncertainty about whether that state of affairs will come about, uncertainty even about how it might be brought about. There is also a decision that is motivated by that desired state of affairs and that cannot be justified according to present circumstances: there is insufficient reason (or precedent) to make the decision. Because of this, the decision will certainly be criticized. When judicial hope "succeeds," societal consensus catches the vision of the Court at some future time resulting in a general acceptance of the decision despite societal opposition at the time the decision was made. There is something like a leap of faith involved here, a leap that sometimes works and sometimes fails (*Roe v. Wade*, I will suggest below, is an example of its failure). There is an array of available options for the Court to take, but the Court refuses them all, acting as if the law is something it is not—and so, potentially, making the law something new.

It is tempting to read the scenario I described above, the scenario of *Brown*, as a classic conflict between positive law jurisprudence and natural law jurisprudence. The justices have moral views that conflict with the law; the justices change the law to match morality. I would argue, however, that morality introduces a contingent, not necessary, element into this scenario. It is simply necessary for the Court, or for a justice, to desire a certain future state of affairs; what motivates that desire is not important. Cases such as the decision about the 2000 election, *Bush v. Gore*, and about the Affordable Care Act, *National Federation of Independent Business v. Sebelius*, can be read as relying on a desire that is not moral but political or pragmatic. These cases may belong to a lesser class of judicial hope, however, because the desired state of affairs is not so entirely different from the current world. In other words, such cases may be classed as instances of secular hope rather than theological hope.

It should also be noted that another feature of hope in the Christian theological tradition is that hope is oriented by the good, or God (this is less evident in Jewish writers such as Walter Benjamin and Ernst Bloch).[11] When this specifically Christian clause is added to a definition of theological hope the effect is to make theological hope a feature of natural law jurisprudence, but the question of hope would remain distinct. Hope, as I am describing it here, is expressed in a court decision. A hopeful ruling does not explicitly appeal to morality that would trump law. In the logic of the hopeful ruling, even if its hopefulness is motivated by morality, Justice Taney was correct when writing, in *Dred Scott*, "It is not the province of the court to decide upon the justice or injustice, the policy or impolicy, of these laws . . . The duty of the court is to interpret the [laws] with the best lights we can obtain on the subject, and to administer it as we find it, according to its true intent and meaning when it was adopted."[12] Judicial hope, to potentially "catch," is expressed not by abandoning precedent but by engaging with precedent just as any other decision would, even though there necessarily remains a gap between what is justified by precedent and the court's ruling. That gap is not grounded explicitly in a hopeful decision, but careful reading of such decisions reveals an appeal to the rhetoric of hope, in some guise, to fill the gap. In *Brown*, as is typical, children function as a rhetorical figure of hope, offering a hopeful lens through which to read precedent in order to justify a decision that unfiltered precedent would not support. We now examine this rhetorical trope of the child more closely.

II. Hope in *Brown*

Bruce Ackerman recently and rightly observed, "There is something very curious about *Brown*'s current status: none of the protagonists take Chief Justice Warren's opinion seriously. Whatever else they disagree about, lawyers and judges all fail to study Warren's words with care, choosing instead to see the opinion as a way station on the route to some far more glorious principle."[13] I will look for judicial hope in the rhetoric of decisions, not as a moral principle or in a feeling motivating decisions. To find judicial hope, then, we must read decisions closely. Even in a text as canonical and well-worn as the *Brown* decision, there remains more to be said. In fact, precisely because the case is so canonical and well-worn, the text itself is often forgotten.

The *Brown* decision is frequently understood as using the Equal Protection Clause of the Fourteenth Amendment to invalidate laws that treat racial groups unequally. More recently, conservatives, including those on the Court, have treated *Brown* as ensuring that individuals not be treated on the basis of race; for example, as a cudgel against affirmative action policies.[14] The second round of oral arguments in *Brown* focused on the intention of the authors of the Fourteenth Amendment. Yet on these grounds the arguments of segregationists were the strongest because segregated education had, indeed, been part of the social landscape before the Fourteenth Amendment was ratified, and the amendment's passage did not prompt school integration. Warren begins the substantive portion of his decision by recalling this debate over the meaning of the Fourteenth Amendment and states that, despite looking "exhaustively," the results were not decisive. "This discussion and our own investigation convince us that, although these sources cast some light, it is not enough to resolve the problem with which we are faced. At best, they are inconclusive" (489).[15] Warren writes that some of the amendment's authors supported segregation and others did not. Moreover, nineteenth-century education was organized much differently than education in the 1950s: most education of whites was private and few educational opportunities for Blacks existed; sometimes, educating Blacks was illegal. In short, "We cannot turn the clock back to 1868 when the amendment was adopted, or even to 1896 when *Plessy v. Ferguson* was written" (492). History is inconclusive; an additional ingredient is necessary.

Plessy v. Ferguson itself cites the long history of segregation laws found to be consistent with the Fourteenth Amendment. While *Plessy* was about segregated trains in particular, the segregation laws that the Court cites include intermarriage laws, laws segregating theaters, inns, and trains, and laws segregating schools (including in the North, where there was a longer tradition of free public education). The crucial distinction drawn in *Plessy* is between "social equality" and "political equality." The Court affirmed the latter but not the former and found this distinction in the amendment itself: "The object of the amendment was undoubtedly to enforce the absolute equality of the two races before the law, but, in the nature of things, it could not have been intended to abolish distinctions based upon color, or to enforce social, as distinguished from political, equality, or a commingling of the two races upon terms unsatisfactory to either."[16] For the *Plessy* Court, this meant that, for example, jury membership could not be restricted based on race because a fair trial is central to political equality, but marriage, schools, and transportation could be segregated because they had to do with social equality.

The astounding fact about the *Brown* decision that has been largely forgotten is that it does not contest the foundation of *Plessy*, the distinction between social and political equality. Rather than attacking this distinction, *Brown* reclassifies schools as political rather than social institutions.[17] While education at the time of the adoption of the Fourteenth Amendment was largely private and, where public, uneven and unsystematic, by 1954 education had become "perhaps the most important function of state and local governments" (493). School had become universal and mandatory. This demonstrated, according to Warren, the central importance of education to political life: "It is the very foundation of good citizenship" (493). Warren demonstrates how what seemed like the social sphere is actually part of the political sphere; left intact by *Brown* are state segregation laws affecting only the social sphere.

It was the Southern states' contention that their schools were equal, that the same financial resources were offered to both Black and white schools, and that the same curricula were used, at least in the recent years relevant to the case. Warren appealed, famously, to the "intangible" factors that reduce the quality of Black education in segregated schools. "To separate [school children] from others of similar age and qualifications solely because of their race generates a feeling of inferiority as to their status in the community that may affect their hearts and minds in a way unlikely ever to be undone" (494). Here, Warren cites psychology experiments purporting to demonstrate the detrimental effects of segregation on children. According to Michael Klarman, it was social science that bridged the gap between the law as it stood and the decision the Court reached.[18] Indeed, Warren describes the social scientific research he cites as "modern authority" that may not have been available at the time *Plessy* was decided. Rather than explicitly overturning *Plessy*, Warren writes, immediately after citing the social science research, "Any language in *Plessy v. Ferguson* contrary to this finding is rejected" (494–495). In other words, law must be read in light of science, and science has changed. *Plessy* was not overruled; it was updated.

Instead of seeing the gap between established law and the *Brown* decision filled with social scientific evidence, as Klarman and Warren himself would have it, I see that gap filled by hope. Hope is not a feeling invoked by Warren in the text. Rather, hope arrives in the figure of the child. By conjuring the "hearts and minds" of children, the decision taps into a social imaginary that views children as representing a better, brighter future. Indeed, Warren sets aside the "tangible" equality of funding and facilities to focus on these "hearts and minds" that will, he worries, be irreparably damaged by segregation. The justices desire a dramatically different world, a world without segregation. They are not sure how that world might be achieved; they have no illusions that one ruling of the Court will achieve it. Yet they hope. To express this hope, to use it as a principle guiding their interpretation of the law, they need a figure of hope. The child is the paradigmatic figure of hope, and the "hearts and minds" of children are at the center of the *Brown* decision.

Indeed, children are effectively used as a bridge to move from an attack on political segregation to an attack on social segregation. Warren describes the rapid changes in public education as effectively justifying the switch of education from the social to the political domain, but he makes an argument that is broader than necessary for those purposes. Education, he writes, "is a principal instrument in awakening the child to cultural values, in preparing him for later professional training, and in helping him to adjust normally to his environment" (483). This description goes far beyond the domain of the political. It refers to the values of a future society, the society of the next generation and of generations to come. Current practices stymy the possibility of a different, better future. This is rhetoric; it is above and beyond the line of argument needed for Warren to make the point that education has come into the political domain. It also opens the door to incorporating other segregation laws into the political domain. Surely it is difficult to transmit cultural values to Black children and to help them adjust normally to their environment when their families are not permitted to live in the same neighborhoods as whites, when they are not permitted to sit in the same theater seats as whites, and even when they are not permitted to sit in the same train cars as whites. When we think of the children, the social becomes thoroughly political. And when we think of the children, we can hope for a world dramatically different from the present.

For judges, the authority of hope is dependent on the pretense that hope is not involved, that a judicial decision is strictly clear-headed and rational. This is how Warren represents the *Brown* deliberations: "We discussed all sides dispassionately week after week, testing arguments of counsel, suggesting various approaches, and at times acting as 'devil's advocates.'"[19] Warren insists that the justices were always unanimous in their decision and that the five months it took to produce a decision was spent considering the possible reasoning of a decision and its implications rather than building consensus. As Warren puts it, "In my entire public career, I have never seen a group of men more conscious of the seriousness of a situation, more intent upon resolving it with as little disruption as possible, or with a greater desire for unanimity."[20]

In reality, and as Warren's final phrase suggests, unanimity was an achievement rather than a given. By 1954, the strongest forces against integration were justices who saw the case in strictly positive law versus natural law terms. Felix Frankfurter, for example, was vehemently opposed to segregation personally, but he was equally vehement in his belief that it was "the compulsions of governing legal principles" that must guide the judge, not "the idiosyncrasies of merely personal judgment."[21] Such commitments had prevented the Court from ruling for integration earlier. However, when Warren was appointed chief justice and signaled his support for an integration decision, Frankfurter and those aligned with him found themselves in the minority. Klarman argues that opinions based on the notion that law should trump politics or morality happen most frequently when such opinions are in the majority, or when the Court is nearly evenly split.[22] When it gets down to one or two justices potentially dissenting despite their own personal convictions, those convictions are more often allowed to have the day. Thus, the result was ultimately unanimous not because careful deliberation revealed the best arguments, as Warren would have it, but because the potentially dissenting justices did not want to find themselves in such an unseemly position, one that ran counter to their personal convictions. Rather than viewing such choices in terms of personal convictions, as Klarman does, I am proposing that they ought to be viewed in terms of judicial hope. Frankfurter did not set aside "the compulsions of governing legal principles"; rather, he counted hope as one of those governing legal principles, as a principle of interpretation. By reading the Fourteenth Amendment and the laws before the Court with hope, Frankfurter was able to sign on to Warren's unanimous decision.

Warren's discussion of *Brown* constructs a division between the dispassionate Court and the passionate public. The chapter of his memoirs in which he describes *Brown* is titled "A Case of Emotional Impact," but the emotional impact is certainly not on Earl Warren. He describes a "wave of emotion" that "swept the room" when he stated that the Court's decision was unanimous.[23] He describes the "emotional opposition to the Decision" in the South.[24] At the interface between the passionate public and the staid Court, according to Warren, was his decision. "It was not a long opinion, for I had written it so it could be published in the daily press throughout the nation without taking too much space. This enabled the public to have our entire reasoning instead of a few excerpts from a lengthier document."[25] Warren saw himself communicating to a divided and emotional public, and he wanted to communicate directly. If the public could access the cool reasoning of the Court, passions would be less inflamed. But Warren here is also acknowledging that the decision was a rhetorical document, aimed at a specific audience, the public. In a sense, Warren is admitting that the decision *performs* dispassion in the hope that it will foster acceptance of the decision in the public. While it was crucial that the decision appear to conform to judicial norms, with careful reasoning based on established law, it was not necessary, from Warren's perspective, to conform to those norms in substance, in what would have been "a lengthier document."

Curiously, rather than using his memoir to defend the legal reasoning of *Brown*, Warren presents himself as a consistent opponent of segregation. Indeed, Warren brings the reader back to his California childhood, where he attended integrated public schools and the integrated University of California. He "sat in classrooms with blacks and members of almost every minority group. I never gave it a second thought."[26] It is the memory of the young Warren, the child Warren, that justifies *Brown* in this text, not reasoning from precedent. Communicating directly with the public, in a decision he imagined would be published in "the daily press," Warren appealed to the same hopeful figure, the child, that he himself once was. He remembered his hopeful youth, his youth as a figure of hope, integrated, and he projected it into the centerpiece of the *Brown* decision.

Kenneth Karst has documented the way children are often at the center of legal conflicts over cultural values. He suggests that the concern for children, or for the figure of the child, is due to "the hope that a child will continue to self-identify as one of 'Us,' or at least not as one of 'Them'" and, further, "the hope that children will act in accordance with 'Our' values, and the fear that they may not."[27] In other words, while we ostensibly hope for children, we are really expressing hope as such: hope for a future in which we ourselves will continue, even after our deaths. Karst goes on to argue that legal invocations of the child are fomented by the politicization of the figure of the child, for example, in campaign ads.

My suggestion is that hope, and the child, need not only be considered representative of continuity, of reproducing "Us." The child is not "Us" but a better "Us," fulfilling the dreams that go unfulfilled in our own lifetimes. The first person plural is important here, for children represent collective dreams and the possibility for collective improvement: leaving a better world for the next generation. Children are essential for a family, for a nation—and for a race.[28]

Karst concludes that "political operatives go on offering the promise of law to achieve their constituents' preferred cultural orthodoxies."[29] His worry is that this politicized image of the child, and hope for the child, may have destructive effects when it enters law. I have suggested that there is another, less conservative dimension of hope for children when invoked by judges, a hope for a different, better world. But are political and judicial hope really so different? When hope grows out of an image of the child, might it always be fostering a brighter future for a specific "Us"? The Southern states also were invested in transmitting their cultural values to the next generation; they just had different views from the Court on what those cultural values were.

Queer theorist Lee Edelman launched a broadside attack on the privileged figure of the child in his book *No Future*.[30] In short, Edelman argues that "the Child," as he puts it, secures the interests of the powers that be. Orienting us toward a future secure for the Child makes us act in essentially conservative ways, perpetuating the status quo and with it the interests of the powerful. The Child is essentially innocent and in need of protection—by parents, by society, and by laws. Edelman argues that queers fundamentally threaten the status quo by their refusal to organize their lives around the Child, by their embrace of pleasure in the moment rather than pleasure deferred into the indefinite future, into generations to come.

The *Brown* Court relies on hope, but it is hope that only appears theological; it is actually secular hope. Hope for the generations to come is hope that is this-worldly, not other-worldly. It is hope that advances the interests of an elite, and a race, a certain "Us," in the name of the universal, of a better world for all. It is not hope that grows out of despair, nor is it hope cultivated in communities of the marginalized. Such secular hope appears to take great moral courage—to think of the children even if it causes difficulties for us in the present—but it actually advances the desires of the parents in the name of the children, as so many parents are wont to do. Barack Obama rose to national prominence invoking the "audacity of hope," with a memoir detailing the promise of the multicultural American Child, yet this audacity manifested in his presidency in an era not of racial progress but of racial stagnation, perhaps racial regression. And it manifested not in leadership that reframes issues and reveals new possibilities but in leadership that was calculating and pragmatic. We thus see the rhetorical figure of the child as a cover for the continuing legitimation of white domination inscribed in American law and political practices. We will next turn to this problem in *Skinner v. Oklahoma* and other cases, which reveal the arbitrary nature of juridical hope, and how its greatest "success" is, at best, deceptive, and at worst a calculated attempt to maintain the status quo, while its greatest failure is continued social and political conflict.

III. The Child Figure and the Vagaries of Juridical Hope

In *Skinner v. Oklahoma*, the 1942 case that largely outlawed forced sterilization for those convicted of crimes, Justice William O. Douglas begins his unanimous decision by boldly stating, "This case touches a sensitive and important area of human rights."[31] This is another case, like *Brown*, that involves judicial hope. That it begins not by invoking law but by invoking moral principle (even international human rights laws were still in the future) primes the audience for a decision that will leap beyond established law. The case involved Jack T. Skinner, a man who had been convicted of three crimes and so, in accordance with Oklahoma law, was to be sterilized.[32] The three crimes were chicken theft, in 1926, robbery, in 1929, and robbery again, in 1934. Despite beginning its ruling with the banner of human rights, the Court did not, in fact, spare Skinner from the vasectomy blade because of these rights, though he was spared the blade. As in *Brown*, the Court in *Skinner* seems to have a desire for a world without involuntary sterilization, but it lacks the legal (not to mention political and social) resources to move from here to there. The Court sidestepped Skinner's claim that he was being subjected to cruel and unusual punishment because, as Justice Douglas pointed out, there was a much more blatant problem with the law. Specifically, the law treated crimes unequally. Theft was considered in the class of crimes warranting sterilization but embezzlement was not. A thief could steal farm animals thrice and be subject to sterilization while an employee of the same farm who steals thousands of dollars in cash, also thrice, would be considered an embezzler and exempt from sterilization.

Like *Brown*, *Skinner* was decided based on the Equal Protection clause of the Fourteenth Amendment, a text that seems to particularly attract hopeful decisions. Justice Douglas compares the discrimination against a certain class of criminals, in *Skinner*, with discrimination against those of a certain race or nationality.[33] Further, even more directly than in *Brown*, the image of the child is invoked to fill a legal gap. So the Court declared the practice of sterilization unconstitutional. Justice Douglas explains:

> We are dealing here with legislation which involves one of the basic civil rights of man. Marriage and procreation are fundamental to the very existence and survival of the race. The power to sterilize, if exercised, may have subtle, far-reaching and devastating effects. In evil or reckless hands, it can cause races or types which are inimical to the dominant group to wither and disappear. There is no redemption for the individual whom the law touches.[34]

The right to have a child is a basic civil right, Douglas argues. In a sense, it means we have a right to a future; we have a right to have hopes. In quite religious language, Douglas refers to the redemption of the criminal, a return from the status of criminal to the status of citizen, but he also simultaneously associates redemption with the potential child, with our hopes for the future. Without such hopes, an individual can never be redeemed. But this is also a group right: that a group can continue to exist for future generations through procreation. All Americans are entitled to hopes, and they are entitled to their own hopes. Preventing certain classes of people from having children might make all Americans have the same hopes—hopes in the same (e.g., white, blond, blue-eyed) children.

This sounds like a pronouncement of deep and enduring moral truths, but in fact it is essentially unrelated to the Court's decision. The Court's decision permits sterilization, it just requires sterilizing both chicken thieves and embezzlers, or neither. This weak result is based on even weaker legal reasoning. As Chief Justice Harlan Stone points out in his concurrence, if the Court allows Oklahoma to sterilize any criminals based on the state's view of science, it ought to defer to Oklahoma to decide which criminals science shows to require sterilization. Chief Justice Stone made explicit the belief that goes unspoken in the majority opinion: "the state may protect itself from the demonstrably inheritable tendencies of the individual which are injurious to society."[35] In other words, the question about how to define classes subject to sterilization is already invested in a hoped-for figure of the child: the healthy, innocent child. While Stone ultimately agrees with Douglas and the rest of the Court, his argument leans on the Due Process Clause. In a sense, Stone is not hopeful but realistic, offering reasoning that is more appropriate to the case than the majority's reasoning. But, in that realism, Stone affirms the state interest in children and so affirms the power of the status quo—those deemed beneficial rather than injurious to society.[36]

What happens when children, as figures of hope, cannot be invoked when a court makes a hopeful ruling? In some cases, an alternative figure of hope may be invoked to do the same work as the figure of the child. This occurs most famously in *Lawrence v. Texas*, the hopeful ruling that proclaimed to a divided country the legality of sodomy. Justice Anthony Kennedy, writing for the majority, shifted the Court's approach to homosexuality away from interrogating whether there is a right to homosexual conduct. Instead, Kennedy focused on intimate relationships, of which sexual expression is one component.[37] The freedom to engage in intimate relationships is essential, Kennedy argued, and it is guaranteed by the right to privacy located in the Due Process Clause by contemporary jurisprudence. In circumstances where the figure of the child is unavailable (indeed, invoked occasionally by opponents of gay rights), a related figure is deployed: romantic intimacy. Nothing should stand in the way of romantic relationships, Kennedy asserts: in effect, our hope for true love is as strong as our hope for a child. Once again, hopeful rhetoric stands apart from the legal reasoning, which alone would not quite reach the hoped-for conclusion. For example, Kennedy asserts that previous decisions have "overstated" the degree of historical evidence of sodomy prohibitions. Kennedy cites an early opinion that he also authored: "History and tradition are the starting point but not in all cases the ending point of the substantive due process inquiry."[38] Here, made explicit, is the opening for hope: both the judge's hope for a different, better world and the decision's rhetoric of hope used to push toward that world.

The cases discussed above all involve hope that succeeds in the following sense. At the times they were decided, it was unclear whether, some years in the future, they would be treated as obviously right—but they were. Segregation, forced sterilization, and increasingly homophobia are recognized as clear wrongs, both morally and legally. The mere fact that the Court so ruled did not change public or scholarly opinion. Many, varied events intervened, most of them unrelated to the Court's decision, and eventually the nation came around to the view that the justices had hoped would prevail. In *Brown*, the Court's decision increased social discord around segregation for two decades before the Court's view ultimately prevailed.[39] But the dramatic transformation in the social world that judges hope for does not always materialize, even after much public debate. The most famous such example is *Roe v. Wade*.[40]

Roe is an example of hope failed, and I suspect this has to do with the Court's failure to find a substitute figure of hope, given the unavailability of the child. The rhetorical tropes called up by abortion are the opposite of those called up by hope: potential life is ended, opportunities are lost, futures are foreclosed. Justice Harry Blackmun begins his decision by acknowledging how emotionally charged abortion is and offering assurances that the Court will "resolve the issue by constitutional measurement, free of emotion and of predilection."[41] Like all cases involving judicial hope, precedent does not offer sufficient reason to reach the Court's decision; there is a gap that can only be filled by hope, ordinarily manifested in rhetorical figures of hope. Blackmun expends considerable effort in his decision showing the complicated history of abortion laws and so demonstrating the insufficiency of precedent. After rehearsing this history, he proceeds to quickly list the sequence of cases developing the right to privacy from the Due Process Clause before stating, "This right of privacy . . . is broad enough to encompass a woman's decision whether or not to terminate her pregnancy" (153). He then lists problems that may arise when abortion is prohibited, including medical problems, psychological harm, and the stigma attached to unwed mothers. There is no explanation of how these effects are connected to the right to privacy, or how the right to privacy is related to the earlier history of abortion regulation that Blackmun rehearsed. In a sense, they function as rhetorical flourish in the same way that the image of the child does in *Brown*. In *Roe*, however, the child is hopeless, unwanted: "there is the problem of bringing a child into a family already unable, psychologically and otherwise, to care for it" (153). The mother, too, becomes another figure of hopelessness: "Maternity, or additional offspring, may force upon a woman a distressful life and future" (153). Even when, later in the decision, Blackmun is justifying limits on abortion, he does not invoke a hopeful child but rather cold science: "at some point the state interests as to the protection of health, medical standards, and prenatal life, become dominant" (155).

Justice Blackmun and six of his colleagues hoped that, eventually, somehow, a consensus would develop that *Roe* was rightly decided. The ruling failed to achieve their hopes in part, I would argue, because the hopeless language of the decision misaligned with the justices' hopes. They envisioned a dramatically different world, but Blackmun was not able to conjure this world in the language of his decision. He appealed to medicine, and to images of destitution and unhappiness. It may seem odd, and opposed to the spirit of Bell's work, to position *Brown* as a successful decision and *Roe* as a failed decision. As Bell and others have aptly demonstrated, *Brown* was a failure in several ways, and its present renown should not blind us to its shortcomings. As Gerald Rosenberg has shown in his aptly titled book *The Hollow Hope*, it was not *Brown* but actions of the legislative and executive branch of the federal government that integrated schools.[42] As Bell and many others have shown, segregation persists to the present, even in schools.[43] Moreover, new, grave injustices are faced by Blacks in the United States created by an out of control drug war and a race to incarcerate.[44] My point, however, is that *Brown* did transform public consciousness, or at least public rhetoric, around segregation. That is the greatest potential effect of secular hope, of hope anchored in this world through the figure of the child, or the analogous figure of romance.[45] My attempt has been to show how judicial hope often functions and why it is alluring—so as to inoculate us against its allure.

Conclusion

Law is not the place to look for hope in the fullest sense, for hope that opens new horizons of possibility, challenging entrenched systems of domination. The sort of hope that we find in law, even in *Brown*, ultimately falls back on precisely those group interests that Bell so aptly diagnosed. Specifically, hope in American law depends on figures of the child and the family that are very much invested in racial domination. Bell has rightly urged that to look for hope in the fullest sense we must look elsewhere. For example, Bell points out that in hope, "We can accept the dilemmas of committed confrontation with evils we cannot end. We can go forth to serve, knowing that our failure to act will not change conditions and may very well worsen them."[46] We must continually refocus on the most marginalized, taking their experience as authoritative, humbling ourselves to them. But we—we Black lawyers and academics—also have the opportunity and challenge of forging our humanity ourselves, with "imagination, will, and unbelievable strength and courage," in a world that denies the possibility of Black humanity.[47] Crucially, hope in the sense Bell commends, in the deepest, genuinely justice-oriented sense emerges not alone, in chambers, but in community, and particularly in the aesthetic expressions of the most marginalized communities.

With critical race theory institutionalized, or at least part of institutional memory, do new possibilities for hope in law open up? Might Bell's lessons provide means for a younger generation of lawyers and judges to bring hope cultivated at the margins into the courtroom? One Supreme Court justice in particular, of that younger generation, offers a tantalizing response. Sonia Sotomayor's memoir is animated by the questions, "How is it that adversity has spurred me on instead of knocking me down? What are the sources of my own hope and optimism?"[48] Sotomayor's book is a coming-of-age story, tracking both the depths of despair she faced (an alcoholic father, a distant single mother, unsupportive teachers, cultural alienation) and her own resilient spirit that led her from housing projects to the Supreme Court. On the one hand, Sotomayor's narrative finds hope in despair, and in the experiences of those at the bottom of the well, as it were. On the other hand, Sotomayor closely associates hope and optimism, and she finds both in the privileged image of the child (herself) coming of age. Such a narrative seems close to the judicial hope of earlier generations, to those stories of American progress that Bell rejects—and to Obama's audacious but ultimately pragmatic hope.

Notes

1. For an overview of Bell's use of religion, see George H. Taylor, "Racism as 'The Nation's Crucial Sin': Theology and Derrick Bell," *Michigan Journal of Race & Law* 9 (2004): 269–322.

2. See especially Søren Kierkegaard, *The Sickness Unto Death: A Christian Psychological Exposition for Upbuilding and Awakening* (Princeton, NJ: Princeton University Press, 1980).

3. Derrick Bell, *Faces at the Bottom of the Well: The Permanence of Racism* (New York: Basic Books, 1992), 197.

4. See Derrick Bell, *Silent Covenants: Brown v. Board of Education and the Unfulfilled Hopes for Racial Reform* (New York: Oxford University Press, 2004).

5. For example, Kathryn Abrams and Hila Keren, "Who's Afraid of Law and the Emotions?" *Minnesota Law Review* 94 (1997): 1997–2074; Martha C. Nussbaum, *Hiding from Humanity: Disgust, Shame, and the Law* (Princeton, NJ: Princeton University Press, 2006); Eric A. Posner and Cass R. Sunstein (eds.), *Law and Happiness* (Chicago: University of Chicago Press, 2010).

6. Kathryn Abrams and Hila Keren, "Law and the Cultivation of Hope," *California Law Review* 95.2 (2007): 319–381.

7. Derrick Bell, "Racial Realism," *Connecticut Law Review* 24.2 (1992): 363–379.

8. Bell, *Faces*, 197. Italics removed and punctuation corrected.

9. A point explored by James Martel in *Divine Violence: Walter Benjamin and the Eschatology of Sovereignty* (New York: Routledge, 2012).

10. For background, see Michael J. Klarman, *From Jim Crow to Civil Rights: The Supreme Court and the Struggle for Racial Equality* (Oxford, UK: Oxford University Press, 2004).

11. For a fuller account of the Jewish tradition of reflection on hope, albeit one that moves it toward Christianity, see Akiba Lerner, "Otherness and Liberal Democratic Solidarity: Buber, Kaplan, Levinas and Rorty's Social Hope" in *Thinking Jewish Culture in America*, ed. Ken Koltun-Fromm (Lanham, MD: Lexington Books, 2014), 31–70.

12. *Dred Scott v. Sandford*, 60 U.S. 393, 405 (1857).

13. Bruce Ackerman, *The Civil Rights Revolution: We the People*, vol. 3 (Cambridge, MA: Harvard University Press, 2014), 128.

14. Reva B. Siegel, "Equality Talk: Antisubordination and Anticlassification Values in Constitutional Struggles over *Brown*," *Harvard Law Review* 117 (2004): 1470–1547.

15. *Brown v. Board of Education*, 347 U.S. 483 (1954).

16. *Plessy v. Ferguson*, 163 U.S. 537, 544 (1896).

17. On the specificity of educational institutions in *Brown*, see Risa Gobuloff, *The Lost Promise of Civil Rights* (Cambridge, MA: Harvard University Press, 2007), chap. 9.

18. Klarman, *From Jim Crow to Civil Rights*, 303.

19. Earl Warren, *The Memoirs of Earl Warren* (Garden City: Doubleday and Company, Inc., 1977), 2.

20. Ibid., 2–3.

21. Klarman, *From Jim Crow to Civil Rights*, 303. Klarman further argues that politics enters when the law is indeterminate (308), though this would seem to be true for every case that reaches the Supreme Court.

22. Klarman, *From Jim Crow to Civil Rights*, 303.

23. Warren, *Memoirs*, 3.

24. Ibid., 4.

25. Ibid., 3.

26. Ibid., 4.

27. Kenneth L. Karst, "Law, Cultural Conflict, and the Socialization of Children," *California Law Review* 91.4 (2003): 970.

28. See Jacqueline Stevens, *Reproducing the State* (Princeton, NJ: Princeton University Press, 1999); Vincent Lloyd, "Of Fathers and Sons, Prophets and Messiahs," *Souls: A Critical Journal of Black Politics, Culture, and Society* 16.3-4 (2014): 209-226.

29. Karst, "Law, Cultural Conflict, and the Socialization of Children," 1028.

30. Lee Edelman, *No Future: Queer Theory and the Death Drive* (Durham, NC: Duke University Press, 2004).

31. *Skinner v. Oklahoma*, 316 U.S. 535 (1942).

32. For an account of the case for a general audience, see Victoria F. Nourse, *In Reckless Hands: Skinner* v. *Oklahoma and the Near Triumph of American Eugenics* (New York: W.W. Norton & Co., 2008).

33. *Skinner*, 316 U.S. at 541.

34. Ibid.

35. Ibid. at 545.

36. On this and the connection between *Skinner* and gay marriage cases, see Ariella R. Dubler, "Sexing *Skinner*: History and the Politics of the Right to Marry," *Columbia Law Review* 110.5 (2010): 1348-1376.

37. For a development of this point, see Katherine M. Franke, "The Domesticated Liberty of *Lawrence v. Texas*," *Columbia Law Review* 104.5 (2004): 1399-1426.

38. *Lawrence v. Texas*, 539 U.S. 558.

39. Klarman, in *From Jim Crow to Civil Rights*, argues that the polarization effected by *Brown* fueled the social movements that would lead to federal civil rights legislation that ultimately settled the issue; in short, *Brown* was the indirect cause of a consensus for integration. I do not think such a causal story is necessary or helpful: hope is defined by uncertainty. See also Gerald Rosenberg, *The Hollow Hope: Can Courts Bring About Social Change?* (Chicago: University of Chicago Press, 1991).

40. On the public reaction to *Roe*, see Robert Post and Reva Siegel, "Roe Rage: Democratic Constitutionalism and Backlash," *Harvard Civil Rights–Civil Liberties Law Review* 42 (2007): 373-433.

41. *Roe v. Wade*, 116.

42. Rosenberg, *Hollow Hope*.

43. Bell, *Silent Covenants*.

44. Michelle Alexander, *The New Jim Crow: Mass Incarceration in the Age of Colorblindness* (New York: New Press, 2011).

45. The conservative, "homonormative" wake of *Lawrence* has been persuasively shown, for example, by Jasbir Puar, *Terrorist Assemblages: Homonationalism in Queer Times* (Durham, NC: Duke University Press, 2007), chap. 3.

46. Bell, *Faces*, 198.

47. Ibid. Bell's commitments here resonate strongly with both strands of Black existentialism—see, e.g., Lewis Gordon, *Existentia Africana*—and, more recently, the Afro-pessimist tradition synthesized by Frank Wilderson in *Red, White, and Black*.

48. Sonia Sotomayor, *My Beloved World* (New York: Alfred A. Knopf, 2013), viii.

Works Cited

Abrams, Kathryn, and Hila Keren. "Law and the Cultivation of Hope," *California Law Review* 95.2 (2007): 319–381.

Abrams, Kathryn, and Hila Keren. "Who's Afraid of Law and the Emotions?" *Minnesota Law Review* 94 (1997): 1997–2074.

Ackerman, Bruce. *The Civil Rights Revolution: We the People*, vol. 3. Cambridge, MA: Harvard University Press, 2014.

Alexander, Michelle. *The New Jim Crow: Mass Incarceration in the Age of Colorblindness*. New York: New Press, 2012.

Bell, Derrick *Silent Covenants: Brown v. Board of Education and the Unfulfilled Hopes for Racial Reform* (New York: Oxford University Press, 2004).

Bell, Derrick. "Racial Realism," *Connecticut Law Review* 24.2 (1992): 363–379.

Martel, James. *Divine Violence: Walter Benjamin and the Eschatology of Sovereignty*. New York: Routledge, 2012.

Bell, Derrick. *Faces at the Bottom of the Well: The Permanence of Racism*. New York: Basic Books, 1992.

Brown v. Board of Education, 347 U.S. 483 (1954).

Dred Scott v. Sandford, 60 U.S. 393 (1857).

Dubler, Ariella R. "Sexing Skinner: History and the Politics of the Right to Marry," *Columbia Law Review* 110.5 (2010): 1348–1376.

Edelman, Lee. *No Future: Queer Theory and the Death Drive*. Durham, NC: Duke University Press, 2004.

Franke, Katherine M. "The Domesticated Liberty of *Lawrence v. Texas*," *Columbia Law Review* 104.5 (2004): 1399–1426.

Gobuloff, Risa. *The Lost Promise of Civil Rights*. Cambridge, MA: Harvard University Press, 2007.

Gordon, Lewis R. *Existentia Africana*. New York: Routledge, 2000.

Karst, Kenneth L. "Law, Cultural Conflict, and the Socialization of Children," *California Law Review* 91.4 (2003): 970.

Kierkegaard, Søren. *The Sickness Unto Death: A Christian Psychological Exposition for Upbuilding and Awakening*. Translated by Howard V. and Edna H. Hong. Princeton, NJ: Princeton University Press, 1980.

Klarman, Michael J. *From Jim Crow to Civil Rights: The Supreme Court and the Struggle for Racial* Equality. Oxford, UK: Oxford University Press, 2004.

Lawrence v. Texas, 539 U.S. 558.

Lerner, Akiba. "Otherness and Liberal Democratic Solidarity: Buber, Kaplan, Levinas and Rorty's Social Hope," in *Thinking Jewish Culture in America*, ed. Ken Koltun-Fromm. Lanham, MD: Lexington Books, 2014. 31–70.

Lloyd, Vincent. "Of Fathers and Sons, Prophets and Messiahs," *Souls: A Critical Journal of Black Politics, Culture, and Society* 16.3–4 (2014): 209–226.

Nourse, Victoria F. *In Reckless Hands:* Skinner v. Oklahoma *and the Near Triumph of American* Eugenics. New York: W.W. Norton & Co., 2008.

Nussbaum, Martha C. *Hiding from Humanity: Disgust, Shame, and the Law*. Princeton, NJ: Princeton University Press, 2006.

Plessy v. Ferguson, 163 U.S. 537 (1896).

Posner, Eric A., and Cass R. Sunstein (eds.). *Law and* Happiness. Chicago: University of Chicago Press, 2010.

Post, Robert, and Reva Siegel. "Roe Rage: Democratic Constitutionalism and Backlash," *Harvard Civil Rights–Civil Liberties Law Review* 42 (2007): 373–433.

Puar, Jasbir. *Terrorist Assemblages: Homonationalism in Queer Times*. Durham, NC: Duke University Press, 2007.

Rosenberg, Gerald. *The Hollow Hope: Can Courts Bring About Social Change?* Chicago: University of Chicago Press, 1991.

Siegel, Reva B. "Equality Talk: Antisubordination and Anticlassification Values in Constitutional Struggles over *Brown*," *Harvard Law Review* 117 (2004): 1470–1547.

Skinner v. Oklahoma, 316 U.S. 535 (1942).

Sotomayor, Sonia. *My Beloved World*. New York: Alfred A. Knopf, 2013.

Stevens, Jacqueline. *Reproducing the State*. Princeton, NJ: Princeton University Press, 1999.

Taylor, George H., "Racism as 'The Nation's Crucial Sin': Theology and Derrick Bell," *Michigan Journal of Race & Law* 9 (2004): 269–322.

Warren, Earl. *The Memoirs of Earl* Warren. Garden City, NY: Doubleday and Company, Inc., 1977.

Wilderson, Frank. *Red, White, and Black: Cinema and the Structure of U.S. Antagonisms*. Durham, NC: Duke University Press, 2010.

Chapter 6

Between Hope and a White Body
The Challenge of Racial Realism and Interracial Love

Desirée H. Melton

> When a love relationship is at its height, there is no room left for any interest in the environment; a pair of lovers are sufficient to themselves.
>
> —Freud, *Civilization and Its Discontents*[1]

Introduction

Institutional racism has the power to affect where one lives, the quality of one's education, whether one receives proper health care, whether one gets a callback for a job, and whether one calls the police for help or avoids interacting with them in any way. Its depth and breadth are astonishing. Its de facto resiliency and malleability, startling. Racial justice has evaded blacks for so long, it is understandable why those fighting for justice would fall into despair. Why continue to fight such a formidable foe? Why hold onto hope that racial justice would ever be achieved? It is easy to fall into despair at the seeming futility at fighting against such a formidable foe. Derrick Bell argues that one way to avoid slipping into despair is for Blacks to—perhaps counterintuitively—accept their permanent subordination to whites.

Bell argues that Racial Realism, a perspective where blacks continue to resist racial injustice while holding that racism is permanent, can prevent blacks from falling into despair. Untethered from the fantasy of racial equality, the mind is free to imagine new and novel forms of resistance against racial injustice that can be fulfilling in and of themselves, unconnected to the goal of racial equality.

In this chapter, I argue that Racial Realism is a pragmatic, appropriate perspective for blacks to take against enduring systemic inequality, but it poses challenges for the racial realist in a romantic, egalitarian relationship with a white person. A racial realist can accept that her institutions will not treat her as equal to whites. She can accept that racial injustice will persist. However, as I will show, there will be challenges to holding a racial realist perspective while simultaneously being in an egalitarian romantic relationship with a white person. Her experience of egalitarianism with her partner may actually make it difficult for her to continue to hold an institutional racial realist perspective. Her egalitarian life with her partner that continually reinforces her equality could make the possibility of achieving institutional equality alluring once again.

If it's true that our romantic relationships are our most important relationships in that they affect how we see the world, what we imagine is possible, and help support and fuel our dreams, then a successfully egalitarian romantic relationship between a Black racial realist and a white person can pose a challenge to resist hoping for racial equality—one of the psychological moves necessary for the racial realist. Experiencing equality in her relationship could do the opposite. It could cause a shift in mindset that renews hope for racial equality leaving the racial realist at risk once again of despair.

I. "Locked-In" Black Inequality

Slavery laid a foundation for black inequality so effective, that the legacy continues over a century after the Thirteenth Amendment was ratified. Income and wealth gaps between blacks and whites continue to grow, as well as rates of unemployment. Health disparities between blacks and whites have not narrowed. Whites serve shorter prison sentences than blacks for committing the same crime—if they are convicted at all. Law enforcement officers are much more likely to suspect black women and men of criminal activity without probable cause than white women and men. Police who interact with whites tend to better follow standard police procedure than they do with blacks.

Whites are much more likely than blacks to live in decent neighborhoods with good public schools that are well resourced. More whites tend to own their own homes. If they hold a mortgage, it likely has a reasonable interest rate and terms. Since residency determines which public school one attends and the wealth of the neighborhood determines how well resourced the schools are and whether neighbors can assist one another, whites have a significant advantage that gives them a boost in all of the areas that make the greatest impact on life.

Education, Employment, and Income

The number of college-educated African Americans—particularly women—is increasing. Typically, a college education allows one to land a job with a higher income. However, a college education is not foolproof protection from unemployment. In fact, black college graduates do not fare much better than blacks without one. John Schmitt, senior economist at the Center for Economic Policy and Research, reports that recent black college graduates are almost as likely as the unskilled black worker to be unemployed.[2] The unemployment rate for all college graduates from 2010 to 2013 was 5.6 percent. For black graduates, the unemployment rate during this same period was 12.4 percent. In 2013, the unemployment rate for whites who did not complete high school was lower than the unemployment rate for blacks with some college education.[3] The Labor Department reports that the joblessness rate is higher for blacks than whites across all education levels, from the low-skilled to the high-skilled positions. Consider that in 1983 the weekly wage for white workers was 18.4 percent higher than the weekly wage for blacks.[4] In a 2016 report by the Economic Policy Institute, in 2015, black men's hourly wage was 31 percent lower than that of white men.[5] The gap between black women's earnings and white women's earnings has grown from 9 percent in 1979, to black women now earning 19 percent less than white women.

Health, Wealth, and Residency

The Centers for Disease Control reported that in 2015[6] the overall death rate declined for both blacks and whites, but blacks are still twice as likely as whites to die from diabetes, stroke, or heart disease. Blacks are 50 percent more likely than whites to have high blood pressure. Baltimore, Maryland, is a perfect case of a city whose segregated past and rampant racial inequality continues to this day. In the poorest neighborhood in Baltimore, Clifton/Berea—also predominantly black—the life expectancy is 66.9 years. The infant mortality rate is 14.8 percent. Nine miles away in Cross Country/Cheswolde, a predominantly white neighborhood, the infant mortality rate is 5.4 percent. If those infants survive, and they likely will, they can expect to live on average to 87, 20.1 years longer than blacks who live less than ten miles away in the same city. In Baltimore city, black children are more likely than white children to live in homes with lead paint and suffer cognitive deficits and behavioral problems as a result of the exposure. They are more likely to have at least one incarcerated parent, and they are more likely to remain at the same socioeconomic level as their parents, assuming their socioeconomic status does not continue to diminish over time.

II. The Power of Invisible Networks

In a 2016 report by the Pew Research Center, researchers found that black households headed by someone with at least a bachelor's degree had a median net worth of $26,300 in 2013. White households held eleven times more wealth with a median household net worth of $301,300.[7] Twenty-seven percent of black households have zero net wealth. All households experienced a decrease in net wealth after the Great Recession of 2007, but white households bounced back more quickly. In fact, the wealth gap between middle-income white families and black families has increased since the recession. And the upper-income earners? They now have more wealth than ever before. What accounts for these disparities? In most cases, poverty, stress, and the enduring effects of racism. In 2013, four times more black children lived in poverty than white children, while the numbers of children rising from poverty steadily increased in other racial groups. Nancy Krieger of The Harvard School of Public Health sums it up this way: "We literally embody, biologically, the societal and ecological conditions in which we grow up and develop and live." Several studies have concluded that the black mother's experience of racism affects their infant's birth weight, health, and mortality. Babies are born with their mother's experience of racism in their bodies.[8]

In her book *Reproducing Racism: How Everyday Choices Lock In White Advantage*,[9] Daria Roithmayr argues that black inequality and white advantage is locked into our institutions so deeply and so broadly that, barring radical intervention, it is likely to continue indefinitely. The justifications for slavery, discrimination, and oppression of blacks were intentionally racist, but as Roithmayr explains, unless radical steps are taken to unlock white advantage, inequality will certainly persist and likely worsen absent any intentional white racism. She details the hidden networks and positive feedback loops that advance whites and disadvantage blacks. This is alarming on its own, but coupled with the fact that a recent poll revealed that 38 percent of whites believe the nation has done enough to eradicate inequality, and the problem feels intractable.[10] If whites believe the necessary covert and overt institutional changes have been made for racial justice, how difficult will it be to convince whites of *hidden* advantages that give them a considerable edge over blacks, how likely are they to accept that "there are non-racially discriminatory hidden systems at work that perpetuate—and will continue to perpetuate—black inequality, indefinitely."[11]

Roithmayr reveals that *nonracist* white intraracial interaction in the education system, in the workforce, and in residential neighborhoods is one of the primary reasons for steady white advancement. Whether whites live in predominantly white neighborhoods or diverse neighborhoods, they tend to limit their interactions to other well-connected whites like themselves. All racial groups tend to interact intraracially more frequently than interracially, but since whites are far better off socioeconomically, these segregated positive networks result in a wealth of benefits for whites and a dearth of benefits for blacks.[12]

Predominantly white neighborhoods enjoy the benefits of a higher tax base that fund good public schools, provide financial security, and, most importantly, provide access to a network of people who can help them continue to advance. The higher population of well-connected, college-educated parents with secure jobs and a rich network of connections, including neighbors and friends of friends, create a pool of resources they can draw from to give their children a leg up in education, job searches, and internships. They are better able to buy their child a car or hand one down, provide a college education, and contribute to a down payment for their first mortgage. When those children have families of their own, their children enjoy the same benefits and more since they can rely on their parents and grandparents for financial support, as well as formal and informal connections to other well-connected whites.

The picture is different in black neighborhoods. They tend to have smaller homes that do not appreciate at the rate that whites homes do. Even houses comparable in size to white homes are worth less than ones in white neighborhoods.[13] Because homes low in value generate a smaller tax base, the public schools tend to be under-resourced staffed with poorly skilled, overwhelmed teachers. The majority of residents tend to be unskilled or low-skilled, with only a small number of high-skill workers who can connect neighbors to high-skill, better paying jobs. Residents in black neighborhoods tend to rely on public transportation. If you do not have a car, you cannot join the community carpool and informally network with other parents. Since residents are not in a position to help one another because everyone is equally worse off, blacks in majority black neighborhoods are at a disadvantage compared to whites in white neighborhoods; they do not have the luxury of offering a helping hand to one another.

There is no one to give application advice to the high school graduate who aspires to be the first in the family to attend college. There is no neighbor with connections to admissions officers, or who owns a software firm and can offer an internship to a new computer science graduate. There are few if any neighbors with connections to hiring offices, or who can put in a good word with friends at their law firm. This lack of positive feedback loops prevents them from advancing like their white counterparts.[14]

A college degree is not an equalizer; it does not close the gap between young black adults fresh out of college and young white adults. Black parents often struggle to give their children a head start when they embark on their own. Their children often hobble from the family nest, weighed down with their own debt and the burden of helping family who then look to them for financial support. When those young adults become older adults, they are more likely to be "sandwiched" between caring for the parents who sacrificed their own meager financial health to help them as much as they could, and providing for their own families.

If it is true that the quality of one's networks is by far the greatest indicator of whether someone will advance and pass on their advantage to the next generation or whether they will fall farther behind, then the next generations of white children will actually surpass—not maintain—their parents' achievements. Young, white adults, beneficiaries of institutional advantage, de facto racism, and hidden positive feedback loops of privilege, can soar from the family nest with less financial burden than their black peers. Indefinite successive generations of blacks will be at a grim disadvantage.[15]

III. Racial Realism

Given the above, it is clear why Bell concludes that racism is permanent. Accepting this fact and adopting a racial realist perspective will relieve Blacks from perpetual frustration, dashed hopes, and despair. Bell writes:

> Black people will never gain full equality in this country. Even those herculean efforts we hail as successful will produce no more than temporary "peaks of progress," short-lived victories that slide into irrelevance as racial patterns adapt in ways that maintain dominance. This is a hard-to-accept fact that all history verifies. We must acknowledge it and move on to adopt policies based on what I call: "Racial Realism." This mind-set or philosophy *requires us to acknowledge the permanence of our subordinate status.* That acknowledgement *enables us to avoid despair, and frees us to imagine and implement racial strategies that can bring fulfillment and even triumph.*[16] (emphasis mine)

Bell's "Racial Realism is to race relations what Legal Realism is to jurisprudential thought."[17] Legal Realism, a perspective formed by scholars in the early decades of the twentieth century, asserts that the law is "instrumental, not self-evidently logical and 'made' by judges."[18] Bell claims that this position "changed the face of American jurisprudence by exposing the result-oriented, value-laden nature of legal decision-making."[19] As a lens, Legal Realism afforded a view of jurisprudence obscured by a traditional, formalist approach and allowed for new and better ways to evaluate the legal system.[20] Racial Realism, a lens not obscured by "equality ideology," frees African Americans from the exhausting, frustrating fight for racial justice. Whereas Legal Realists had the goal of "challenging the entire jurisprudential system," racial realists' goal was more modest. Bell envisioned it as a "legal and social mechanism" that challenges "the principle of racial equality."[21]

Optimists who believe blacks will eventually reach equality often cite the de jure progress blacks have made over the years, in particular the momentous 1954 *Brown v. Board of Education* ruling that outlawed school segregation and overturned *Plessy v. Ferguson*. Bell sees it differently, however. In *Silent Covenants: Brown v. Board of Education and the Unfulfilled Hopes for Racial Reform*, Bell argues convincingly that school segregation was not ruled unconstitutional because our justice system was persuaded that Jim Crow's "separate by equal" policy on school segregation was unjust to blacks, but primarily because white interests converged with black interests.

Blacks had an interest in school desegregation and whites had an interest in portraying the United States in a favorable light in comparison to the Soviets during the Cold War. The Supreme Court outlawed school segregation because the United States had an interest in winning the war against Communism, not rectifying an injustice against African Americans. The Soviets were gaining world support in part by shaming the United States and its claim of equality for all while it held blacks under Jim Crow laws. The U.S. government did not end Jim Crow because it had an interest in gaining justice for blacks, Bell argues.[22] The U.S. government's interest in winning the war against Communism and blacks' interest in school desegregation converged, thus the Supreme Court ruled in favor of plaintiff Oliver Brown, bringing an end to *Plessy v. Ferguson*'s decision that separate public schools are constitutional as long as they are equal.[23]

De jure efforts toward racial justice, however, have been ineffective long term. In 1857, the U.S. Supreme Court upheld slavery in the court case *Dred Scott v. Sandford*. The Emancipation Proclamation that outlawed slavery was signed in 1863. *Plessy v. Ferguson*, the case that upheld segregation, was signed in 1896. Segregation was ruled unconstitutional in *Brown v. Board of Education* in 1954. The Civil Rights Act in 1964 outlawed discrimination by race, color, religion, sex, or national origin. Despite these de jure advances in black equality, in 2018, African Americans are disadvantaged in our health care system, educational system, and workforce. Positive feedback loops perpetuate racial inequality even when there is no intentional institutional racism. They are set to continue indefinitely unless radical measures are taken, and there is no reason to believe that the United States will take those measures, since we refuse to take even modest ones.

I doubt I am alone in finding a racial realist perspective simultaneously appealing and troubling. It is deflating to say the least that it may be more beneficial for blacks to accept their subordination to whites and give up hoping that they will ever reach the goal of ending racial oppression. It is also demoralizing to accept that blacks have not reached the social or economic equality they should have since the end of Jim Crow. After all, twenty-six years after Bell concluded that blacks are better off adopting a racial realist perspective, and eight years after the United States had first elected a black president, America chose a populist, racist, sexual-abuser of women and enemy of brown immigrants, the disabled, and LGBTQ people to succeed him.

Racial Realism can offer a shield against the pessimism and despair of sinking time and energy into fighting for racial equality that, despite our best efforts, has evaded us for centuries. The racial realist continues to fight against racial injustice but with a new goal in mind. A racial realist fights because it is good for one's humanity to fight against subordination, and because it can help the realist to reimagine a future for blacks apart from "traditional, integration-oriented remedies" that "seem to work only when it is in the interest of whites for them to work."[24] It is an irrefutable fact, Bell claims, that past efforts to achieve racial equality—efforts spanning centuries—have not managed to fully wrest power from whites through legislative efforts or social ones. Racial Realism opens the imagination to new and creative ways to push against our social subordination that will be more fulfilling than chasing a goal we are unlikely ever to reach. Despite how disheartening it is to even consider accepting one's permanent subordination, thankfully, a racial realist can turn to her relationships—particularly her romantic ones—for support and fulfillment.

IV. Our Most Important Relationship

Bell's marriage to his first wife was his "most important relationship."[25] In his 2002 memoir, *Ethical Ambition*, Bell tells of challenges he faced, competing obligations, the fear of standing alone for something one believes is right, and the beauty of committing oneself to living a principled life and advancing causes that try to improve society. The loving, supportive bond he shared with his first wife, Jewel Hairston Bell, his "confidant, advisor, and best friend"[26] provided the foundation and stability for many of his accomplishments. Citing a pamphlet on marriage written by John Hope Franklin and Aurelia Whittington Franklin that he believes sums up a successful marriage, Bell notes:

> [The couple] saw themselves as members of a team: The good of one was the good of the other; harm or hurt to one was harm or hurt to the other. The basis of the relationship was an empathy enacted through respect. In short, the partnership enhances the couples' humanity by challenging each person to

become more sensitive to and better able to rely on, respect, and cherish the other.[27]

The Franklins and the Bells had long, successful marriages built on love, mutual respect, equality, a sensitivity to the other, an investment in each's well-being, and the desire to join their partner in advancing their goals. A relationship that lacks any of these qualities might not last, although relationships end for many other reasons.

Relationships suffer when couples do not communicate well or often. Couples could have satisfying sex and mistake that for genuine intimacy. Couples marry too young, long before they know themselves, much less what they want in a partner. How and if to care for one's aging parents can stress a relationship to its breaking point, as can different ideas on how to raise children and what to spend money on and how much to save. Whether to move the family for one's job or stay put for the partner's career can tear apart a couple. If a partner is dishonest, trust could be so shattered that the relationship never recovers. Some couples are just deeply incompatible and the relationship is doomed from the start, even if the couple decides to stay together in lifelong misery or disappointment. These issues are not peculiar to any race. Both intraracial and interracial relationships can end for any of these reasons, but when one member of the relationship is white and the other is black, they have an additional stressor or challenge that intraracial ones do not have.

Interracial marriage has been legal in the United States since laws prohibiting it were ruled unconstitutional in the 1967 court case *Loving v. Virginia*. The approval rate of these unions continues to increase, yet it remains uncommon for people of different races to marry.[28] In the case of blacks and whites, limited access and exposure could be one reason. Even when blacks and whites live, work, and gather in racially diverse spaces, they tend to interact more with people of their own race. If they do interact with one another, it tends to be superficial and not in the meaningful way that fosters deep interracial friendships, much less interracial romantic relationships. Another reason is that blacks and whites have very different experiences and perspectives that can make compatibility a challenge. At times, it can seem like whites and blacks live in different worlds.

A 2016 survey by Pew Research Center shows that blacks and whites hold polar views on racial inequality and how much race impacts one's life.[29] Most of the whites polled, 70 percent, believe that individual racism is a bigger problem than institutional racism, while only 19 percent of blacks share that view. Sixty-six percent of blacks polled believe that blacks are treated unfairly by the police, compared to 26 percent of whites. The gulf between whites and blacks is far more telling, though, on questions about how the country has responded to racial inequality and whether it will ever be reached. Forty percent of whites say the United States will eventually make the changes necessary for blacks to have equal rights to whites. Forty-three percent of blacks say the United States will not make the necessary changes. Whites disagree. As mentioned earlier, 38 percent maintain that the necessary changes have already been made.

The rate of interracial black-white marriage is increasing, however, despite limited exposure to one another, and the fact that there are still those on both sides who remain apprehensive about dating outside of their race.[30] For African Americans, most of the wariness stems from moral concerns about what it reveals about oneself and what it communicates to family and community to enter into a romantic relationship with a white person, given our long history of discrimination, oppression, and subordinate status.

Anita Allen explores these concerns in "Interracial Marriage: Folk Ethics in Contemporary Philosophy."[31] Out of "respect and care" for community, family, and oneself, blacks may experience entering into interracial relationships with whites as a moral failing. Intraracial marriage affirms the value of the black community, solidifies one's connection to family and friends, and expresses pride in one's race. Blacks who couple interracially run the risk of appearing to not respect or care for their community, family and friends, or self. Allen acknowledges that these are compelling reasons for blacks to be wary of entering into a romantic relationship with whites. Blacks may be untroubled or indifferent about living, working, or socializing with whites. However, given the history of slavery, Jim Crow, individual and institutional racism, white men's historical sexual access to black women, and the mortal risk black men face in some regions for merely interacting with or appearing to interact with white women, it is evident why some blacks may find inviting them into one's bed morally repugnant.[32]

V. Racial Realism and Interracial Love

Given the many obstacles to interracial relationships succeeding, what happens when an additional obstacle arises? What happens when the black partner adopts a racial realist perspective and accepts her permanent subordination to white people?

An African American in an intraracial relationship who adopts a Racial Realist perspective will not face the same sorts of obstacles as she would in an interracial relationship. Accepting one's permanent subordination to whites does not disturb the equality between two black partners. Other tensions may arise around Racial Realism, however, particularly if one partner changes her perspective to or from Racial Realism and her partner does not. It could cause a great deal of pain if their shared perspective on racism guided their activities as a couple, informed their discussions, and bonded them to one another. They are likely to feel abandoned or betrayed if their partner is no longer "in it" with them. There are likely to be disagreements, accusations of pessimism, and accusations of misplaced optimism. Their difference in perspectives may even drive a wedge between them.

A racial realist who couples romantically with a white person will have a different experience. Adopting that outlook will have consequences on how she views her place in the world and will certainly affect her involvement in liberatory efforts. How will Racial Realism affect her relationship with her white partner? To get a better sense of how an interracial relationship could be affected, let us consider a hypothetical couple, Deidre and Sean.

Deidre is black and Sean is white. To make them as egalitarian as possible and isolate how racial inequality could affect them, let us suppose they are a lesbian couple.[33] Soon after Deidre and Sean met, they discovered that in each other they had found their person. They share the same interests, values, and sense of humor. There is no tacit understanding that one's job demands or career aspirations take precedence to the others'. Housework is not divided along gender lines, as is typical in heterosexual relationships, but divided according to preferences or individual schedules.

Their occupations overlap and they are fortunate enough to work together on projects when time allows and it is appropriate. They are competitive, but not with one another; success for one is success for both. They are best friends and communicate well and often. In short, they share the deep compatibility that is so vital for a successful, fulfilling, romantic relationship. They experience the same occasional miscommunications, hurt feelings, and small slights all couples do, but their relationship is as strong as one could be. Deidre and Sean both consider their relationship the most fulfilling and important relationship in their lives. And this is how it should be. Allen puts it aptly when she says, "romantic love is typified by a placement of the object of love at the center of the universe: nothing and no one matter more than the beloved."[34]

Deidre surveys the racial landscape and notes that police brutality against blacks has not abated, mass incarceration of blacks continues,[35] the opioid epidemic receives the attention it deserves once it touches white families, and black women bring home 63 cents on the dollar compared to 75 cents for white women.[36] She reflects on the arc of racial inequality over the course of her life. She considers the progress and setbacks, the gains achieved, the losses suffered, and the justice work she has engaged in to achieve racial equality. She recalls the votes cast for candidates who promised to advance black equality but then promptly reneged once they took office. She thinks of the phone calls and the letters she has written to her senators and representatives on issues that concern black equality. She sees that if any of it had a positive effect on racial justice, it was not an appreciable difference and was certainly not long lasting. She thinks of the protests she engaged in, the laws passed but for the wrong reasons, the steps backward the country took on race—and other issues—after the Trump administration took office in 2016. She concludes that racial injustice is deep, infused in every American institution, and permanent. She acknowledges the progress blacks have made, but she also believes that any gains blacks have made were dependent on white interests.

She abandons the belief that racial equality will be achieved, and decides it is in her psychological interest to accept that she is permanently subordinate to whites. This conclusion does not sadden her. Rather, she is relieved to be disabused of the notion that black racial justice will be achieved. It frees up mental space and reallocates her energy toward other projects that are more worthwhile and less dispiriting than trying to break through a wall of injustice that is as deep as the centuries of black inequality are long.

There are two "moves" to adopting a racial realist perspective. The first is to accept that blacks are permanently subordinate to whites. The second is to continue resistance efforts against racial oppression, detached from the goal of achieving equality. The first move involves the realist understanding and accepting that she will never rise above her subordinate status in a white supremacist society. The second move calls for the realist to resist oppression using new strategies, but not with the expectation of *achieving* racial justice. The first move accomplishes two things: it aids in avoiding despair and it frees the mind to imagine new ways of resisting racism that could "bring fulfillment and even triumph."[37] Those new ways are implemented in the second move of Racial Realism, continuing to resist injustice.

Deidre makes the first "move." She does not *believe* she is subordinate to whites, but *accepts* that she will always be treated as inferior and subordinate to whites. She thinks she may as well accept that fact. She settles into a racial realist perspective. Racial Realism asks African Americans to *acknowledge* and *accept* their subordinate status, not to believe that they deserve or are inferior to whites. Critics of Racial Realism can easily argue that it is harmful for blacks to accept their subordination to whites. Indeed, it can be harmful for anyone to accept subordinate treatment. Deidre accepts that institutions like health care and the workforce will always treat her as inferior. She accepts that she will never earn as much as her white peers (nor will she earn as much as her black male peers). She accepts that if she were to tell her primary care physician that she is in pain, her doctor may not believe her, or not believe it is as severe as she says it is. She accepts that she must be extra careful to always use the same pharmacy, or she will give the appearance of drug shopping. She accepts that she will be followed around stores, and that when she goes car shopping, her creditworthiness will not be assumed as it would be if she were a white woman.

She decides that she must find new ways to resist racial injustice, because it is good for her humanity to continue to fight against it, not because she thinks it will work. Rather than feeling despair, she feels unburdened by unfulfilled expectations and freed from disappointment. However, Deidre is in a romantic relationship with a white person. While it could be beneficial for her to acknowledge and accept her subordinate status to whites in general, it will be challenging in the context of being romantically coupled with Sean, her white partner.

Bell says "we need a mechanism to make life bearable in a society where blacks are a permanent, subordinate class."[38] Deidre's realist institutional perspective may make it bearable for her to work alongside a white peer who earns more than she does, or run errands alongside white strangers at the store who are not aware that their every move is not being watched. But, she cannot accept that she is subordinate to the person with whom she makes herself vulnerable and shares secrets. How can she be subordinate to the person she relies on, makes love to, and plans a life? Racial realists in intraracial relationships do not run into this trouble. Their relationship with their black partner could be unequal in other ways, like class or gender, but white supremacy does not subordinate one of them to the other. This fact is actually one of the reasons why some blacks are against interracial relationships. Who else but another black person can empathize and understand the black experience? Black racial realist partners may actually find that their shared perspective on the permanence of institutional racism draws them closer to one another. Couples have certainly bonded over matters much more superficial.

Does Racial Realism succeed in making life bearable for Deidre? It may help Deidre avoid despair as she refuses to take part in what she concludes is the fantasy of expecting racial justice, but if she is in a relationship with a white person, things get complicated if she takes on a realist perspective. The egalitarian dynamic she and Sean have cultivated may make it impossible not to feel at least some small measure of optimism about the possibility of achieving racial justice. Her experience of egalitarianism with a white individual may renew her hope that racism is not permanent. Cracks may form in her realist perspective in proportion to how egalitarian her relationship is; the better things are with Sean, the more hopeful she becomes and the less firm her realism is.

VI. Institutional Inequality, Individual Equality

A racial realist in an interracial relationship either held the perspective prior to entering the relationship or adopted it during. What happens when a black person becomes a realist while in an interracial relationship with a white person? Does her change in perspective change her view of her relationship? Does her view of herself change? Our most important relationship touches every corner of our lives. The beloved is our confidante, our best friend, our life partner, and our lover. They challenge, cheer, soothe, support, nurture, respect, and love us. How can her abandonment of the hope for racial equality *not* affect her most important relationship, her view of herself as an individual, and herself in her relationship? Let us return to Deidre and Sean and consider some of the troubles they encounter if Deidre adopts Racial Realism sometime during her relationship with Sean.

Sean wants racial justice. If Sean continues to believe it will be reached and fights for it with that goal in mind, have not she and Deidre now reached an impasse over something profound? How should Sean address this? Does she continue her usual justice efforts, the one that the realist no longer engages in, or does she drop them and join Deidre? Sean cannot adopt Racial Realism, for obvious reasons, but is it not troubling if Sean *does* join Deidre in accepting her permanent inferiority? Let us say she does not join her, but she supports Deidre, since she is a good partner and that is what good partners do. Is it not also a repugnant thought that Sean would *support* Deidre's acceptance of her inferiority? Should not Deidre's realism—one that she arrived at in defeat—motivate Sean to resist and fight with even greater resolve, so horrified is she that society has driven her beloved to this perspective? And is there not a hint of condescension when Sean, from her position of advantage, continues to hold out for racial justice despite her partner Deidre, weary of being disadvantaged, concluding that enough is enough? Should Deidre's perspective take precedence over Sean's? But if it does, then Sean is back in the troubling situation of either supporting Deidre's subordination, attempting to join her, or both.

And what of Deidre? She adopts a racial realist mindset that accepts her permanent subordination to white people. The wisdom of her decision is confirmed daily in the systemic injustice all around her in all the institutions with which she interacts. Yet, she comes home to the protective cocoon of a loving and supportive relationship where she is an equal alongside her white partner. Deidre must accept permanent subordination systemically while experiencing equality individually. Surely there is a mental and emotional cost to the effort. And what of the effect of bouncing between equality and subordination? She must hold two truths constant that affect one another and are in opposition to one another: she is subordinate to white people systemically and equal to this white person individually. The love and support she experiences in her relationship—her most important relationship—gives her the strength to keep fighting against racial injustice with no expectation justice will be achieved. However, because the right person loving and supporting us can also give us hope, she may also begin to hope again for racial equality. If she does, she will be hoping against hope. Hoping against hope can lead one to despair. And that is precisely what racial realism is meant to guard against.

For the reasons above, it is clear that it must be challenging for blacks whose beloved is white to hold the perspective that our institutions will never treat them as equal to whites while simultaneously experiencing equality with their white partner. There is an emotional cost to holding a racial realist perspective and experiencing an egalitarian interracial relationship. The racial realist attitude relieves stress and the egalitarian interracial relationship—like all egalitarian relationships—also relieve stress. The experience of equality undermines Racial Realism, and Racial Realism undermines the experience of equality.

Conclusion

I do not know if racism is permanent, but there are good reasons to believe that it will not end soon. Abandoning an unobtainable goal and accepting the permanence of systemic black inferiority frees us from holding a false hope of achieving racial justice. However, a black person in a loving relationship with her white partner may find that it is challenging to keep the realms separate. Experiencing equality with her partner may make it hard to continue to hold the perspective that she will always be subordinate. The love, respect, and equality between her and her white partner may rekindle her hope for racial justice and thus expose her to the risk of again falling into despair—the opposite of what a racial realist perspective should afford.

Notes

1. Sigmund Freud, *Civilization and Its Discontents*, ed. and trans. J. Strachey (New York: W.W. Norton, 1961), 65.

2. John Schmitt, "A College Degree Is No Guarantee," Center for Economic Policy and Research, www.cepr.net/documents/Blackgrads_infographic.pdf

3. U.S. Bureau of Labor Statistics, "Labor Force Statistics from the Current Population Survey," www.bls.gov/cps/cpsaat07.htm

4. U.S. Bureau of Labor Statistics, www.bls.gov/emp/ep_edtrain_outlook.pdf

5. Valerie Wilson and William M. Rogers III, "Black-White Wage Gaps Expand with Rising Wage Inequality, Economic Policy Institute, September 20, 2016, www.epi.org/publication/black-white-wage-gaps-expand-with-rising-wage-inequality

6. "African American Health: Creating Equal Opportunities for Health," Centers for Disease Control and Prevention, www.cdc.gov/vitalsigns/aahealth/index.html

7. "On Views of Race and Inequality, Blacks and Whites Are Worlds Apart," Pew Research Center, June 27, 2016, www.pewsocialtrends.org/2016/06/27/on-views-of-race-and-inequality-blacks-and-whites-are-worlds-apart

8. J.W. Collins, R.J. David, A. Handler, S. Wall, and S. Andes, "Very Low Birthweight in African American Infants: The Role of Maternal Exposure to Interpersonal Racial Discrimination," *American Journal of Public Health* 94.12 (2004): 2132–2138; M.R. Kramer and C.R. Hogue, "What Causes Racial Disparities in Very Preterm Birth? A Biosocial Perspective," *Epidemiologic Reviews* 31 (2009): 84–98; Tyan Parker Dominguez, "Adverse Birth Outcomes in African American Women: The Social Context of Persistent Reproductive Disadvantage," *Social Work in Public Health* 26.1 (2011): 3–16.

9. Daria Roithmayr, *Reproducing Racism: How Everyday Choices Lock In White Advantage* (New York: New York University Press, 2014).

10. "On Views of Race and Inequality."

11. Roithmayr, *Reproducing Racism*.

12. Ibid., 71.

13. Ibid., 67.

14. Ibid., 64–68.

15. Ibid., 57.

16. Derrick Bell, "Racial Realism," *Connecticut Law Review* 24.2 (1992): 363–379, 373–374.

17. Ibid., 364.

18. Ibid., 364.

19. Ibid., 368.

20. Ibid. Bell cites *Board of Regents of the University of California v. Bakke* as a "paradigm" case of the legislature's formalist approach that presumes the law is "transcendent" and comprised of "ultimate principles." Had the Justices taken into consideration the many social disadvantages blacks typically faced that explained the low numbers of minority applicants to medical schools, perhaps they would have decided the case differently.

21. Bell, "Racial Realism," 364.

22. *Brown v. Board of Education*, 347 U.S. 483 (1954).

23. Derrick Bell, *Silent Covenants: Brown v. Board of Education and the Unfulfilled Hopes for Racial Reform* (New York: Oxford University Press, 2004), 67.

24. Derrick Bell, "Racism Is Here to Stay: Now What?" *Howard Law Journal* (Thurgood Marshall Commemorative Issue) 35 (1991): 89.

25. Derrick Bell, *Ethical Ambition: Living a Life of Meaning and Worth* (New York: Bloomsbury, 2002), 96.

26. Ibid.

27. Ibid., 99.

28. *Loving v. Virginia*, 388 U.S. 1 (1967).

29. "On Views of Race and Inequality."

30. I am using relationship and marriage interchangeably. Whether a couple is in a long-term relationship or married, these issues are the same.

31. Anita Allen, "Interracial Marriage: Folk Ethics in Contemporary Philosophy," in *Women of Color in Philosophy*, ed. Naomi Zack (Malden, MA: Blackwell, 2000), 183.

32. Ibid., 182–183.

33. Housework, responsibility for childcare, and work demands tend to be shared more equally between lesbians in relationships than between a man and a woman or between two men. Of course, I am not claiming that all heterosexual relationships are inegalitarian and that all lesbian relationships are. I am merely pointing to the tendency of lesbian relationships overall to be more egalitarian compared to both heterosexual and male same-sex relationships. R.-J. Green, M. Bettinger, and E. Zacks, "Are Lesbian Couples Fused and Gay Male Couples Disengaged? Questioning Gender Straightjackets," in *Lesbians and Gays in Couples and Families: A Handbook for Therapists*, eds. J. Laird and R.-J. Green (San Francisco: Jossey Bass, 1996), 185–230.

34. Allen, "Interracial Marriage," 196.

35. It has slowed down, however. See E. Ann Carson, "Prisoners in 2016," Bureau of Justice Statistics, January 9, 2018, www.bjs.gov/index.cfm?ty=pbdetail&iid=6187

36. "The Simple Truth about the Gender Pay Gap," American Association of University Women, 2019, www.aauw.org/research/the-simple-truth-about-the-gender-pay-gap

37. Bell, "*Racial Realism*," 374.

38. Ibid., 377.

Works Cited

Allen, Anita. "Interracial Marriage: Folk Ethics in Contemporary Philosophy," in *Women of Color in Philosophy*, ed. Naomi Zack. Malden, MA: Blackwell, 2000.

American Association of University Women. "The Simple Truth about the Gender Pay Gap," 2019. www.aauw.org/research/the-simple-truth-about-the-gender-pay-gap

Bell, Derrick, *Ethical Ambition: Living a Life of Meaning and Worth*. New York: Bloomsbury, 2002.

Bell, Derrick. "Racial Realism," *Connecticut Law Review* 24.2 (1992): 363–379.

———. "Racism Is Here to Stay: Now What?" *Howard Law Journal*. Thurgood Marshall Commemorative Issue 35 (1991): 89.

———. *Silent Covenants:* Brown v. Board of Education *and the Unfulfilled Hopes for Racial Reform*. New York: Oxford University Press, 2004.

Board of Regents of the University of California v. Bakke 438 U.S. 265 (1978).

Brown v. Board of Education, 347 U.S. 483 (1954).

Carson, Ann E. "Prisoners in 2016," Bureau of Justice Statistics, January 9, 2018. www.bjs.gov/index.cfm?ty=pbdetail&iid=6187

Centers for Disease Control and Prevention, "African American Health: Creating Equal Opportunities for Health." www.cdc.gov/vitalsigns/aahealth/index.html

Collins, J.W., R.J. David, A. Handler, S. Wall, and S. Andes. "Very Low Birthweight in African American Infants: The Role of Maternal Exposure to Interpersonal Racial Discrimination," *American Journal of Public Health* 94.12 (2004): 2132–2138.

Dominguez, Tyan Parker. "Adverse Birth Outcomes in African American Women: The Social Context of Persistent Reproductive Disadvantage," *Social Work in Public Health* 26.1 (2011): 3–16.

Freud, Sigmund. *Civilization and Its Discontents*. Edited and translated by J. Strachey. New York: W.W. Norton, 1961.

Green, R.J., M. Bettinger, and E. Zacks. "Are Lesbian Couples Fused and Gay Male Couples Disengaged? Questioning Gender Straightjackets," in *Lesbians and Gays in Couples and Families: A Handbook for Therapists*, ed. J. Laird and R.-J. Green. San Francisco: Jossey Bass, 1996. 185–230.

Kramer M.R., and C.R. Hogue. "What Causes Racial Disparities in Very Preterm Birth? A Biosocial Perspective," *Epidemiologic Reviews* 31 (2009): 84–98.

Loving v. Virginia, 388 U.S. 1 (1967).

Pew Research Center, "On Views of Race and Inequality, Blacks and Whites Are Worlds Apart," June 27, 2016. www.pewsocialtrends.org/2016/06/27/on-views-of-race-and-inequality-blacks-and-whites-are-worlds-apart

Roithmayr, Daria. *Reproducing Racism: How Everyday Choices Lock In White Advantage*. New York: New York University Press, 2014.

Schmitt, John. "A College Degree Is No Guarantee," Center for Economic Policy and Research. www.cepr.net/documents/Blackgrads_infographic.pdf

U.S. Bureau of Labor Statistics. "Labor Force Statistics from the Current Population Survey." www.bls.gov/cps/cpsaat07.htm

U.S. Bureau of Labor Statistics. www.bls.gov/emp/ep_edtrain_outlook.pdf
Wilson, Valerie, and William M. Rogers III. "Black–White Wage Gaps Expand with Rising Wage Inequality, Economic Policy Institute, September 20, 2016. www.epi.org/publication/black-white-wage-gaps-expand-with-rising-wage-inequality

PART IV
RACIAL REALISM AND THEOLOGY

Chapter 7

Rethinking Hope

The Importance of Radical Racial Realism for Womanist Theological Thought

Keri Day

This chapter focuses on how Derrick Bell's idea of radical racial realism helps womanist religious thought rethink its language of hope in response to racial injustices. Within much of womanist religious studies, the language of hope in relation to racial injustice has been grounded in a vocabulary of eradication. In part, this assumption that racisms can be eradicated is associated with womanist eschatological visions, which are rooted in the real possibility of alternative social worlds marked by love and justice. The idea of hope, for some womanist scholars, involves the belief in the emergence of future worlds *free* from structural racism. However, Bell's idea of racial realism in relation to racism challenges this language of eradication and debunks this belief in an alternative world free from structural racism. Racial realism argues that race is not an anomaly to American structures but constitutive of American sociopolitical life. Racism is a *permanent part of the DNA of America*. Consequently, racism cannot be eradicated, as it constitutes the foundation of American political life. However, racism can be *defied*. One can infer that Bell does not think of racial resistance in terms of eradication; rather, he thinks of racial resistance as *defiance*.

I think that Bell's idea of racial realism invites womanist theological thought to rethink its language of hope. Much of womanist theological discourse tends to frame hope through the language of eradication instead of the language of defiance. Taking its cue from Bell's racial realism, I argue that womanist thought can better theorize resistance to structural racism by employing the language of defiance. Defiance as a mode of resistance is not impotent or a "giving up" in the face of racial injustice. Instead, defiance functions as a disruptive ethics to structural (re)productions of racism, perpetually dislodging the theoretical and practical force of racial logics and practices that denigrate black subjects. Moreover, defying racisms allows oppressed "raced" subjects to claim their humanity within the objectifying, dehumanizing matrices of racial oppression. Defiance does not allow structural racisms to "have the last say" over black life. Defiance then can be construed as a *theological good* in relation to hope. My proposal is that Bell's idea of racial realism allows womanist theological language of hope to move away from the idea of eradication to defiance, enabling womanist theological thought to theorize *diverse* modes of resistance that reclaim black humanity.

I. Confronting Racism from Multipositionality: Womanist Ideas of Hope

Black womanist theological thought has an intellectual commitment to deconstructing racial logics and practices in the United States and around the world. Specifically, womanist thought in the United States has addressed the structural production of racism and how racist practices inhibit the liberation and flourishing of black communities, particularly black women.[1] However, womanism has critiqued black liberation thought and critical race theory for their emphasis on structural racism to the exclusion of gender, sexual, and class oppressions. Black women's experiences of racial oppression cannot be accounted for when race *overdetermines* how one theorizes black oppression. Race and racism do not operate in a vacuum. Instead, race articulates itself with gender/sexuality/class in structuring the experiences of black women. Because black women sit at the center of womanist discourse, a theory of multipositionality is essential. Black women are racialized subjects with multiple positionalities in relation to their gender, class, sexuality, and so forth. As a result, womanist theological thought has sought to demonstrate how racial logic is linked to intersectional oppressions (such as class, gender, etc.) for black women.

For instance, the historical and contemporary racialization of black women has been tied to interpreting black women as hypersexual beings.[2] During slavery, the insidious sexual violence that black women endured (i.e., rape) at the hands of white slave masters discloses how the black female racial subject was constructed: through the hypersexualization of her body. Black women were read *pornotropically*,[3] in which their bodies were interpreted and treated as sites of sexual pleasure and conquest.[4] This hypersexualization of the black female body grounded black women's experiences as racialized subjects. One cannot understand the black female as racial subject without interrogating the gender and sexual forms of violence that constituted their experiences of racial oppression in the United States. Consequently, gender, sexual, and economic forms of violence have been constitutive of how black women experience structural racism in America. This move toward multipositionality in womanist theological studies has served as a corrective to early black liberation thought.[5]

One cannot confront anti-black racism in this country without acknowledging the ways in which gender and sexuality shape experiences of structural racisms among black women. We better understand the multiple and diverse ways in which structural racism operates upon black bodies when we consider issues of gender, sexuality, class, and more. I do acknowledge the multiple critiques of intersectionality, particularly the problem of how the concept of gender tends to imply an essentialized category of woman within early intersectional theories. Although the scope of this chapter is *not* to nuance arguments surrounding the limits of intersectionality, my idea of multipositionality within womanist theological thought considers the importance of diverse gendered and sexual identities in articulating the category of woman.

Intersectional oppression for black people (in particular, black women) is a *theological problem* for womanist discourse. What is unique about womanist theological thought is that it does not merely see black oppression as social injustice. It interprets racial oppression as *sin*. Many womanist scholars identify Black women's subordination as the *sin* of racist hetero-patriarchy. Such racist hetero-patriarchy is not merely a social problem but sin (violation against God and one's neighbor) that is addressed through God's delivering and redemptive character. The interpretive/conceptual categories of Black women's intersectional oppression and liberative activity are tied into a grand cosmic narrative of the Divine God who offers quality of life to the most marginalized and oppressed with a redemptive word of hope that extends within *and* beyond history.

For instance, womanist theologian Delores Williams uses theological categories in describing Black women's intersectional oppressions and experiences of hope in her text *Sisters in the Wilderness: The Challenge of Womanist God-Talk*. She likens Black women's oppression to the biblical story of the servant Hagar (Genesis 16) who is exploited both by Sarah (in which white women are the contemporary equivalents of Sarah) and Abraham (in which Black men are the contemporary equivalents of Abraham) when she bears them a child but is forced into destructive wilderness conditions due to Sarah's insecurities and abuse. It is God's liberating activity that offers survival and quality of life to Hagar and her son, Ishmael. Likewise, it is this same God who speaks a word of hope to Black women in America who are trying to survive and have quality of life despite their racially oppressive experiences. This pursuit of survival, liberation, and quality of life for Black women is always seen against the eschatological horizon of hope that does not reduce liberation from racist, hetero-patriarchal structures to a mere human goal. Liberation is also a divine "reaching toward," which locates liberation not only within history but also beyond history.

Many womanist theological projects of hope reflect a *realized eschatology* rather than a strict apocalyptic eschatology.[6] For some womanists, such as Karen Baker-Fletcher and Monica Coleman, apocalyptic eschatological visions have been used as tools by the powerful to maintain control. Such otherworldly visions reinforce the internalization of oppression among marginalized persons. In Alice Walker's novel *The Color Purple*, we meet Celie, an abused young black woman who lives in the rural South. At the beginning of Celie's marriage to Mr. __ , she internalized the patriarchal abuse she endures, even accepting herself as ugly and unworthy of love. Walker demonstrates the dangers associated with the otherworldly ideas Celie possessed, which prevented her from exercising her own agency against her abusive husband. In the novel, we hear Sophia say to Celie in response to the domestic violence they both endured, "You ought to bash Mr. __ head open . . . Think about heaven later."[7] Over the course of the novel, we witness Celie shift her religious perspective to a God or Divine force that seeks the moral transformation and wholeness of individuals, societies, and all of creation. Celie moves away from traditional ideas of the afterlife, which kept her from developing the courage to resist her oppression in the present. She decides to embrace a religious perspective that sees the transformation of the present order as a possibility.

Instead of apocalyptic visions, many womanist thinkers employ realized eschatological visions of hope. Realized eschatology does not necessarily see redemption as being contingent on some final act that comes outside of history (Jesus coming, Messiah's return, etc.). Rather, realized eschatology points to the possibilities for rebirth, renewal, and "becoming" in the present as the seeds of hope have already been planted in the past that await to be actualized. Within liberationist, womanist, and postcolonial theologies, Jesus's ministry is seen as paradigmatic of how redemption and hope can be actualized in the present. As Williams suggests, we do not need to wait until some final culminating act outside of history to experience redemptive hope.[8] This realized eschatology provides rich, fertile ways of re-thinking moral imagination in the present order.

Womanist theologian Karen Baker-Fletcher also captures this eschatological vision of hope that seeks the moral transformation of hearts and oppressive structures in the present. She states, "For womanists, eschatology does not have to do with the 'last things' or 'end time' in any far-off, abstract, otherworldly sense. Rather, eschatological hope and envisionment have to do with the daily, moment-by-moment business of living."[9] For Baker-Fletcher, the "Reign of God" stands at the center of personal and social salvation. She employs a liberationist hermeneutic in how she reads the Christian gospels and other scriptures, arguing that these scriptures point to the actualization of God's reign of love on earth (within individuals, communities, and societies). The complete transformation of social structures is possible through the inauguration of God's kin-dom.[10] Baker-Fletcher echoes a Social Gospel vision of the kin-dom of God being "at hand."

While Social Gospel reformers such as Walter Rauschenbusch and Washington Gladden are known for this nineteenth-century message, African Americans were certainly responsible for the birth and shaping of the Social Gospel movement as this movement's realized eschatology could be found in black religious writings, songs, prayers, and more. Black female religious and social leaders such as Anna Julia Cooper and Ida B. Wells grounded their ideas of social transformation in an interpretation of salvation as social—that salvation comes to morally transform not just individuals but societies. This argument of social transformation is rooted in a realized eschatology that interprets Jesus life and ministry as an example of *why* social transformation must remain a possibility: because it inaugurates love, peace, justice, and reconciliation into the present world (which are central to the gospels). New worlds marked by justice and love are concretely possible when turning to the gospel narratives. Womanist ideas of hope are grounded in this possibility that social structures can be transformed. As a result, the language of eradication tends to be inferred from much of womanist discourse on hope in which old worlds of oppression are destroyed in order to inaugurate new peaceable and loving societies.

Before demonstrating how Bell's racial realism throws womanist ideas of hope (as eradication) into question, I do not want to dismiss the practical force of hope (as eradication) within much of womanist theological thought. For many womanist thinkers, the concrete possibility of transforming social structures of oppression (racism, heteropatriarchy, classism, etc.) reflects their *theological point of view* in which human beings co-partner with a God who secures liberation and flourishing for all of creation within and beyond the human histories of this world. This faith in a God who liberates and offers quality of life *guides what is morally possible in the present and future*. In other words, humans are not proscribed to the social structures that they construct and inhabit, as God ultimately works in and through human history to bring the world into right relationship. Consequently, a belief in the eradication of oppressive institutions is not a statement about what humans alone can attain within society but a *theological statement* about a sovereign God who co-partners with humanity to inaugurate new worlds of flourishing potentially free from radical injustices. These visions then provide regulative ideals toward which womanist thinkers creatively imagine alternative worlds to the present order of inequity and inequality.

While womanists' realized eschatological visions provide creative imaginative powers on what is morally possible in relation to justice and love, these visions often do not consider the contradictions and paradoxes in fashioning modes of resistance to multiple forms of oppression associated with structural racism. Hope is reduced to eradicating oppressive evils instead of asking what might be diverse ways in which hope may be expressed among oppressed subjects. I think that Bell helps womanist theological discourse ask this important question as it theorizes the multiple forms of resistance to racial evil. Moreover, Bell's racial realism invites womanist discourse to question the utility in maintaining the language of eradication as the primary and/or only form of language associated with hoping against racial sin.

II. Radical Racial Realism: The Problem of Eradication

Bell's radical racial realism complicates and complexifies womanist concepts of hope and their language of eradication. How does Bell's racial realism throw into question this language of eradication? In *Faces At the Bottom of the Well*, Bell asserts, "Black people will never gain full equality in this country. Even those herculean efforts we hail as successful will produce no more than temporary 'peaks of progress,' short-lived victories that slide into irrelevance as racial patterns adapt in ways that maintain white dominance. This is a hard-to-accept fact that all history verifies."[11] This hard-to-accept fact is the foundation of Bell's racial realism, a viewpoint that sees racism as a permanent reality in the United States. In *Faces at the Bottom of the Well*, Bell introduces his radical realist position through his usage of allegorical stories or "chronicles" that emphasize the contradictions associated with racial themes such as the status of the civil rights movement as well as contemporary problems of racial relations. Bell reintroduces Geneva Crenshaw, a heroine of his earlier text, *And We Are Not Saved*. Geneva is a fictional civil rights attorney who dialogues with the anonymous narrator who is a legal scholar/teacher (presumably Bell) in order to explore the limits and impossibilities of eradicating racial injustice in America. Bell uses fiction to probe racial complexities and contradictions in order to understand that the resolution of racism is necessary yet impossible.

In the introductory chapter of *Faces at the Bottom of the Well*, Bell contends that although civil rights gains over the last several decades led to desegregation in housing, education, employment, and more, these "gains" are slowly being eroded. For example, Bell cites major disparities that continue to exist between white and black Americans, such as the unemployment rate for black people being two times that of whites.[12] Bell suggests that civil rights activism has proffered a *false hope* as such activism claims that racial justice is achievable through litigation as well as protests/demonstrations. The civil rights' assumption that racial inequalities can be eradicated misrepresents the insidious ways in which racism re-invents itself in order to uphold American "democratic" ideals. The failure of traditional civil rights strategies to see racism as a permanent feature (not an aberration) of the American democratic republic has prevented more realistic strategies aimed toward transcending racial injustice. For Bell, civil rights strategies need to be grounded in a racial realism, which sees resistance to racial injustice in terms of defiance rather than eradication.

What is also important to note about Bell's idea of racial realism is his "interest-convergence theory." For him, white Americans will advance the cause of racial justice only when doing so is consistent with their own socioeconomic and political interests. In *Faces at the Bottom of the Well*, Bell presents a short story, "Racism's Secret Bonding," that challenges the idea that education is the solution to eradicating racial bigotry and discrimination. In this story, Geneva, the female protagonist, offers a tale that promotes the view that education about racism (and its deleterious effects) can compel white Americans to deconstruct and reject their racial bigotry, becoming more empathetic toward the racial experiences of African Americans. In this tale, Geneva tells the story of how "racial data storms" rained down from heaven, penetrating the minds of white Americans.[13] Through the storms (and the penetration of the data), white Americans are able to ascertain historical and contemporary firsthand knowledge of the racist conditions and experiences of African Americans. This firsthand knowledge is both cognitive and affective, enabling white Americans to *feel* the effects of structural racism upon black bodies. The result of this enlightenment is new laws addressing structural racism, leading to greater equality and equity. However, because white Americans now contain the intellectual and emotional knowledge of black's experiences of racism, laws become less needed. White Americans have gained empathy for blacks who were grossly violated by structural forms of racism.[14]

Using an anonymous law professor as the narrator, Bell throws into question this liberal assumption that education leads to the eradication of racism, an assumption that undergirds Geneva's tale. In this tale, there is a belief that education leads to enlightenment and ultimately empathy and solidarity with blacks. However, Bell contends that we are intellectually dishonest "when we argue that whites do not know what racial subordination does to its victims."[15] Structural racist ideologies and practices are maintained by white supremacy and white privilege, which are intentional discursive practices meant to keep whites "on top." For Bell, socioeconomic and political interests undergird the continuation of anti-black racism because whites benefit from such interests. The "education leads to eradication" argument ignores and/or dismisses what is really at stake in confronting racism for whites. For white Americans, ending racist structures in the United States means they are forced to give up the privileges that accrue to them due to such structures. White Americans gain material privileges through their whiteness, which means that structural racism lifts them up above those at "the bottom of the well."

From a radical realist position, Bell persuasively argues that addressing racism is not simply about education. In fact, the call for greater education actually conceals the covert ways in which racial logics and practices operate and persist in America. One need only gain more knowledge to know how to empathize with oppressed racial subjects. To the contrary, racial realism acknowledges that *interest* is at the heart of racial oppression. In fact, oppressors are aware of how racial oppression affects black bodies but provides moral rationalizations to legitimate such systemic behavior. Consequently, Geneva's tale comes up short. It does not grapple with how racial complexities are grounded in the (re) production of racial hierarchy and power. Eradicating racism, then, does not simply happen due to education. Racism remains present due to hegemonic interests and power.

Most interesting within Bell's notion of racial realism is his ethic of "trickery for trickery" in *Faces at the Bottom of the Well*. In the short story "Space Traders," Bell discloses the moral complexities and ironies associated with addressing racial injustice in the United States. The story opens with a futuristic group called Space Traders who come to the United States with a trade proposal. The space traders offer the United States unlimited gold to pay off U.S. debt along with unlimited renewable energy sources (to solve the problem of fossil fuels) in exchange for every African American citizen.[16] The President and most white voters approve the departure of African Americans. However, some African Americans vehemently protest this proposed plan, describing it as inhumane. Professor Golightly is an educated African American who publicly protested the plan at first but later argues that African Americans need to alter their strategy in order to succeed in thwarting this proposal.

Golightly argues that instead of rejecting the plan to go to space, blacks need to embrace the proposal by framing it as a plan of "affirmative action," which would send blacks to an "interplanetary biblical land of milk and honey."[17] Golightly argues that white supremacy and privilege could be used by blacks to influence whites to reject this plan, as whites would see the proposal as an act of "reverse discrimination" against whites. Golightly explains that the white voters will be "so jealous of blacks based on race-based prerogatives that they will oppose it."[18] Professor Golightly promotes an ethic of trickery in efforts to derail the space traders' inhumane plan, as whites have historically shown that they tend to vote *according to their political and economic interest* despite any moral conviction they may possess to the contrary.

Not all African American leaders agree with Professor Golightly's strategy. The black spiritual leader Rev. Jasper is concerned that using deceit and trickery "may preserve the body at the sacrifice of the soul."[19] Although Rev. Jasper concedes that Golightly might understand the psychology of white hegemonic thinking, this tactic does not ultimately save blacks or whites in terms of facilitating the moral transformation of hearts and minds. Through the conflicting strategies of Golightly and Jasper, Bell lifts up whether black communities need to depend on the same forms of moral protest (represented through Jasper) or think in more shrewd, savvy ways about black resistance to racism (represented through Golightly). Professor Golightly mutters, "faith in God is fine," but "God expects us to use the common sense he gave us."[20] Bell seems to be communicating through Professor Golightly that strategies to resist racisms must take account of the moral complexities and paradoxes associated with racial relations in the United States. White groups will not concede their privilege within racist structures on moral grounds because their privilege is deeply tethered to their sociopolitical and economic interests. Interestingly, African Americans, linked by chains, end up boarding the alien vessel at the end of the story.

In "Space Traders," I understand Bell to be invoking a reevaluation of moral values (ideas of right and wrong, good or bad) within *contexts of survival*. The moral weighing of actions (trickery) become highly contextual questions and may even be morally weighed differently from the meaning any white normative gaze would ascribe to such actions. Professor Golightly offers a plan that will promote survival of his people against the racial hegemony of white structures, despite the fact that this plan may depend on trickery of sorts. The point here is that moral resistance can be re-thought outside of the normative categories of the white gaze, in which "trickery" can be viable forms of defiant resistance within already deceitful matrices of white institutional power.

For certain, Bell invites the reader to rethink the language of eradication in relation to racism in the United States. Hope in relation to racial evil is not necessarily about our ability to eradicate such evil (although this desire is understandable). Hope can be defying inhumane racist structures, not allowing such structures to define black humanity and agency. The two aforementioned short stories insist on the permanence of racial logics and racism. As Bell argues, our civil rights strategies will continue to fail when strategies do not account for the permanence of racism. While we can defy and subvert racism, we cannot eradicate racism as such. His rejection of the eradication of racism can be understood not as hopelessness or a "giving up" in the face of racial evil. Instead, Bell intimates that *salvation lies in the struggle itself against racist structures*. Bell encourages anti-black racist activists to "accept the dilemmas of committed confrontation with evils we cannot end."[21] Bell's radical racial realism allows one to both skeptically interrogate the political liberal ideal of equality while remaining committed to the struggle for racial justice. Bell's challenge to the language of eradication *seeks to enlarge one's understanding on the ongoing, permanent struggle for racial justice*.

Bell also wants to expand how we think of civil rights strategies in relation to race. Most civil rights strategies tend to focus on legal and activist tactics that can end all forms of structural racism, which always puts racial justice beyond reach. However, Bell wants to argue that the task of racial justice is ultimately the struggle for agency, which includes the struggle against "objectification" as the "other" within the context of white supremacy. A critical part of the struggle for agency involves developing a decolonized consciousness among the oppressed in order to reject the "master's tools" (images and rationalities of race within white structures).[22] Agency must be reclaimed among racially oppressed communities because this provides one condition toward the possibility of alternate, subversive epistemologies.

Self-knowledge is essential to how oppressed communities resist objectification and reclaim their humanity within inhumane matrices of white power. Internalized racial oppression always produces self-deprecation and self-doubt in the oppressed. For instance, when African Americans speak publicly about racial harms, they are interpreted as lacking credibility or standing, as white society interprets blacks as exaggerating such harms in service to "preferential treatment." As a result, African American's articulation of racial harms is not taken seriously. When blacks are not given full voice to articulate their experiences of racial injustice in the United States, their struggle against objectification is thwarted, obscuring racial harms. This denial of racial standing then produces doubt within marginalized black subjects themselves over time. Consequently, the struggle for self-knowledge is the quest against the objectification of black people's humanity.[23]

As discussed earlier, I think it is important to explore the limits of Bell's radical racial realism. While he speaks of a lack of racial standing in white society, he stops short of offering *gender standing* for black women within black communities and broader society. Gender injustice is not a separate discourse as black women experience gender and sexual harms *in and through* structural racisms. As discussed, the conceptualization of black flesh in the white imagination has differed between black men and black women. The construction of "black female flesh" has included gross gender injustices and sexual harms. Black women's oppression is not a matter of gender alone; it is also a matter of racism within white society. Black women's racial subjugation reflects intersectional oppressions, which means that race, gender, class, sexuality, and more must be given full articulation in any quest for racial justice.

This was a blind spot in Bell's earlier work. For example, in *Faces at the Bottom of the Well* he criticizes Alice Walker and Ntozake Shange for not privileging the racial struggle over gender aspirations. While Bell acknowledges that black women must not wait until racism ends to address patriarchy, he nevertheless attributes the problem of black communities to the inability for black men to occupy traditional patriarchal leadership roles within the family. In *Faces*, Bell tends to treat race as the primary category through which to interpret black oppression and liberation, which leaves gender (as well as class, sexuality, etc.) as a peripheral or tangential matter.

However, in Bell's latter work, he recognizes the tensions between gender and race more fully, noting the intersectional ways black women experience racial logics and practices. For example, in his book *Gospel Choirs* he offers a parable entitled "Women to the Rescue." In this dialogue, the woman protagonist Geneva Crenshaw is the subject of conversation between two black men, brother Jesse Semple and the Professor. Semple vocally assumes that the Professor is sleeping with his assistant Geneva, based on an entire array of sexist assumptions. The Professor calls out Semple's patriarchy and asserts that "women are far more than sexual vessels for men." The Professor then turns toward the movement for racial justice and notes, "For a long time, I thought race and sex were separate agendas, but I have slowly come around the agreeing with my women students—white as well as black—who have been telling me for years that we blacks must deal with sexism and patriarchy in our communities before we can address effectively the continuing evils of racism."[24] The Professor then concludes with: "our greatest strength, our survival hope . . . is black women."[25] For Bell, he is citing a growing awareness that gender parity and liberation also ground the racial struggle. In fact, hope for Bell is embodied in the *figure of the black woman*, which one could *theologically* construe as a womanist position.

Bell's radical realist argument on the permanence of racism does not seek to create apathy and hopelessness in relation to racial resistance. His argument does not deny hope. Instead, his argument on the permanent state of racism is meant help readers rethink our strategies of resistance and languages of hope. Acknowledging the permanence of racism allows one to let go of the false hope in returning to some Edenic way of living within the United States through destroying the "aberration" of racism. Because racism is permanent, prospects of racial justice must be grounded in transcending racism instead of eradicating racism. This transcending task is related to de-legitimating racial logics/practices that conceal their harmful, cancerous nature.

This transcending task is about *defiance*. Such defiance acknowledges the danger but engages in order to unmask the machinations and duplicitous operations of racism. It disrupts racist cycles of violence and refuses to let racial/gender/sexual forms of oppression "have the last say" over black life. Moreover, this defiance reclaims black humanity and agency within a white racist system that attempts to silence black racial pain and wounding. Through an ethics of defiance, Bell eliminates both racial apathy and racial victory (if victory is understood as the ending of racial oppression). Instead, he paves a middle ground between the two, asserting that our "victory" against racist forces must be rethought in light of agency and defiance. Bell asserts a different kind of hope—a defiant hope.

III. A Defiant Hope

Bell offers a hope that can be properly understood as defiance. This hope is a disruptive ethics committed to not letting racism/sexism/heterosexism "have the last say." For certain, Bell's idea of radical racial realism invites womanist theological thought to rethink its language of hope in response to structural racism (and its relation to gender and sexuality). Womanism's eschatological visions of hope often articulate the "eradication" or "ending" of racism as the *telos* of racial resistance and hope. I have already discussed that womanist thought tends to speak of hope through the language of eradication—that racism will be eradicated in order to make room for radically new worlds marked by radical justice, free from oppressive structures such as racism. I acknowledge that the creative force of this language (eradication) enables womanist thought to imagine alternative modes of being and relating grounded in radical care and compassion. However, this language forecloses other modes of resistance as *equally viable* such as a politics of defiance. Defiance can be seen as a form of hope when the discourse of eradication is decentered.

Defiance, in this sense, is not merely bold disobedience. It also functions as a disruptive ethics to structural (re)productions of racism, perpetually dislodging the theoretical and practical force of racial logics and practices that denigrate black subjects. Defying racisms allows oppressed "raced" subjects to claim their humanity within the objectifying, dehumanizing matrices of racial oppression. While acknowledging the intractability of systemic racist forms of violence, defiance does not allow structural racisms to define black life. Defiant hope provides meaning for oppressed racialized communities to reclaim their humanity and agency as they envision better worlds. However, current language of eradication that is found within much of womanist thought *often positions this reclamation of humanity as a proximate end to the ultimate end of eradicating racial injustice*. However, the reclamation of the oppressed's humanity and agency in a dehumanizing system can be construed as the ultimate end toward transcending the power of racist structures. Some womanist discourses do not consider human transcendence as an ultimate end in relation to a politics of hope against racial/gender/class oppression.

Pragmatic philosophers and theologians such as Victor Anderson and Vincent Lloyd identify human transcendence as a religious good that remains important to how we articulate ideas of hope. Human transcendence as a form of religious resistance to racial injustice involves the ability for oppressed groups to make meaning within incurable systems of injustice and exploitation. In talking about transcendence to racial oppression, the ultimate end may not be eradication of such systems. Instead, the ultimate end may be defying and refusing to let racial structures define the subjectivities and agency of oppressed communities. For instance, enslaved African Americans certainly did not *solely* express hope in a one-dimensional way as eradicating the institution of slavery (although that desire was indisputably there). Rather, many grounded their sense of hope in defying and transcending the inhumanities of the slave institution itself. Many enslaved persons made meaning through their experiences of joy, meaningful sex, deep friendship, peace of mind, and more, so that slavery did not have the last say over how they exercised their full humanity. Through acts of defiance in the face of an institution that attempted to "break the souls" of enslaved blacks, the enslaved articulated a profound sense of hope by defying and disrupting their inhumane social order.

Even today, defiant hope has theological meaning as it allows blacks to interpret the reclamation of their humanity as acts of love and justice. The Ferguson protests after the killing of Mike Brown by Ferguson police officer Darren Wilson demonstrates the theological importance of defiant hope. Black youth activists organized and mobilized around the nation and persistently marched in Ferguson, Missouri, in order to categorically declare that racist, violent institutions such as law enforcement would not denigrate black life. For these activists, religious rhetoric shaped how they understood their subversive acts in which this rhetoric drew its meaning from defiance as a form of hope that the police department would not have the last say over the God-given value and worth of black bodies. In this movement, *defiance was hope* as these young activists asserted *why* black freedom and flourishing are unequivocal rights rather than options within this country. In Ferguson, defiant hope exposes the exploitation and injustice present so that new possibilities of care, respect, and inclusion can be discerned. Ferguson continues to be an excellent example of why defiance is *theologically important* to womanist theological ideas of hope. What would it mean to see a politics of defiance as central to how black Christians articulate hope, as we navigate and defy the permanent (re)productions of classist, hetero-patriarchal racism in the United States?

However, one may offer a rebuttal. Much of the womanist discourse I have referred to emerges out of Christian traditions. Would this "defiant hope" still be Christian within womanist thought? If womanist discourse removes the *singular, absolute telos* of ending all forms of injustice in the "coming age," is womanist theological thought then untethered from its Christian moorings? Womanist theological thought employs the language of eradication based on its eschatological commitments that the "Reign of God" or "God's Kin-dom" can be actualized within our present order. God's kin-dom of love, nonviolence, and justice can create and fashion new social orders marked by radical right relationships. Consequently, the language of eradication is not merely a social statement about human progress but a theological statement about a God who co-partners with humanity to effect social and moral transformation within and beyond the histories of the world. Without this eschatological commitment, critics of my argument may assert that womanist theological thought is untethered from its explicit grounding of Christian hope.

This is a fair critique. However, I think my proposal could still be properly understood as "Christian," although I am proposing a pragmatic reconstruction of hope within Christian traditions, foregrounding the richly textured world of social practices among racially oppressed subjects—practices that disclose defiance as more in keeping with projects of hope among diverse black forms of activism. Religious scholar Vincent Lloyd does well in arguing how redefining ideas of hope within Christian traditions critiques and expands what we mean by the term "Christian." So, I am certainly trying to disrupt what can be properly understood as "Christian hope" in rethinking ideas of hope within womanist theological thought. Christian hope can be understood as defiance, which secures human value and meaning in the present against death-dealing forces of darkness that come to rob the oppressed of their goodness, trust, faith, love, joy, and so forth.

One might also critique my argument and maintain that it offers no preferable future. Although defiant hope does not affirm a universal, grand telos toward which history is moving, I do envision a diverse set of conditional, preferable futures that practices of hope (as defiance) might be oriented toward. Yet, these conditional futures are grounded in social practices of defiance in the here and now and not in articulations of one grand universal future of ending hetero-patriarchal racism. Defiant hope moves this discourse along by inviting womanist scholars to theorize the importance of resisting forms of racial violence while acknowledging the permanence and insolvability of racial evil. It invites womanism to theologically think within the context of this unresolved tension. Rethinking hope as defiance within womanist discourse is certainly provocative and even tedious to accept in light of Christian eschatological presuppositions that womanist discourse employs. Yet, womanist discourse must be sure to pay attention to the richly textured world of social practices among oppressed subjects in the present to actually *see how they are hoping*. For certain, many racially oppressed subjects are hoping through a politics of defiance.

Notes

1. Refer to the plethora of womanist theological literature on racism in the United States and how it impacts black women. For a beginning discussion, refer to Jacquelyn Grant, *White Women's Christ and Black Women's Jesus: Feminist Christology and Womanist Response* (Atlanta, GA: Scholars Press, 1989); Katie Cannon, *Black Womanist Ethics* (Eugene, OR: Wipf and Stock Publishing, 2006);

Marcia Riggs, *Awake, Arise, and Act: A Womanist Call for Black Liberation* (New York: Pilgrim Press, 1994); Stacey Floyd-Thomas, *Mining the Motherlode: Methods in Womanist Ethics* (New York: Pilgrim Press, 2006); Melanie Harris, *Gifts of Virtue, Alice Walker, and Womanist Ethics* (New York: Palgrave McMillian, 2010); and Monica Coleman, *Making a Way Out of No Way: A Womanist Theology* (Minneapolis: Fortress Press, 2008).

2. Black feminists Hortense Spillers and Traci Sharpley-Whiting provide excellent analyses of histories related to the hypersexualization of black women's bodies in the United States. Refer to Hortense Spillers, "Mama's Baby, Papa's Maybe: An American Grammar Book," in *Black, White, and in Color: Essays on American Literature and Culture* (Chicago: University of Chicago Press, 2003) as well as Tracy Sharpley-Whiting, *Pimps Up, Ho's Down: Hip Hop's Hold on Young Black Women* (New York: New York University Press, 2007). Also refer to Melissa Harris-Perry, *Sister Citizen: Shame, Stereotypes, and Black Women in America* (New Haven, CT: Yale University Press, 2013).

3. The concept of "porno-tropics" is described by Anne McClintock in *Imperial Leather: Race, Gender, and Sexuality in the Colonial Contest* (New York: Routledge, 1995). In this text, McClintock focuses on British imperialism and how it reinvented hetero-patriarchy through "sexualizing" indigenous cultures in order to "masculinize" British colonization and conquest. British projects of conquest and colonization relied on pornographically "feminizing" the indigenous land and indigenous women as a way to rape and plunder both bodies. The colonized land was interpreted through a pornographic gaze in which such land was described as an extension of indigenous women's bodies, which were hypersexual and "ready for penetration." Hetero-patriarchy in relation to European colonization and conquest were deeply tied to the pornographic interpretation and fetishizing of the land itself.

4. Black women's bodies were sites of sexual pleasure within racial economies of conquest in the United States. Angela Davis certainly offers a pornotropic reading of sexual violence committed against black women's bodies from slavery to the present in *Women, Race, & Class* (New York: First Vintage Books, 1983).

5. In the 1980s and 1990s, Black feminists such as Audre Lorde, bell hooks, and Alice Walker critique how race is privileged above other identity markers such as gender, sexuality, and class when talking about black oppression. During this time, their critiques were directed against black studies and black theology.

6. Delores Williams, *Sisters in the Wilderness: The Challenge of Womanist God-Talk* (Maryknoll, NY: Orbis Books, 1993) is an excellent example of a womanist project grounded in a realized eschatology in which our embodiment of Jesus's ministry is understood as the impetus for redemptive transformation within history. For Williams, we do not need to wait until some sudden act from the outside of history to experience hope and redemption. Rather, redemption

sits in the present by incarnating Jesus's radical actions of love and liberation.

7. Alice Walker, *The Color Purple* (New York: Harcourt Publisher, 1982), 103.

8. Williams, *Sisters in the Wilderness*, 182.

9. Karen Baker-Fletcher, "Strength of My Life," in *Embracing the Spirit: Womanist Perspectives on Hope, Salvation, and Transformation*, ed. Emilie Townes (Maryknoll, NY: Orbis Books, 1997), 127.

10. The term "kin-dom of God" is a feminist concept that challenges the imperialist connotations associated with the term "Kingdom of God," which is used throughout Western theological literature in describing radically egalitarian societies led by love, justice, and reconciliation.

11. Derrick Bell, *Faces at the Bottom of the Well: The Permanence of Racism* (New York: Basic Books, 1992), 12.

12. Ibid., 3.

13. Ibid., 147.

14. Ibid., 147–157.

15. Ibid., 150.

16. Ibid., 333.

17. Ibid., 335.

18. Ibid., 340.

19. Ibid., 341.

20. Ibid., 342.

21. Ibid., 198.

22. Refer to Audre Lorde, *Sister Outsider* (Berkeley, CA: Ten Speed Press, 1984), 112.

23. Refer to Bell's chapter "The Rules of Racial Standing," in *Faces*, 111–126.

24. Derrick Bell, "Women to the Rescue," in *Gospel Choirs: Psalms of Survival in an Alien Land Called Home* (New York: Basic Books, 1997), 154.

25. Ibid., 155.

Works Cited

Baker-Fletcher, Karen. "Strength of My Life," in *Embracing the Spirit: Womanist Perspectives on Hope, Salvation, and Transformation*, ed. Emilie Townes. Maryknoll, NY: Orbis Books, 1997.

Bell, Derrick. "Women to the Rescue," in *Gospel Choirs: Psalms of Survival in an Alien Land Called Home*. New York: Basic Books, 1997.

———. *Faces at the Bottom of the Well: The Permanence of Racism*. New York: Basic Books, 1992.

Cannon, Katie. *Black Womanist Ethics*. Eugene, OR: Wipf and Stock Publishing, 2006.

Coleman, Monica. *Making a Way Out of No Way: A Womanist Theology.* Minneapolis: Fortress Press, 2008.
Davis, Angela. *Women, Race, & Class.* New York: First Vintage Books, 1983.
Floyd-Thomas, Stacey *Mining the Motherlode: Methods in Womanist Ethics.* New York: Pilgrim Press, 2006.
Grant, Jacquelyn. *White Women's Christ and Black Women's Jesus: Feminist Christology and Womanist Response.* Atlanta: Scholars Press, 1989.
Harris, Melanie. *Gifts of Virtue, Alice Walker, and Womanist* Ethics. New York: Palgrave McMillian, 2010.
Harris-Perry, Melissa. *Sister Citizen: Shame, Stereotypes, and Black Women in America.* New Haven, CT: Yale University Press, 2013.
Lorde, Audre. *Sister Outsider.* Berkeley, CA: Ten Speed Press, 1984.
McClintock, Anne. *Imperial Leather: Race, Gender, and Sexuality in the Colonial Contest.* New York: Routledge, 1995.
Riggs, Marcia. *Awake, Arise, and Act: A Womanist Call for Black Liberation.* New York: Pilgrim Press, 1994.
Sharpley-Whiting, Tracy. *Pimps Up, Ho's Down: Hip Hop's Hold on Young Black Women.* New York: New York University Press, 2007.
Spillers, Hortense. "Mama's Baby, Papa's Maybe: An American Grammar Book," in *Black, White, and in Color: Essays on American Literature and Culture.* Chicago: University of Chicago Press, 2003.
Walker, Alice. *The Color Purple.* New York: Harcourt Publisher, 1982.
Williams, Delores. *Sisters in the Wilderness: The Challenge of Womanist God-Talk.* Maryknoll, NY: Orbis Books, 1993.

Chapter 8

Liberalism, Christendom, and Narrative

Paradox and Indirect Communication in
Derrick Bell and Søren Kierkegaard

Timothy J. Golden

"I find myself suddenly in a world in which things do evil; a world in which I am summoned into battle; a world in which it is always a question of annihilation or triumph."

—Fanon, *Black Skin, White Masks*[1]

"Man is mortal. That may be; but let us die resisting; and if our lot is complete annihilation, let us not behave in such a way that it seems justice!"

—Camus, *Resistance, Rebellion, and Death*[2]

"But he, willing to justify himself, said unto Jesus, And who is my neighbor? And Jesus answering him said, A certain man went down from Jerusalem to Jericho."

—*Holy Bible*[3]

I.

Derrick Bell's use of fiction throughout his corpus puts him in good philosophical company. Indeed, fiction's use in the service of truth is a philosophical tradition that reaches back at least as far as Socrates. Recall that Socrates brought his interlocutors down a notch or two from their perches of epistemic certainty by luring them into his razor sharp cross-examinations with his ironic, maieutic communicative methodology. For example, Euthyphro, who begins the dialogue that bears his name absolutely certain of the definition of piety, is left not with absolute certainty as to what piety is, but rather is left only with the now famed "Euthyphro Dilemma."[4] This dilemma is representative of the epistemic conundrums that lead to the aporia of the Socratic dialogues. There is a profound ethical lesson in these aporetic endings that represents the essence of Socratic virtue and the higher truth that Socratic irony helps us to see: that wisdom is found in the epistemic humility of knowing that one does not know.[5] The Socratic method of indirect communication thus has an ethical dimension to it that, among other things, uses the deception of irony to reach the higher moral truth and virtue of epistemic humility. This ethical dimension of indirect communication resurfaces in Plato's account of the "noble lie" from the *Republic*: "What about falsehood in words? When and to whom is it useful and so not deserving of hatred? . . . when any of our so-called friends are attempting, through madness or ignorance, to do something bad, isn't it a useful drug for preventing them . . . By making a falsehood as much like the truth as we can, don't we also make it useful? We certainly do."[6] Based upon this notion of falsehood being a "useful drug," Plato articulates his "Myth of the Metals" in book III of *Republic* as a way to further his principle of specialization within the *Kallipolis* and promote what he thought to be societal stability.[7] With each group of people in the *Kallipolis* made aware of their natural endowments through the myth of the metals, they will proudly maintain their group identity and make meaningful contributions in ways that maintain the status quo *ante*.[8] Plato thus uses fiction to inspire social, political, and cultural stability.

René Descartes also uses fiction to arrive at the truth. Descartes's methodological skepticism in his *Meditations on First Philosophy* enables him to re-imagine a world where all is false so that he could find the *cogito*, which, in his view, is undeniably true. He assumed not only that all was false, but also that there was an "evil genius" deceiving him.[9] So he not only uses fiction in the sense that he assumes all to be false, he also adds a fictitious character, an "evil genius" to help him make his point. Descartes thus leads us to the insight that fiction both conceals and reveals. On one hand, it was the fictions of Aristotelian-infused scholasticism that *concealed* the truths of the natural sciences; on the other, it would be the fictions of the Cartesian methodological skepticism that would *reveal* the a priori truths of the natural sciences.

Kierkegaard, too, worked squarely within this tradition of "noble lies." Through the use of pseudonyms inserted between him and his readers, Kierkegaard sought a religious reawakening in nineteenth-century Denmark. He wanted Christians to realize that their religion was not one of ease and comfort, something attributable to their mere participation in rites and ceremonies, but rather a religion that must be approached with great "fear and trembling."[10] For Kierkegaard, the deception was that one was a Christian because one had been baptized. This sort of objective orientation toward one's religious beliefs "changes Christendom into a baptized paganism."[11] To remove this deception in order to get to what Kierkegaard thought was the truth of Christianity, Kierkegaard, as did Socrates, Plato, and Descartes before him, resorted to fictions in order to reveal truth.[12]

Derrick Bell faced a problem similar to that of Kierkegaard. Like Kierkegaard, Bell lived in a culture that objectivity and abstraction had deceived—a world that saw milestones that many thought were clear indications that America had overcome anti-Black racism. From the Civil Rights Act of 1964, to the Voting Rights Act of 1965, to the national holiday for Dr. King, and all the way to the election of President Barack Obama, our legal and political culture has interpreted each of these events as strong indications of racial progress. In fact, many people have become so convinced of racial progress in America that they have called for a color-blind society, demanding that race not be taken into account even when it is to remedy effects of past racial discrimination. The sooner we eliminate "race talk," the argument goes, the sooner we eliminate racism. Or, in the words of U.S. Supreme Court Chief Justice John Roberts, "the way to stop discrimination on the basis of race is to stop discriminating on the basis of race."[13] But Bell disagrees. For Bell, racism in America is permanent, and he argues that any such gains as those just mentioned are mere racial symbols that provide a false hope for African Americans.[14] Moreover, such "gains" only happened, Bell argues, because the hopes of African Americans coincidentally converged with the interests of whites, and not because whites have been morally persuaded that racism is wrong.[15]

Indeed, for Bell, if such policies were not in the interests of whites, none of the civil rights "gains" would have ever been made.[16] Bell thus wants to remove the deceptions of liberalism's legal and political culture, and to do so he joins the ranks of his philosophical predecessors, who all used fiction to reveal the truth as they understood it to be.

This chapter argues that Derrick Bell's fictional narrative can be interpreted as a form of indirect communication that can both disabuse Americans of liberalism's deceptions of racial progress and reinvigorate a passionate moral struggle against anti-Black racism in America. To make this case, I argue that Bell operates similar to the way that Kierkegaard used indirect communication to disabuse Christians of Christendom's deceptions, such as Christianity being a matter of objective, or "scientific" criteria, and thus attempting to reinvigorate a passionate inward commitment to Christianity in Denmark.[17] In support of this argument, I point to the concepts of paradox and passion in each thinker and try to show how these concepts are related to indirect communication. Taken together, I conclude that paradox, passion, and indirect communication represent the bold attempt, in both Bell and Kierkegaard, to remind us that complacency in moral, political, and religious matters is unacceptable. Throughout Kierkegaard's critical engagement with Christendom, and Bell's critique of what he believes are liberalism's deceptive notions of "equality," and "color-blindness," I believe that both thinkers use indirect communication strategies to remind us that whether it is the task of "becoming" a Christian (Kierkegaard), or resisting America's anti-Black racism (Bell), we have not "arrived"—and indeed we will never "arrive"—as there is an infinite amount of work to be done in each of these spheres.

The second section presents a discussion of the notions of paradox and passion as presented in both Kierkegaard and Bell. Here, I attempt to uncover what I believe to be at the foundation of both Kierkegaard's and Bell's thought: an abiding and emphatic critique of abstraction that manifests itself in both thinkers emphasizing the difference between the objectivity of epistemic certainty and the subjectivity and contingency of human existence. In both Bell and Kierkegaard, subjectivity demands passion in response to an existential problem in a way that knowledge and abstraction, as types of objectivity, do not.

The focus of the third section is Bell's and Kierkegaard's uses of indirect communication. In this section, I argue that, based on the demands of subjectivity that I have discussed in the second section, indirect communication is the most effective means to reach those who are deluded by objectivity and abstraction in both Christianity (Kierkegaard) and law/political theory (Bell). After a discussion of some Kierkegaardian principles of indirect communication, in a brief interlude I contextualize Bell's use of narrative within the larger American legal culture, which demands storytelling due to an epistemologically and judicially diluted notion of "truth" in certain aspects of American law. I then discuss several of Bell's stories and his use of literary criticism in order to show how Bell can be interpreted as using indirect communication in order to achieve an objective similar to Kierkegaard's: to remove the deception from those deluded into liberalism's false hopes through a deceptive communication that encourages what Kierkegaard would call "double reflection" and "subjective appropriation." I conclude in the fourth section.

II.

Paradox figures prominently in the work of both Kierkegaard and Bell.[18] I want to articulate the role of paradox and the role of passion in both thinkers that will lay the foundation for the next section in which I discuss the relationship of indirect communication to paradox and to passion. My aim is to show that paradox, with its attendant epistemic difficulties, and passion, with its sense of subjective moral commitment, as articulated in Bell and Kierkegaard, demand a mode of existing (subjectivity) that both thinkers believe is best reached through indirect communication. I begin with Kierkegaard.

KIERKEGAARD

To fully appreciate the role of paradox in Kierkegaard's work, some background is necessary. Kierkegaard's work takes place in the nineteenth century. At that time, Kierkegaard thought that institutionalized Christianity, what he termed "Christendom," had gone wrong. The problem as he understood it was that the difficulties of Christianity, once so prominent when to be a Christian was to be a pariah, were no more. Being a Christian once entailed great risk and personal sacrifice. But in Kierkegaard's day, it had become a religion of comfort and convenience; it was fashionable to be a Christian. The influence of Hegelian theology and philosophy rendered the most intellectually challenging, paradoxical Christian doctrines easy to understand. For example, in response to theologian Jakob Peter Mynster, who criticized Hegel's logic, Danish Hegelian theologian Hans Martensen argued, in defense of Hegel, that Judaism could not accept the Incarnation of Jesus Christ because of its commitment to Aristotelian logic.[19] By adhering to the principle of the excluded middle, the Jews had to reject the Incarnation because it claimed that Jesus was simultaneously both God and human. According to Martensen, in contrast to Jewish theology, the Christian doctrine of the Incarnation represented the Hegelian principle of mediation, where there is no longer an either/or, but rather an advance on Aristotelian logic that demands the abandonment of the principle of the excluded middle, and explains God's immanence in the world.[20] Kierkegaard sees this kind of conceptual rationalization of Christian doctrine as going hand in hand with a moral complacency that he believes is plaguing Christianity. If Christianity can be easily understood through Hegelian theology, then it is easy to be a Christian. And if it is easy to be a Christian, then one has forgotten the need for faith. Christianity had thus become a matter of objective knowledge. It had become morally and spiritually stale, as the members of the Danish State Church considered themselves to be Christians in virtue of their "understanding" of the most difficult of Christian doctrines, which made them believe that Christianity was a matter of objective knowledge: "Lo, we have become so objective that even the wife of a civil servant argues from the whole, from the state, from the idea of society, from geographic scientificity to the single individual. It follows that the single individual is Christian."[21] The people of Kierkegaard's day had reasoned incorrectly, committing the fallacy of division and reasoning that because the whole was Christian, each constituent part—each individual—was also Christian. They were, in a word, "deceived." To recapture this faith, Kierkegaard needed to reclaim the conceptual and practical difficulties of Christian life. To demonstrate that Christianity was not as easy as many thought, Kierkegaard used pseudonyms to show how the intellectual and moral challenges of the Christian are still very much part of an authentic Christian experience. For example, the pseudonym Johannes Climacus writes *Philosophical Fragments*, which deals with the paradox of the Incarnation, and Vigilius Haufneinsis writes *The Concept of Anxiety*, which deals with the problem of original sin as it relates to freedom and moral action. And Johannes de Silentio writes *Fear and Trembling*, which addresses the issue of Christian faith. Our concern here is *Philosophical Fragments*, because this text is where Johannes Climacus develops the notion of the paradox that is pertinent for this chapter. I discuss the overall significance of the pseudonyms in the next section on indirect communication. But now I turn my attention to the notion of the paradox.

Two concepts are essential for understanding Johannes Climacus in *Philosophical Fragments*: paradox and becoming.[22] Paradox causes tension between two conflicting propositions. If one proposition is true, the other proposition is necessarily false. The maintenance of both propositions is thus nonsensical. To be nonsensical is to be unknowable. For how can anything be "known" if it cannot be understood? But since human beings want to understand things, the paradox cries out for one of three options: (1) a solution, (2) criticism for failing to make sense of it, or (3) embracing it for some deeper level of understanding about oneself. In *Philosophical Fragments*, Johannes Climacus argues that (1) and (2) are not options. For Climacus, (3) is the correct way to understand the paradox.

In *Philosophical Fragments*, Climacus is contrasting two ways of learning what he calls "the truth." The first way of learning the truth is to be reminded of it through recollection. And the second way of learning the truth is through revelation. As for recollection, Climacus wants to show that on this account the truth is already in existence within the learner. Climacus begins with the well-known "learner's paradox" from Plato's *Meno*. The learner's paradox begins with the question, "Can the truth be learned?," and proceeds as follows: if one already knows the truth, one cannot learn what one already knows, and if one does not know the truth, one cannot learn it because one cannot recognize what one does not already know.[23] Plato solves this paradox with his doctrine of knowledge as recollection, arguing that the truth is already present within a person, and that if asked the right questions, the person can recall the truth from the soul's prior kinship with it in the world of Forms. In this way, the person already has the truth, but can still learn it because they merely need to be reminded of it. The truth is thus already in existence, and the moment when one recognizes the truth is incidental, and can be occasioned by anyone who asks the right questions. This was the point of the Socratic interaction with Meno, the slave boy in the Platonic dialogue that bears his name. There is no need to come into the truth; no need for a change of one's condition; no need to *become or move toward truth*. Such a state of becoming is not possible because the truth already is. On this account of knowing the truth, the paradox is solved because the truth already exists; it does not need to become. Climacus calls this way of learning the truth the "Socratic." Knowledge is equated with being—what is already in existence—on this account.

In contrast, Climacus discusses a situation in which the truth is not already within a person, but comes from beyond the person. On this view, the person must come to know the truth. But how can this be possible, given that if one does not know the truth, then how will one know the truth if one is presented with it? One cannot. This is Climacus's point. Unlike the Socratic way of learning the truth, learner's paradox is never solved. Not only is the learner's paradox never solved, but the truth on the second account is brought from beyond the individual, implying that prior to receiving the truth, the individual was in a different condition. So the arrival of the truth from beyond the individual causes a change, or some level of becoming within the individual who received the truth. After receiving the truth, one has *become something different*. Because the paradox is not solved, it remains, and for Climacus it is the "passion of the understanding." The understanding or reason is in constant pursuit of solving the paradox, but it will never be able to solve it. Such a pursuit may seem foolish or ill-advised, but Johannes Climacus cautions against this view: "But one must not think ill of the paradox, for the paradox is the passion of thought, and the thinker without the paradox is like the lover without the passion: a mediocre fellow."[24] There is, then, for Johannes Climacus, a connection between the ever evasive comprehension of that which cannot be understood (the paradox), and the desire (passion) to understand it. The former fuels the latter. The more difficult the paradox, the more passionately one tries to comprehend it.

In the *Concluding Unscientific Postscript to the Philosophical Fragments*, Johannes Climacus writes that one must not only accept the fact of the paradox but also that one must cling to it as though it were objectively true. On this latter view of learning the truth, the individual is on a perpetual quest for understanding that which cannot be understood—but not only that. In addition, the individual thoroughly invests him or herself into the task of understanding the paradox as though it were objectively true although it is not. This is what makes Christianity "unscientific," according to Johannes Climacus: whereas scientific methodology demands that one remove oneself (e.g., one's biases, prejudices, etc.) from an experiment in order to achieve "objective" results, Christianity demands the very opposite: it demands that one must wholeheartedly and passionately throw oneself *into* the task of becoming a Christian without any assurances that it is objectively true. So in opposition to this latter, more dynamic understanding of learning the truth, on the Socratic view, learning the truth is of no real consequence because the truth is already present and known within the individual; there is no real change, no real commitment, and no passion needed in order to attain the truth because the paradox is resolved through recollection.

With this in mind, one can understand the Socratic and, for Climacus, the Christian ways of learning the truth as corresponding to objectivity and subjectivity, respectively. The contrast between the two could not be clearer: the former has no paradox, and is easily understood through the abstractions of Hegelian theology, while the latter is paradoxical, and is never understood, but passionately sought as though it is objectively true when it is not. Objectivity and subjectivity thus form the basis for the difference between abstraction and knowledge on one hand and a difficulty of understanding that generates a wholehearted, passionate, inward commitment on the other hand. With this in mind, we now turn our attention to Derrick Bell, whose paradoxical thesis of racial realism, I argue, bears some striking similarities to Kierkegaard's notions of paradox, passion, inwardness, and commitment.

DERRICK BELL

The historical context in which Bell employs the notion of paradox is crucial to understanding how Bell arrived at his thesis of racial realism and the paradox that is at its core. Bell, a graduate of the University of Pittsburgh School of Law in 1957, worked for the NAACP Legal Defense fund litigating civil rights cases. As a committed civil rights lawyer, Bell practiced law on the assumption that it was through the courts that African Americans would secure equal justice under the law. But as time moved forward, Bell began to question the legitimacy of this view, since, in the 1970s, he observed what he thought was an increased hostility toward civil rights. This hostility came from a number of Supreme Court decisions that he thought undid many of the gains made in the civil rights movement. Among these decisions is *Bakke v. Board of Regents of the University of California*,[25] which first articulated the notion of "reverse" race discrimination. Decisions like *Bakke*, according to Bell, ushered in the advent of a so-called "postcivil rights era," and a "post-racial era," where abstract notions of "color-blindness," and "equality" would invalidate any race conscious policy whatsoever, including those "benign" race-conscious policies that were implemented to redress historical wrongs against African Americans.[26] Individual rights and color-blindness, both characteristics of liberalism, found additional theoretical support beyond Supreme Court jurisprudence in the resurrection of political philosophy in the 1970s with the publication of John Rawls's landmark text, *A Theory of Justice*—a text which, in the words of its author, takes "to a higher level of abstraction the familiar theory of the social contract as found, say, in Locke, Rousseau, and Kant."[27] Rawls demonstrates his commitment to abstraction through theoretical devices such as his "veil of ignorance," and his "original position." Abstracting further from the Hobbsean and Lockean "state of nature," the original position is a theoretical space in which abstract "persons," are completely unaware of their racial, sexual, or socioeconomic identities as they are hidden behind a "veil of ignorance." Thus stripped of their identity, these "persons" select basic principles of justice that will guide them in a free society. This move to a "higher level of abstraction" has been criticized at length for its failure to articulate and to address problems of race and racism in political life.[28] For example, Charles Mills has argued that the failure to address problems of race in political philosophy not only does nothing to redress wrongs but also exacerbates them.[29] Bell would likely agree with Mills on this point, for Bell would argue that abstract notions of "equality" and "color-blindness" are dimensions of liberalism that have found their way into the adjudicative practices of the courts as legal formalism. Legal formalism claims "that judges respond primarily (indeed, perhaps exclusively) to the rational demands of the applicable rules of law and modes of legal reasoning."[30] For the legal formalist, adjudication is a rule-driven endeavor that demands a mechanical, formulaic application of legal rules to a set of facts to achieve predictable outcomes. Abstract notions such as "equality" and "color-blindness" fit in rather well on the formalist account of adjudication because they are abstractions that are inattentive to concrete factual considerations, such as the race of the litigants or the implications of a judicial decision for race relations. On the formalist account of adjudication, Themis's blindfold is secure. Abstractions in liberal political theory thus not only buttressed decisions like *Bakke*, but also contributed to the preexisting formalist theory of adjudication. Together, liberal political theory and legal formalism represent abstractions that characterized a political culture now openly hostile toward race-conscious governmental policies designed to remedy the effects of invidious discrimination against African Americans. Indeed, one sees this sort of hostility today in decisions such as *Shelby County, Alabama v. Holder*,[31] and in Chief Justice Roberts's previously cited profoundly problematic claim that "the way to stop discrimination on the basis of race is to stop discriminating on the basis of race."[32] Bell would likely view such judicial statements as the pernicious notions of color-blindness and racial equality made law through abstraction. For Bell, the notions of color-blindness and equality as articulated in recent Supreme Court jurisprudence such as Justice Roberts's statement from *Parents Involved* are simply adaptations of racist practices that continue to reinforce systems of white domination.[33] The similarity to Kierkegaard is noteworthy here: even as Kierkegaard resisted the abstractions of Hegelian theology, Bell resists the abstractions of liberalism and legal theory. It is in this context of abstraction in the service of continuing oppression that Bell articulated his thesis of racial realism.

According to George Taylor, a paradox lies at the heart of Bell's thesis of racial realism.[34] The paradox is that on one hand Bell claims that racism is permanent, but on the other that we resist racism and that our resistance is somehow meaningful.[35] Bell articulates this proposition rather forcefully throughout several of his books and essays. For example, in his essay "Racial Realism," Bell states the thesis of racial realism in its entirety, which bears repeating here:

> Black people will never gain full equality in this country. Even those herculean efforts we hail as successful will produce no more than temporary "peaks of progress," short-lived victories that slide into irrelevance as racial patterns adapt in new ways that maintain white dominance. This is a hard-to-accept fact that all history verifies. We must acknowledge it and move on to adopt policies based on what I call "racial realism." This mindset or philosophy requires us to acknowledge the permanence of our subordinate status. That acknowledgement enables us to avoid despair, and frees us to imagine and implement racial strategies that can bring fulfillment and even triumph.[36]

Bell makes his point clear: historical evidence suggests that the future will be no brighter for African Americans than the darkness of the past. And, based on this inductive move, Bell believes that our energies are best spent on tactics that will yield better results than what he believes are mere racial "symbols." In 1992, racial realism is paraphrased in the subtitle of his landmark text, *Faces at the Bottom of the Well: The Permanence of Racism.*

As Taylor has pointed out,[37] and as Bell himself admits, Racial Realism demands that one argue "two seemingly irreconcilable points."[38] When Bell makes this point, he is drawing heavily from Frantz Fanon, and also from Albert Camus.[39] Bell argues that Fanon demanded a sort of existential freedom in the face of despair. Bell writes that Fanon's book *Black Skin, White Masks* "was enormously pessimistic in a victory sense. He did not believe that modern structures, deeply poisoned with racism, could be overthrown. And yet he urged resistance."[40] Like Fanon, Bell urges holding two irreconcilable points. First is the belief that racism is permanent, and second is the demand to resist racism. Underlying the demand to resist is the belief that the struggle against racism is somehow meaningful despite racism's permanence.

One can better appreciate Bell's permanence of racism thesis when it is compared to the optimism of integrationist thought within the context of American liberalism. In contrast to Bell, who makes an inductive, empirical, claim about the permanence of racism that is fundamentally uncertain, proponents of liberalism rely on a priori, universalist notions of human reason and rational progress. These proponents argue that abstract principles of "rights" and "equality" lie atop a sort of neo-Platonic hierarchy as transcendent forms that ignore racial particularities. On this view, the further we move away from notions such as "race," the closer we get to equality. This is what Gary Peller has called the "ideology of integration." Peller has argued that integrationist ideology works through a triad of abstract concepts: truth, universalism, and progress. The basic idea behind these three abstract concepts is that the concrete particularities of human beings such as race, which would include historical realities of the sort that are so integral to Bell's analysis and trenchant critique of structural racism, represent a low epistemic and metaphysical status in the neo-Platonic hierarchy—that the particularity of human beings as racially understood are mere shadows in the Platonic cave that will be removed once the ultimate good of universal truth shines its light upon them and exposes them for the illusions that they really are. It is then that real racial progress can be made. Peller writes:

> Integrationists comprehend racism at a high level of abstraction in part because they wish to transcend the bias of particularity that they see at the root of racist consciousness. Integrationism, in short, links with a broader set of liberal images—images that connect truth, universalism, and progress.
>
> A commitment to universalism and an association of universalism with truth and particularism with ignorance form the substructure of American integrationist consciousness.

This universalism is the common theme that connects the integrationist analytic distinctions between reason and prejudice, objectivity and bias, neutrality and discrimination, and integration and segregation. Each dichotomy envisions a realm of impersonality, understood as the transcendence of subjective bias and contrasted with an image of a realm of distortion where particularity and stereotype reign. Integrationist beliefs are organized around the familiar enlightenment story of progress as the movement from mere belief and superstition to knowledge and reason, from the particular (and therefore the parochial) to the universal (and therefore enlightened).[41]

So, unlike Bell's racism is permanent thesis, which is a posteriori, empirical, and probabilistic in nature, the racial progress as connected to integrationist ideology is a priori, conceptual, and certain in nature. The two views are diametrically opposed to one another.

This is where I interpret Bell as making a movie akin to Johannes Climacus, thus causing Bell's paradox to function similarly to the paradox of Climacus's *Philosophical Fragments*. On one hand, the permanence thesis, as an inductive claim, is not true with objective, deductive certainty; it is merely more or less probable. Yet, on the other hand, if one holds to this probabilistic, empirical claim, *as if it is objectively true although it plainly is not*, one can interpret Bell's permanence of racism thesis as a catalyst for passionate moral action against racism, even as one, for Climacus, must hold to the uncertainty of the Incarnation *as if it is objectively certain*, when it plainly is not, and interpret that as the catalyst for an authentic Christian subjectivity. Bell's notion of resistance is, in some sense, dependent upon a notion of despair arising out of the certain belief in the inductive claim that "Black people will never gain full equality in this country," and that the illusion of racial progress is a "hard-to-accept fact that all history verifies." Bell goes on to say not that we ought to acknowledge this, but rather that "We must acknowledge it, not as a sign of submission, but as an act of ultimate defiance."[42] Bell then, as Climacus does, urges the acceptance of the uncertain as if it is objectively certain when it clearly is not. There are, of course, more rational grounds for the belief in the permanence of racism as Bell conceives of it than there are for the Christian belief in the Incarnation. But the pertinent point for my analysis is that although Bell's claim is more believable than the Incarnation, neither is objectively certain and both thinkers argue that despite the objective uncertainty of their claims, embracing them as if they are certain is the impetus for moral action.

So if we can agree with Bell that racism is a perpetual moral wrong, and that perpetual moral wrongs demand a corresponding perpetuity of moral resistance, then Bell is helping us to avoid moral complacency. In this regard, Bell is no different from Immanuel Kant, who argues that an individual never possesses virtue but that "virtue possesses" an individual.[43] Kant also reminds us that, as finite moral beings, we can never attain the moral status of good, but rather that we can only get "better."[44] Indeed, Kant's practical postulate of the immortality of the soul is significant here as well, as one is infinitely involved in the task of achieving moral goodness, which again, for Kant, is impossible.[45] Bell, as does Climacus, claims that clinging to this objective uncertainty as though it was certain demands that one passionately and wholeheartedly commit oneself to the permanence-resistance paradox. Such a commitment demands subjectivity as opposed to objectivity. One must put all of oneself into such a project, as did Mrs. MacDonald, who "lived" to "harass white folks," which is precisely what Bell demands of us. So Bell, like Climacus, demands that we hold fast to an objective uncertainty as though it was objectively certain. Racial Realism, then, requires us to hold fast to the probability that racism is permanent as though the permanence of racism was an objective, deductive, truth. Bell believes that this sort of existential embrace of racism's permanence as though it was objectively true will free us to implement strategies that will demand our continued resistance to racism. As Bell points out in "Racial Realism:"

> I am convinced that there is something real out there in America for black people. It is not, however, the romantic love of integration. It is surely not the long-sought goal of equality under law, though we must maintain the struggle against racism, else the erosion of black rights will become even worse than it is now. The Racial Realism that we seek is simply a hard eyed view of racism as it is and our subordinate role in it. We must realize, as our slave forbears, that the struggle for freedom is, at bottom, a manifestation of our humanity that survives and grows stronger through resistance to oppression, even if that oppression is never overcome.[46]

We all thus become as committed to the struggle against Mrs. MacDonald, the African American exemplar of moral virtue who "lives to harass white folks." For Bell, Mrs. MacDonald understands that the paradox of fighting to eliminate that which cannot be destroyed is not about being solved, but rather is about being committed; about being morally committed to struggle against racism with such passion that resistance becomes our life's work, as it did for Mrs. MacDonald.

To summarize, both Bell and Kierkegaard offer critiques of abstraction. Kierkegaard's critique of abstraction is a theological critique of Hegelian theology. For Kierkegaard, paradoxical Christian doctrines such as the Incarnation are not intellectually resolvable as they are through the Hegelian doctrine of mediation, but rather are epistemic uncertainties that demand our perpetual and passionate pursuit of that which cannot be understood. Kierkegaard tells us that we must cling to the paradox as though it was objectively true when it is not. In similar fashion, Bell's critique of abstraction is a legal and political critique of liberalism that leads him to the paradox of Racial Realism, which demands our perpetual and passionate resistance to racism as though its permanence is objectively certain although it is not. For both thinkers, abstraction falls on the side of an epistemic certainty and objectivity that generates moral complacency, while passion falls on the side of a subjectivity that demands moral action in the form of Kierkegaard's demand for radical Christian faith and Bell's demand for resistance to racist practices.

III.

Thus far, I have concluded that Bell and Kierkegaard each have a specific target that impedes authentic existential engagement and moral responsibility. That target is abstraction. For Kierkegaard, the abstractions of Hegelian theology render Christianity intelligible and thus offer a false sense of epistemic certainty, diluting the dynamism of subjectivity which demands choice, passion, and inwardness. And for Bell, liberalism's pernicious conceptual formations contribute to the abstractions of legal formalism creating, among other things, notions of "color-blindness" that convince us that racism can be eliminated if we stop considering it altogether in our political discourse, even for remedial purposes. But Bell believes that the abstractions of both liberalism and legal formalism actually *perpetuate* rather than eliminate racism. Indeed, such abstractions strike another fatal blow: they deceive us into thinking that our moral obligation to act against racist practices is a thing of the past, to be jettisoned along with the talk of race itself. As I argued in the last section, undergirding the notion of paradox and passion in Bell and in Kierkegaard is the difference between the inactivity of abstract objectivity and the dynamism of an inward subjectivity. It is this subjectivity and this inwardness that both thinkers must reach within their respective audiences—but how?

A clue to answering this question lies in the difference between direct and indirect communication, which are connected to the abstraction of objectivity and to the passionate inwardness of subjectivity. According to Kierkegaard's pseudonym, Johannes Climacus, "Objective thinking is completely indifferent to subjectivity and thereby to inwardness and appropriation; its communication is therefore direct."[47] Direct communication is used to communicate objective and abstract matters of knowledge. So it is that when one wants to communicate an abstract knowledge of ideas, that sort of communication can be made directly. For example, mathematical or historical truths can be communicated from one person to another rather easily. I can tell you that "$2 \times 3 = 6$" or that "Barack Obama was the 44th President of the United States," and both of these statements are objectively true. We can verify them. More importantly, however, these facts demand nothing of you. You only have to digest the statements at the most basic level of hearing them.

But suppose I want to communicate something to you that I hope will cause you to change your behavior in some way through self-reflection? Suppose the message of the communication demands that you act in some way? In the *Concluding Unscientific Postscript*, Climacus writes, "Whereas objective thinking is indifferent to the thinking subject and his existence, the subjective thinker as existing is essentially interested in his own thinking, is existing in it. Therefore, his thinking has another kind of reflection, specifically that of inwardness."[48] Climacus continues with this contrast between abstract thinking and concrete existence: "Whereas objective thinking invests everything in the result and assists all humankind to cheat by copying and reeling off the results and answers, subjective thinking invests everything in the process of becoming and omits the result."[49] "Wherever the subjective is of importance in knowledge and appropriation is therefore the main point, communication is a work of art; it is doubly reflected."[50] If the objective of my communication is to get you to engage in self-reflection, then telling you directly will not accomplish my goal. So, I resort to a method of indirect communication, where I convey the message to you in such a way that upon receiving it you engage in reflection on two levels: first, you hear the message, and second, you appropriate it to yourself in an attempt to change your behavior. In order to access a subjectivity that is deluded by abstraction, both Kierkegaard and Bell employ indirect communication. For Kierkegaard, whether either direct or indirect communication will be necessary depends in part on the condition of the listener: "there is also a difference between writing on a blank piece of paper and bringing out by means of chemicals some writing that is hidden under other writing."[51] He continues: "Now, on the assumption that someone is under a delusion and consequently the first step, properly understood, is to remove the delusion—if I do not begin by deceiving, I begin with direct communication."[52] If one is not deceived, then there is no impediment to their receipt of the truth. A person can simply accept it by hearing it. But, if someone is deceived, there is a need to first remove the "corrosive," or the deception, in order for the person to be able to hear and appropriate what is being said. Double reflection is not possible for a deceived person who receives a direct communication. This is the situation confronting both Kierkegaard and Bell. Both must undo the damage of abstraction. But this is challenging because abstraction plays the role of deceiver in that, while intellectually appealing, it makes people believe either that Christian faith is a matter of merely expressing one's assent to an objective set of beliefs (Kierkegaard), or that racism will end if everyone simply becomes "color-blind" (Bell), and thus is existentially and morally bankrupt. How then, does one in Bell's position deal with this problem? How does Bell reach those whom liberalism has deceived? He does it in a similar manner to Kierkegaard: whereas Kierkegaard used pseudonyms and irony as forms of indirect communication to remove the deceptions of Christendom, Bell uses fictional narrative to remove the deceptions of liberalism. In both Bell and Kierkegaard, abstraction has made the flesh of subjectivity into a word of conceptual objectivity, but both thinkers aim to, through the use of indirect communication, make the word of conceptual objectivity into the flesh of subjectivity and moral action. Before discussing Bell's narratives, I want to contextualize Bell's use of fictional narrative within the larger American legal tradition of storytelling. In doing so, I am attempting to show how epistemologically and judicially driven distortions of the "truth" that are so pervasive in American law demand that lawyers—Bell included—embrace a notion of truth that is wholly distinct from rigorous philosophical epistemic demands in both its conception and its practice. This move is necessary to show that Bell is not haphazardly weaving claims out of whole cloth, but rather is using the power of narrative as a trial lawyer would to persuade a jury, and is thus doing his legal scholarship within the larger tradition of storytelling that is so prevalent in the American legal culture.

INTERLUDE: THE LEGAL DEMAND FOR FICTION

Lawyers like stories. But they do not just like stories, they *need* them. Stories are what keep lawyers open for business. Ask trial lawyers who have ever had a jury rule in their favor in either a civil or a criminal case, and they will tell you that they won because they were able to tell the better story. It is ironic that "verdict" means "to speak the truth," and yet more often than not juries do not know the "truth" about the cases on which they deliberate. And they cannot. For by the time the jury begins deliberations, they are, in most cases, months or years removed from the event that led to their presence in court. The slip and fall of a civil case or the robbery and murder of a criminal case occurred long before the members of the jury ever knew that their responsibilities of citizenship would call them to sit in judgment about the conduct of one or more of their fellow citizens. It is not that the facts of a case do not matter. Indeed, they do. But the epistemological limitations on litigants, juries, and judges mean that all of the facts of a case are subject to interpretation, and it is the interpretation that becomes the story that is told by either side of a case. Therefore, lawyers involved in litigation need to re-create the events that brought the case to court. And this re-creation requires a high level of ingenuity and skill that some lawyers have more than others, which is what separates the excellent trial lawyer from the average one. Moreover, this task of re-creation is supervised by a judge who, through certain evidentiary rulings, may remove the "truth" even further from the jury. For example, a witness with information about the "truth" of the matter brought before the court may, for legal reasons, not be permitted to testify, or, for strategic reasons, may not be called to testify. So it is that by the time the jury gets the case to deliberate, what they know as the "truth" is often either very different from, or at least an incomplete version of what actually happened. Storytelling is thus of paramount importance to good lawyering.

So it makes sense that Bell—a lawyer and widely regarded as the founder of Critical Race Theory—would employ storytelling to help him "make his case" about the permanence of racism in America akin to how a trial lawyer develops a narrative to persuade a jury. In contrast to judicially imposed evidentiary restrictions and epistemic deficits—which take knowledge of the complete "truth" *away from* a jury—Bell *adds* something to well-known historical "truths" by inserting fictional characters in his narratives, which are based upon the actual historical events in America.[53] These historical events are analogous to the events that bring either a civil or a criminal case to court: they are actual events remote enough in time that force us into an epistemic deficit that Bell augments through re-imagining the events creatively in order to persuade his audience about the permanence of racism. Although it is not surprising that Bell would use fictional narrative, what is interesting is that given the epistemologically and judicially driven distortions of objective "truth" in the practice of law, some of Bell's critics—also lawyers—claim that Bell is wrong for using fictional narrative to demonstrate, as Bell tries to do, that racism is the prominent factor in adjudication in cases involving race.[54] Bell argues that Supreme Court decisions such as *Bakke v. Board of Regents of the University of California*[55] and *City of Richmond v. J.A. Croson Co.*[56] resort to legal formalist notions of "equality" not as legitimate applications of an abstract and mechanically applicable "rule of law," but rather as post-hoc justifications for oppressive adjudications based on "color-blindness," which, Bell contends, is a pernicious abstraction that actually perpetuates rather than eliminates racism by maintaining the structural and institutionalized forms of white dominance.[57]

With this legal background and Bell's purposes in mind, I now turn to Bell's narratives and his use of literary criticism. The first two narratives, "Divining a Theory of Racial Realism"[58] and "The Racial Preference Licensing Act,"[59] illustrate the permanence aspect of Bell's racial realism, and "The Afrolantica Awakening"[60] and "Justice Marshall and the Handmaid's Tale"[61] illustrate the resistance aspect of racial realism. As for Kierkegaard, this sort of "deception" is important, because, for Bell, too many people are "mesmerized by the racial equality syndrome."[62] They are "too easily reassured by simple admonitions to 'stay on course,' which come far too easily from those—black and white—who are not on the deprived end of the economic chasm between blacks and whites."[63] Moreover, Bell believes that "the goal of racial equality is, while comforting to many whites, more illusory than real for blacks."[64] Taken together, I argue that these three narratives and this use of literary criticism illustrate the power of the paradox at work in Bell's thought, and that ultimately they do for Bell the same that the pseudonyms do for Kierkegaard: they aim to remove deceptions. Bell thus wants to reawaken a passionate moral resistance to racism through fictional narrative and literary criticism.

Bell on Abstraction and the Permanence Thesis: "Divining a Racial Realism Theory"

Bell's fictional narrative "Divining a Racial Realism Theory" appears in his landmark 1992 text, *Faces at the Bottom of the Well: The Permanence of Racism*. The story begins with the narrator, who is a law professor—perhaps Bell himself—going off into the seclusion of the woods in Oregon to do some writing. Just before he can get settled into his work, Erika Wechsler, a thirty-something white woman, interrupts him. Erika is a member of a paramilitary group called White Citizens for Black Survival (WCBS). The group is based upon two principles: (1) a commitment to racial realism, and (2) an activism that establishes safe houses for African Americans in the event that they become national scapegoats, which, Erika's group believes, is likely.[65] Erika goes on to describe her organization as:

> a collective of whites dedicated to doing what we can to shield blacks from the worst dangers of racism . . . To last in WCBS, one must try to be as sensitive to racial subordination as a member of the oppressor class can be: aware of what went on in the past beyond history's received truths, and cognizant of the fact that slavery, for example, tried to dehumanize blacks, and failed, and didn't try to dehumanize whites, but succeeded.[66]

The law professor/narrator refers to Erika's insightful recitation of slavery's failed dehumanization of blacks and successful dehumanization of whites as "the usual but almost never perceived outcomes of oppression."[67]

Erika then reveals that the name of her brigade within the organization is "Shades of John Brown's Body," referencing John Brown, the white abolitionist who led the slave revolt at Harper's Ferry in West Virginia on October 16-18, 1859. The reference to John Brown derives from WCBS's military training, which is, in turn, based on its belief that WCBS might "have to launch attacks in order to defend blacks in a crisis."[68] Erika points out that WCBS also understands "racism and the role it plays in American law, because law has always been a powerful expression of ruling interests."[69] Erika then says to the law professor/narrator: "when you need us, we hope to be ready whether or not you believe in us."[70] After explaining the aims and purposes of the organization, Erika and the law professor/narrator settle in for a longer conversation. In this conversation, Erika discussed the false hopes of racial equality being achieved through the legal system, the remarkable, chameleon-like adaptability of racist practices to new forms, and that these two realities are undeniable, given America's history with civil rights.[71]

Erika and the law professor then begin discussing jurisprudential differences between legal formalism and legal realism. Erika begins the discussion with a critique of jurisprudence as it is currently taught in law schools. She claims that jurisprudence, as part of contemporary legal education, "is dry and disconnected with the reality of the real world, and it's overly reliant on appellate court opinions that once reflected real problems but now are preserved as legal precedent to be dissected and analyzed, like mummies in a tomb."[72] According to Erika, these abstract legal "rules" that come from precedent "serve to justify preservation of the status quo while tending to bar social reform."[73] The law professor/narrator then points out "that the legal rules regarding racial discrimination have become not only reified . . . but deified. The worship of equality rules as having absolute power benefits whites by preserving a benevolent but fictional self-image, and such worship benefits blacks by preserving hope."[74] Erika then asks the law professor/narrator, "Isn't there a parallel, Professor, between the formalists' reactionary faith in their supposedly apolitical principle and the modern captivation with colorblind neutrality?"[75] And the law professor/narrator replies:

> Of course! I exclaimed, agreeing with her analysis. And, as we have seen, even the laws or court decisions that abolish one form of discrimination may well allow for its appearance in another form, subtle though no less damaging. Thus, the *Brown* decision invalidated "separate but equal," replacing it—as civil rights advocates urged—with "equal opportunity." But given the continued motivations for racism, the society has managed to discriminate against blacks as effectively under the remedy as under the prior law—more effectively really, because discrimination today is covert, harder to prove, its ill effects easier to blame on its black victims.[76]

Here, Bell is pointing to the problem of abstraction in legal formalism showing how its commitment to "rules" as the stimulus for adjudication has been used in the service of maintaining institutionalized racism on the basis of an abstract notion of equality. For Bell, equality is no remedy at all, but rather just another linguistic illusion in the lexical arsenal of those who maintain white supremacy. This false notion of equality, stripped from any historical, sociological, or other empirical data encourage, in Bell's view, "an artificial and inappropriate parity"[77] in judicial reasoning which implies that U.S. Supreme Court jurisprudence has chosen "to ignore historical patterns, contemporary statistics, and flexible reasoning."[78]

In this fictional narrative, Bell wants to remove the deception from those deluded into America's false hopes in the abstract notion of equality through an indirect communication that encourages double reflection and subjective appropriation. Notice that Erika Wechsler, the white character in the narrative, is a member of a paramilitary organization. She is out in the woods in Oregon. In contrast to a sense of contentment stemming from the view that Blacks have somehow attained equality through civil rights gains, as a member of WCBS, she is part of an organization that is as interested in action as it is in policy. This relates to the sort of passion and subjective appropriation that Bell is trying to engender in his reader, for Erika and the other members of WCBS are so passionate about their opposition to racism that WCBS that they actually have a plan of action to do something about racism. Her organization (WCBS) is not only policy driven, but also action driven. According to Bell, notions such as "color-blindness" and "equality" deceive many whites—and others—into believing that there is no need for action because they believe that the American legal system has solved the race problem. But for whites to be able to see someone that looks like them engaged in a passionate struggle against racism is to remove the corrosive of such a deception because it enables whites to see themselves as being resistant to rather than complicit with institutionalized racist practices. By articulating his thesis of racial realism through a white person, Bell gives us a fictional portrayal of what many would seem to be the impossible: a white person being part of a white paramilitary organization that is not organized against Blacks, but rather in their favor! In giving us this sort of character, Bell is encouraging whites to see themselves not as contributors to the racial problem, but rather as active agents of change fighting against the racial problem. Bell is thus not just communicating with us directly about the moral wrong of racism. No. He is doing much more than that. He is painting a picture for us of a world in which whites join together with Blacks in a passionate struggle against institutionalized racist practices.

Bell's message, however, is twofold: for not only does the depiction of a white person enable us to see a world in which whites actually care about resisting American racism, it also enables Blacks to see themselves existing in a world where whites are more passionate about ending racism than Blacks. In painting this picture, Bell arguably intends for his fictional narrative to have some shock value for Blacks, who likely have become complacent with the so-called "civil rights victories" in the courts that they feel a need to "move beyond" race. Thus it is that Erika and the law professor have the following exchange:

> You—and other blacks as well—need to *get* serious. What precisely would you do if they came for you? How would you protect your family? Where could you go? . . . You have money. Could you get access to it if the government placed a hold on the assets in your checking and savings accounts? I thought I was paranoid about whites, but you, Erika, a white, and a lawyer at that! Your paranoia is unnerving.[79]

The "corrosive" in the way of whites accepting his thesis of racial realism is not only the notion that racism is no more, but also that it is a problem that affects only Blacks and not whites. This notion is, however, plainly debunked in the story because Erika points out that the whites in WCBS "believe that America's race problem is a white problem. We have determined to take personal responsibility for racism."[80]

Through the use of fictional narrative in "Divining a Racial Realism Theory," Bell provides a portrayal of a world through the use of indirect communication where whites are more passionate about ending racism than many would believe that they could be. This passion represents a departure from abstraction and knowledge and toward passionate resistance. The fictional character's critique of legal formalism is a critique of abstraction and the action oriented aims of WCBS, the historical allusion to John Brown's slave revolt, and the chastisement of Blacks all lead the reader to see themselves otherwise: whites are led to see themselves as allies rather than as obstacles in the fight against racism, and Blacks are led to see themselves as being in need of a wake-up call to confront the hard reality of racism's permanence, rather than to avoid responsibility for addressing racism because of the deception that racism is no more. So it is that Bell, like Kierkegaard, uses a deception to remove a deception by facilitating double reflection: the deception of indirect communication is used to remove the deception of abstraction such that people will not only read the story, but will apply it to themselves and be changed. In removing this deception, Bell wants to engender a passionate, inward commitment in his reader to resist racism, just as Kierkegaard sought to engender such a commitment in Danish Christendom.

"The Racial Preference Licensing Act"

Also in *Faces* is Bell's fictional narrative, "The Racial Preference Licensing Act."[81] In this story, the President of the United States announces that he is signing a bill into law that will allow employers and merchants to discriminate against Blacks if they choose to do so. In exchange for their ability to discriminate, they would first pay a licensing fee to the government, and they would also pay a 3 percent tax on all income derived from "whites employed, whites served, or products sold to whites during each quarter in which a policy of 'racial preference' was in effect."[82] The license was to be prominently displayed, and it prohibited businesses from tokenism; from hiring Blacks as immunization from liability under the Act. If a business was illegally discriminating on the basis of race without having the license, then the party alleging the racial discrimination is required to prove their case and, if successful, would be entitled to ten thousand dollars per instance of discrimination, plus attorney's fees.[83] The revenue generated from the licensing fees and from the 3 percent tax "would be placed in an 'equality fund' used to underwrite Black businesses, to offer no-interest mortgage loans for Black home buyers, and to provide scholarships for Black students seeking college and vocational education."[84] The President urges the nation to come to the realization that moral policing does not work. Prior approaches to equality through civil rights were therefore as doomed as prohibition because they seek to enforce a social morality rather than provide enforceable, concrete, and workable solutions to the problem of racial inequality.[85]

Bell himself has pointed out that "I have long tried, with Geneva Crenshaw's help, to convey the basic truth about the ineradicableness of racism not as a scary premonition but as a challenge to think about the law and race in new ways, a challenge that would, whether won or lost, bring peace to the mind and solace to the soul."[86] And this is precisely what Bell is attempting to do with Geneva Crenshaw in "The Racial Preference Licensing Act," where he uses fictional narrative "to think about the law and race" in a "new" way. Specifically, Bell puts a subtle, but powerful critique of legal positivism in the voice of the President of the United States that is intended to provoke the reader into a passionate sense of moral obligation to fight against racism. In reciting the history of civil rights laws and the history of the *Brown* decision, Bell wants to remove the deception that the legislative process and the judiciary alone can provide relief from racism. So when the President makes the claim that "the Court determined that laws requiring cessation of white conduct deemed harmful to blacks are hard to enforce because they seek to 'police morality,'" Bell is making the point that the outward gains that many consider to be evidence of real racial progress are actually incapable of inwardly reforming the hearts of the people. Although the letter of the law may change, unless the spirit of moral treatment toward African Americans is based on a renewed inward commitment, then we simply have symbols of progress that are of no long-term use in the struggle against racism. Liberalism, then, invokes legislative and judicial processes to accomplish from without what can only be accomplished from within the human heart: a genuine moral conviction of the wrongness of anti-Black racism. Laws can be changed outwardly, but true morality must be lived inwardly; it cannot merely be legislated. Outward changes to the law, without a corresponding inward moral change, are not only ineffective in eliminating anti-Black racism, but actually perpetuate it. Thus it is that Bell points to civil rights laws and to the *Brown* decision as mere "symbols" that do not actually represent racial progress. When reading "The Racial Preference Licensing Act," Bell wants us to move away from the objectivity of the legal positivism or the "law on the books" and toward a deeper moral commitment that recognizes that since the moral evil of racism is internal to American social and political life, its solution must also be internal. The American legal system only provides window dressing that makes it appear as though we have had real racial progress. And it also provides fodder for those who would argue that because of landmark civil rights legislation and *Brown*, racism is no more. Such arguments are entirely too objective and are deceptions of liberalism that an indirect communication in the form of "The Racial Preference Licensing Act" can help remove by helping us to see a world in which morality is taken seriously. The passion needed to combat anti-Black racism in a liberal democracy can be reached through a deceptive communication that helps us see ourselves, and helps us to transform ourselves not from the outside in, but rather from the inside out. And this is precisely what Bell provides in "The Racial Preference Licensing Act."

Some may argue that "The Racial Preference Licensing Act" moves us deeper toward racist practices rather than away from them. But this assertion is myopic. For, as the President points out in his closing remarks about the Act, "It maximizes freedom of racial choice for all our citizens while guaranteeing that people of color will benefit either directly from equal access or indirectly from the fruits of the license taxes paid by those who would choose policies of racial exclusion."[87] Recall that unlike Jim Crow, where discrimination was lawful but not taxed, Blacks were discriminated against yet without any financial remuneration. But under the Racial Preferene Licensing Act, each instance of discrimination results either in a fine for discriminating without a license, or, if one has a license, there is a licensing fee. Either by fine or licensing fee, the "equality fund" grows and exists for the benefits of Blacks as outlined in the President's remarks. For Bell, this is true equality: not an abstract concept used to legitimate and sediment racist practices, but rather a concrete plan of action used to impose a direct financial burden on the discriminator and to confer direct financial benefits on those who are on the receiving end of anti-Black racial discrimination.

Through the fictional narrative of the Racial Preference Licensing Act, Bell is attempting, as did Kierkegaard, to lead us to a higher moral ground—a moral ground far from the most crass forms of objective legal positivism and toward the most genuine form of moral obligation that demands an investment of oneself in the fight against anti-Black racism. The mere existence of laws must be buttressed by an inward moral sense that represents a genuine recognition of racism as a moral evil and demands nothing less than a passionate struggle against it.

On the Resistance Thesis

"The Afrolantica Awakening"

Bell's fictional dialogue, "The Afrolantica Awakening," in *Faces* is a lesson about the indomitability of the human spirit. It is the story of an island that emerges "in the middle of the Atlantic Ocean, some nine hundred miles due east of South Carolina."[88] Americans began to follow the rising of this land mass on their televisions and "then, one evening, a vast body of land roared into view like an erupting volcano."[89] According to the narrative, the new land was "complete with tall mountains that sheltered fertile valleys and rich plains already lush with vegetation."[90] The description continues: "The new Atlantis was surrounded by beautiful beaches punctuated by deep water harbors. From all indications, the land—roughly the size of the New England states—was uninhabited, though from afar you could see that fish filled its streams and animals in great abundance roamed its fields."[91] Scientific testing confirmed that "the earth on this Atlantis contained substantial deposits of precious minerals, including gold and silver."[92]

Given the beauty of the new land and the richness of the treasures beneath its soil, the story tells of how "The United States and several other countries wasted no time in dispatching delegations to claim the land or portions of it."[93] The problem with the new land, however, was that the people sent to claim the land were unable to breathe: "The crew members had a hard time breathing and managed to take off just as they were beginning to lose consciousness."[94] Apparently this was because scientific experiments showed that "the air pressure—estimated at twice the levels existing at the bottom of the sea—threatened human life. One survivor explained that it was like trying to breathe under the burdens of all the world."[95] On one of the failed submarine explorations was a Navy crew chief named Martin Shufford. An African American, Shufford was not only able to breathe without the aid of any breathing apparatus, he also "felt really invigorated by the new land's waters. And a medical check found him normal."[96] At first this was thought to be insignificant, but further testing confirmed that African Americans were capable of survival—and even thriving—on the new island that emerged from the sea. They reported experiencing "feelings they explained upon their reluctant return . . . as unlike any alcohol—or drug-induced sensations of escape. Rather, it was an invigorating experience of heightened self-esteem, of liberation, of waking up."[97] The black explorers agreed that they felt "free" during their visit to what they were now calling "Afrolantica."[98]

A lengthy debate ensued between what became known as the Afrolantica emigration movement and those opposed to the emigration. Both sides marshalled historical evidence and made various arguments, drawing from African American social and political philosophers. For example, some relied on the emigration arguments of Martin Delany and Marcus Garvey, and those in opposition relied on some of the statements of Frederick Douglass.[99] Despite opposition and criminal charges akin to those lodged against Marcus Garvey, the "Afrolantica Armada" was formed. It was a fleet of a thousand ships "of every size and description loaded with the first wave of several hundred thousand black settlers." The armada left the U.S. shores on the Fourth of July. Unfortunately for the would-be settlers, as they approached Afrolantica, the island descended back into the sea as mysteriously as it arose from it. The armada then returned to the shores of the United States. Upon the return of the armada, "One returning black settler spoke for all: 'It was worth it just to try looking for something better, even if we didn't find it.'"[100]

In this fictional narrative, Bell shows us something powerful: how an elusive goal builds morale and unity in an oppressed community, for the Afrolantica Armada was successful not in what it attained, but rather in what it attempted. In this regard, the would-be settlers are no different from the enterprise of philosophy itself, which subsists on a desire to know all things but cannot. And yet philosophy never stops trying. Indeed, it was the Milesians, that ancient school of pre-Socratic cosmologists that is remembered as "important, not for what it achieved, but for what it attempted."[101] But this is where the similarity ends. For the would-be settlers of the Afrolantica Armada are not mere philosophers. They do not seek a comprehensive metaphysical explanation of all that is. Instead of epistemic and metaphysical desires, theirs are moral and political. They are interested in a land where they can thrive and a land where there is justice. Unlike the long sought after epistemic certainty that further guarantees an all-encompassing explanation of reality, what evades the would-be settlers is the moral treatment and the justice that they so desperately seek. Just as they arrive at the shores of Afrolantica, it disappears beneath the depths of the Atlantic Ocean. This relates to the African American struggle for justice: no sooner do African Americans admire the gains of landmark court decisions and civil rights laws and think themselves to be "free" having reached "the other side," than they are reminded that what they really want is actually unattainable. But African Americans must not despair. To the contrary, it is in the struggle itself that African Americans are successful, despite the permanence of racism: "Blacks discovered that they themselves actually possessed the qualities of liberation they had hoped to realize on their new homeland. Feeling this was, they all agreed, an Afrolantica Awakening, a liberation—not of place, but of mind."[102] It is, then, in the resistance to racism; in the struggle for something better that people most fully realize the indomitable nature of the human spirit, which is what Bell is attempting to get across through this work of fiction. Bell wants people who struggle against something that is impossible to overcome to realize that the elusiveness of the goal should not in the least bit deter the sincerity of the efforts to attain it. For it is in this effort that we see the humanity's greatest triumph. To attain this triumph, to make this effort, demands a departure from stale, objective certainty toward a passionate inward subjective moral commitment. Bell attempts to reach this side of us through his use of this fictional narrative.

"JUSTICE MARSHALL AND THE HANDMAID'S TALE"

Bell's book *Afrolantica Legacies* begins with a council that convenes after the return of the Afrolantica Armada. Published six years after *Faces*, *Afrolantica Legacies* uses the end of "The Afrolantica Awakening" as its point of departure. The prologue of the book is an attempt to describe how, because of a need for the would-be Afrolantica settlers "to nourish the continuing effort to transform the subordination of the body into triumph of the spirit," "committees worked to fashion fundamental standards that would offer both inspiration as well as specific advice for every-day living."[103] The committee eventually adopted what they hoped would serve as rules of racial preservation. They called them "Afrolantica Legacies."[104] The fifth of these legacies is set forth here in its entirety, as it is essentially a restatement of Bell's resistance thesis: "Continued resistance by the powerless eventually triumphs over power, and thus oppression must be resisted, even when opposition seems useless."[105]

To illustrate this Afrolantica Legacy as it relates to the African American quest for equality, Bell interprets Margaret Atwood's novel *The Handmaid's Tale*, which is the story of a woman named Offred. Offred is not her original name. Her original name was taken away from her because she lived "in Gilead, a repressive, dictatorial, post-American regime centered on the campus of what had been Harvard University."[106] The leadership of Gilead, according to Bell, has "absolute control over the citizenry."[107] As a totalitarian regime, Gilead will punish "the least manifestation of heresy" with "a cruel death."[108] In the interest of reproducing white children, Offred and other women "are pressed into service as subjugated breeders for the leaders whose wives are barren."[109] In what Bell views as a courageous attempt to forge meaning out of a meaningless situation, Offred narrates her life story by making audiotapes that tell of her life experiences. It is this courageous act of self-interpretation that is the focal point of Bell's interpretation of *The Handmaid's Tale*. Many years later when scholars of color gather at an academic conference to discuss Gilead and Offred's role in the society, they realize that the tapes lack the information that the scholars need in order to make any sense of them, and the scholars of color dismiss the tapes as lacking in any real historical or anthropological value. But, according to Bell, the academics miss the point: her achievement is not based on the ability of future generations to "understand" her or to study her, but rather on the fact that she made the attempt to tell her story at all. For in attempting to tell her story, she demonstrated courage in the face of despair and hopelessness that makes her victorious despite the odds against her. So her achievement was not in winning, but in her resistance to the oppression that surrounded her.

Likening Offred's experience to the African American struggle for racial equality, Bell readily acknowledges the differences between Offred's world and the world of African Americans. Bell writes:

> Life is less than a picnic for persons of color in this land where whiteness is the deeply assumed norm. But it is not a totalitarian regime. Without fear of official sanction, we can gather and offer commendation to black leaders who have served their people well. Some of these have been lawyers and judges, a group with the difficult task of disproving Audre Lorde's warning that one cannot dismantle the master's house with the master's tools. When at some far distant time, historians and anthropologists review the records of our era, there should be no mistake about them or the tremendous efforts they mounted to gain constitutional protection for our rights.[110]

According to Bell, many of these Black leaders are people like Charles Hamilton Houston and Thurgood Marshall.[111] They are African American heroes, who, like Offred, resisted in the face of oppression. And though their work was unsuccessful in that they did not achieve their goal of racial equality, this is simply not the point. Instead of being victorious because they achieved their goal, their real victory is in their resistance—in the story of their struggle. Bell then explains the deeper connection between Offred and Justice Marshall:

> Like the character Offred in *The Handmaid's Tale*, Thurgood Marshall relied on the power of telling stories to change minds and events. In remarking on what Justice Marshall added to the Court, Justice Sandra Day O'Connor recalled in one interview his ability to use personal examples to convey the human realities behind the cold legal principles the Court debated. But like those at the conference who undervalued poor Offred's story,

the Court's majority—and especially Justice O'Connor whose votes and opinions committing the Court to a nonexistent color-blind society have helped demolish so many civil rights precedents—was unable to get beyond the humor in Justice Marshall's anecdotes to his deeply serious messages—now relegated to his dissenting opinions.[112]

In this passage, Bell illustrates the intention of storytelling generally: "to change minds and events."[113] According to Bell, for both Offred and for Justice Marshall, telling a story is an attempt to create meaning in a meaningless world. The point is not that Offred succeeded in conveying her story such that the totalitarian regime in which she lived was transformed and she was liberated. For Bell, Offred's victory is in the story of her struggle—a struggle unique to herself and to her situation. And this was precisely what Justice Marshall aimed to do: through the story of his struggle to attain equality for African Americans, he and Offred are worthy of our admiration "not because they won, but because they persevered."[114]

IV.

Bell's use of fiction to access what he believes to be the truth is part of a longstanding philosophical tradition. From Socrates and Plato to Descartes and Kierkegaard, fictions have been employed to arrive at what their users have considered to be the truth. Bell can be situated squarely within this tradition of philosophical storytellers, especially Kierkegaard. Even as Kierkegaard sought to remove the deceptions of nineteenth-century members of the Danish State Church that Christianity was easy or simply a matter of church membership, Bell sought to remove the deceptions of twentieth and twenty-first-century liberalism that abstractions such as "equality" and "color-blindness" will eliminate racism. Paradox figures prominently in both Kierkegaard and Bell, as it is the paradox that generates a move away from abstract conceptual thinking to meaningful moral action. Both Kierkegaard and Bell grapple with paradoxical thought through the use of indirect communication; Kierkegaard through pseudonyms and Bell through fictional narrative. This communicative strategy is designed not only to pull us away from abstractions but also to help us access the interior of our humanity such that we are prompted toward the creation of meaning in a world where although racism is permanent it must be resisted. And it is through this resistance that we are victorious against racism despite its seeming intractability.

Notes

1. Frantz Fanon, *Black Skin, White Masks* (New York: Grove Press, 1967), 228.
2. Albert Camus, *Resistance, Rebellion, and Death* (New York: Random House, 1988), 26.
3. *Holy Bible*, Luke 10:29–30.
4. *Euthyphro*, 10e–11b.
5. *Apology*, 29b.
6. *Republic*, 382c–d.
7. *Republic*, 414b–c.
8. Ibid.
9. René Descartes, *Meditations on First Philosophy*, 3rd ed., trans. Donald A. Cress (Indianapolis, IN: Hackett Publishing, 1993), 16.
10. See Kierkegaard's pseudonymous essay *Fear and Trembling*, written by Johannes de Silentio.
11. Søren Kierkegaard, *Concluding Unscientific Postscript to the Philosophical Fragments*, ed. and trans. Howard V. and Edna H. Hong (Princeton, NJ: Princeton University Press, 1992), 368.
12. See especially Kierkegaard's *The Point of View for My Work as an Author*, ed. and trans. Howard V. Hong and Edna H. Hong (Princeton, NJ: Princeton University Press, 1998), 53.
13. *Parents Involved in Community Schools v. Seattle School District*, 551 U.S. 701, 728 (2007).
14. See Derrick Bell, *Faces at the Bottom of the Well: The Permanence of Racism* (New York: Basic Books, 1992), especially "Racial Symbols: A Limited Legacy," 15–31.
15. See Derrick Bell, *Afrolantica Legacies* (Chicago: Third World Press, 1998), especially "Chiara's Enlightenment," 39–59.
16. Ibid.
17. Hence the use of the term "Unscientific" in the title of Kierkegaard's *Concluding Unscientific Postscript to the Philosophical Fragments*. For Kierkegaard's pseudonym, Johannes Climacus, Christianity ought not to be treated as the natural sciences, where *one must remove oneself* from laboratory experiments in order to arrive at the objective truth in support of a hypothesis. In contrast, Climacus argues that Christianity demands that *one throw oneself into it*. And Bell demands the same of us in the struggle against anti-Black racism: we must immerse ourselves

in the struggle, rather than employ "scientific," conceptual abstractions such as "equality," and "color-blindness" to avoid responsibility for anti-Black racism. I discuss this in greater detail later in the chapter.

18. For Kierkegaard, see his pseudonymous work *Philosophical Fragments*. And for an excellent commentary on paradox in the work of Derrick Bell, see George H. Taylor, "Racism as 'The Nation's Crucial Sin': Theology and Derrick Bell," *Michigan Journal of Race & Law*, 9 (2004): 269–322.

19. See Hans Lassen Martensen, "Rationalism, Supernaturalism, and the *principium exclusi medii*," in *Mynster's "Rationalism, Supernaturalism" and the Debate about Mediation*, ed. and trans. Jon Stewart (Copenhagen, Denmark: Tusculanum Press, 2009), 130–131.

20. Ibid., 135.

21. Kierkegaard, *Concluding Unscientific Postscript*, 51.

22. For an excellent discussion of these concepts, see Claire Carlisle, *Kierkegaard's Philosophy of Becoming: Movements and Positions* (Albany, NY: SUNY Press, 2005).

23. Søren Kierkegaard, *Philosophical Fragments*, trans. Howard V. Hong and Edna H. Hong (Princeton, NJ: Princeton University Press, 1985), 9.

24. Ibid., 37.

25. *Bakke v. Board of Regents of California*, 438 U.S. 265 (1978).

26. See *City of Richmond v. J.A. Croson Co.*, 488 U.S. 469 (1989).

27. John Rawls, *A Theory of Justice* (Cambridge, MA: Harvard University Press, 1971), 10.

28. See Charles Mills, *The Racial Contract* (Ithaca, NY: Cornell University Press, 1997), 77, and Charles Mills, "Rawls on Race / Race in Rawls," *Southern Journal of Philosophy* 47 (2009): 161–184.

29. Mills, "Rawls on Race / Race in Rawls."

30. Brian Leiter, "Rethinking Legal Realism: Toward a Naturalized Jurisprudence," *Naturalizing Jurisprudence: Essays on American Legal Realism and Naturalism in Legal Philosophy* (London, UK: Oxford University Press, 2007), 23.

31. *Shelby County, Alabama v. Holder*, 570 U.S. 529 (2013). As I discussed in the introduction, in this case, the Supreme Court declared Congress's renewal of Section 5 of the Voting Rights Act of 1965 under the standards of §4(b) unconstitutional as a violation of the Tenth Amendment, and also as a violation of congressional enforcement power under the Fourteenth and Fifteenth Amendments. Section 5 required federal oversight of proposed changes to local election laws in those jurisdictions with a history of racial discrimination in voting as determined by §4(b). Thus it is that in one fell swoop, the Supreme Court disregarded the efforts of those—both Black and white—who fought and died in order for African Americans to have access to the democratic process. For Bell, a decision such as *Shelby County* puts the Voting Rights Act of 1965 in that class of legislation that has "been undermined by both unenthusiastic enforcement and judicial decisions construing its provisions more narrowly" (Bell, *Faces*, 29). Indeed, *Shelby County*

does not merely give us a narrow construction, but because of the relationship between §4(b) and §5, eliminates federal oversight of state elections altogether, which is especially troubling in jurisdictions with a history of racial discrimination in electoral politics.

32. *Parents Involved in Community Schools*, 551 U.S. at 701, 728. For an excellent critique of Justice Roberts's claim, see Mills, "Rawls on Race / Race in Rawls," 180–181.

33. See also Mills, "Rawls on Race / Race in Rawls," 180.

34. Taylor, "Racism as 'The Nation's Crucial Sin,'" 269–270.

35. Derrick Bell, "Racial Realism," *Connecticut Law Review* 24.2 (1992): 363–379.

36. Ibid., 373–374.

37. Taylor, "Racism as 'The Nation's Crucial Sin,'" 569–570.

38. Derrick Bell, "The Racism is Permanent Thesis: Courageous Revelation or Unconscious Denial of Racial Genocide," *Capital University Law Review* (1993): 571–588.

39. Ibid., 584.

40. Ibid., 584.

41. Gary Peller, *Critical Race Consciousness: Reconsidering American Ideologies of Racial Justice* (New York: Routledge, 2016), 5–6.

42. Bell, *Faces*, 12.

43. See Immanuel Kant, *The Metaphysics of Morals*, trans. Mary Gregor (Cambridge, UK: Cambridge University Press, 1996), 406.

44. See Immanuel Kant, "Critique of Practical Reason," in *Practical Philosophy*, trans. Mary Gregor (Cambridge, UK: Cambridge University Press, 1996), 122.

45. Ibid.

46. Bell, "Racial Realism," 378.

47. Kierkegaard, *Concluding Unscientific Postscript*, 75.

48. Ibid., 73.

49. Ibid.

50. Ibid., 79.

51. Kierkegaard, *Point of View*, 54.

52. Ibid.

53. Consider, for example, the Constitutional Convention of 1787, which Bell uses as the historical event for "The Chronicle of the Constitutional Contradiction," and where Bell creatively inserts the fictional heroine of his narratives, Geneva Crenshaw, a Black woman, to try and persuade the framers of the Constitution that they were doing irreparable harm in ratifying the Constitution without bringing an end to American Chattel Slavery in *And We Are Not Saved: The Elusive Quest for Racial Justice* (New York: Basic Books, 1987), 26–50.

54. See Daniel Farber and Suzanna Sherry, *Beyond all Reason: The Radical Assault on Truth in American Law* (London, UK: Oxford University Press, 1997).

55. See, "The Racial Preference Licensing Act," in Bell, *Faces*.
56. *City of Richmond*, 488 U.S. 469 (1989).
57. See Bell, "Racial Realism."
58. Bell, *Faces*, 89–108.
59. Ibid., 47–64.
60. Ibid., 32–46.
61. *Afrolantica Legacies*, 123–135.
62. Bell, *Faces*, 13.
63. Ibid.
64. Ibid.
65. Ibid., 93.
66. Ibid., 94.
67. Ibid.
68. Ibid.
69. Ibid.
70. Ibid., 94–95.
71. Ibid., 97.
72. Ibid., 99.
73. Ibid.
74. Ibid., 101.
75. Ibid., 103–104.
76. Ibid., 104.
77. Ibid., 102.
78. Ibid.
79. Ibid., 93–94.
80. Ibid.
81. Ibid., 47–64.
82. Ibid., 48.
83. Ibid.
84. Ibid., 48–49.
85. Ibid., 51.
86. Derrick Bell, *Gospel Choirs: Psalms of Survival in an Alien Land Called Home* (New York: Basic Books, 1996), 11–12.
87. *Faces*, 52.
88. Ibid., 32.
89. Ibid., 32–33.
90. Ibid., 33.
91. Ibid.
92. Ibid.
93. Ibid.
94. Ibid., 33–34.
95. Ibid., 34.

96. Ibid.
97. Ibid., 35.
98. Ibid.
99. Ibid., 37, 40.
100. Ibid., 46.
101. Bertrand Russell, *The History of Western Philosophy* (New York: Simon and Shuster, 1972), 28.
102. Ibid., 46.
103. *Afrolantica Legacies*, xii.
104. Ibid., xii–xiii.
105. Ibid., xiii.
106. Ibid., 123.
107. Ibid.
108. Ibid.
109. Ibid.
110. Ibid., 124.
111. Ibid. See also my discussion in chapter 3 of Justice Marshall's 1988 speech in which he claimed that racial equality in America was impossible. There, my discussion emphasizes the resistance thesis of Bell's Racial Realism in the face of Racial Realism's permanence thesis. Here, Justice Marshall's speech is pertinent here for my discussion of the "Handmaiden's Tale" and its emphasis on the value of narrative.
112. Ibid., 129.
113. Ibid.
114. Ibid., 135.

Works Cited

Bakke v. Board of Regents of California, 438 U.S. 265 (1978).

Bell, Derrick. *Afrolantica Legacies*. Chicago: Third World Press, 1998.

———. *Gospel Choirs: Psalms of Survival in an Alien Land Called Home* (New York: Basic Books, 1996), 11–12.

———. "The Racism is Permanent Thesis: Courageous Revelation or Unconscious Denial of Racial Genocide," *Capital University Law Review* (1993): 571–588.

———. *And We Are Not Saved: The Elusive Quest for Racial Justice*. New York: Basic Books, 1987.

———. *Faces at the Bottom of the Well: The Permanence of Racism*. New York: Basic Books, 1992.

Camus, Albert. *Resistance, Rebellion, and Death*. New York: Random House, 1988.

Carlisle, Claire. *Kierkegaard's Philosophy of Becoming: Movements and Positions.* Albany, NY: SUNY Press, 2005.
City of Richmond v. J.A. Croson Co., 488 U.S. 469 (1989).
Descartes, René. *Meditations on First Philosophy,* 3rd ed. Translated by Donald A. Cress. Indianapolis, IN: Hackett Publishing, 1993.
Fanon, Franz. *Black Skin, White Masks.* New York: Grove Press, 1967.
Farber, Daniel, and Suzanna Sherry. *Beyond all Reason: The Radical Assault on Truth in American Law.* London: Oxford University Press, 1997.
Holy Bible, Luke 10:29–30.
Kant, Immanuel. "Critique of Practical Reason," in *Practical Philosophy.* Translated by Mary Gregor. Cambridge: Cambridge University Press, 1996.
———. *The Metaphysics of Morals.* Translated by Mary Gregor. Cambridge: Cambridge University Press, 1996.
Kierkegaard, Søren. *Concluding Unscientific Postscript to the Philosophical Fragments.* Edited and translated by Howard V. and Edna H. Hong. Princeton, NJ: Princeton University Press, 1992.
———. *Philosophical Fragments.* Translated by Howard V. and Edna H. Hong. Princeton, NJ: Princeton University Press, 1985.
———. *The Point of View for My Work as an Author.* Edited and translated by Howard V. and Edna H. Hong. Princeton, NJ: Princeton University Press, 1998.
Leiter, Brian. "Rethinking Legal Realism: Toward a Naturalized Jurisprudence," in *Naturalizing Jurisprudence: Essays on American Legal Realism and Naturalism in Legal Philosophy* London: Oxford University Press, 2007.
Martensen, Hans Lassen. "Rationalism, Supernaturalism, and the principium exclusi medii," in *Mynster's "Rationalism, Supernaturalism" and the Debate about Mediation.* Edited and translated by Jon Stewart. Copenhagen, Denmark: Tusculanum Press, 2009.
Mills, Charles. *The Racial Contract.* Ithaca, NY: Cornell University Press, 1997.
———. "Rawls on Race / Race in Rawls," *Southern Journal of Philosophy* 47 (2009): 161–184.
Parents Involved in Community Schools v. Seattle School District, 551 U.S. 701, 728 (2007).
Peller, Gary. *Critical Race Consciousness: Reconsidering American Ideologies of Racial Justice.* New York: Routledge, 2016.
Plato, "Republic," in *Plato, Complete Works.* Edited by John M. Cooper. Translated by G.M.A. Grube. Indianapolis, IN: Hackett Publishing, 1997.
———. "Apology," in *Plato, Complete Works.* Edited by John M. Cooper. Translated by G.M.A. Grube. Indianapolis, IN: Hackett Publishing, 1997.
———. "Euthyphro," in *Plato, Complete Works.* Edited by John M. Cooper. Translated by G.M.A. Grube. Indianapolis, IN: Hackett Publishing, 1997.
Rawls, John. *Theory of Justice.* Cambridge, MA: Harvard University Press, 1971.

Russell, Bertrand. *The History of Western Philosophy* (New York: Simon and Shuster, 1972).
Shelby County, Alabama v. Holder, 570 U.S. 529 (2013).
Taylor, George H. "Racism as 'The Nation's Crucial Sin': Theology and Derrick Bell," *Michigan Journal of Race & Law* 9 (2004): 269–322.

Epilogue

Critical Race Theory as Paradox
The Propositional and the Poetic

TIMOTHY J. GOLDEN

"What if Truth itself should perish? Will it not be true that Truth has perished? . . . Truth can, then, in no way perish?"

—Augustine[1]

I.

As I have discussed throughout the final chapter, Bell's Racial Realism is paradoxical. Its claim of racism's permanence is at odds with its demand to resist it. Again, why resist the inevitable? This antagonism creates both philosophical and moral problems with attempts to "eliminate" racism. Such attempts often reject the permanence thesis of Racial Realism, either denying the existence of racism by claiming that it once existed but that now all is well, or that the best way to eliminate racism is to deny its existence altogether. Such approaches manifest a moral laziness that simply wants to "move on." And in "moving on," white supremacy is bolstered due to the blatant disregard of America's racist past—a past that, if eliminated, not only erases significant parts of African American history and identity but also relieves whites of accountability for centuries of injustice and oppression, in turn laying the groundwork for whites to demand that everyone is now "free" and "equal," despite American history, which plainly shows the opposite. Hence the danger of retreats into color-blind liberalism, which has such a robust conception of the individual that accountability for racism can easily be avoided by individual denials of racism with no regard for the centuries of oppression that generated institutional norms and practices that benefit whites and burden Blacks even today. Indeed it is liberalism and its abstract notions of "individual rights" and "equality" that allow many American institutions to maintain rather than eliminate racist practices, as I discuss below. Liberal political theory thus allows for the disregard of history in ways that perpetuate white dominance. Events in contemporary American history and politics illustrate this point. For example, during the early days of the Trump administration, a Jeff Sessions-led Justice Department attempted to nullify consent decrees for police reform that the Obama administration secured and instead decided that a top priority of the Department of Justice would be to eliminate race-based admissions practices at Ivy League colleges and universities. Anti-Black racism asserts itself here with a bizarre reshuffling of political priorities from a real need for police reform due to police killings of African Americans with no legal accountability to a pseudo problem of race-based university admissions. The latter is a "problem" simply because it fits into the false narrative that we must forget about race and racism because we are all "free" and "equal." Such a false narrative reared its head again during the final year of the Trump administration in 2020 when Trump signed an executive order banning the pedagogical use of Critical Race Theory in any federally funded diversity training program. So, bookending the racial politics of the Trump administration are events that present themselves to us as though they leaped off the pages of one of Bell's short stories—stories that illustrated, among other things, the permanence of racism in virtue of the futility of attempts to "eliminate" or to "get beyond" it. In other words, recent attempts to eliminate race from American social and political life show the strength of the permanence thesis of Bell's Racial Realism.

It is thus fitting to close this book with a final tribute to Bell in the form of a short story that illustrates what I am calling "Racism as Paradox." What I mean by this is that the recent and current events in which some whites see themselves as ridding the world of racism by ridding the world of Critical Race Theory bear a strong resemblance to a philosophical problem about the nature of truth, which is that the very attempt to deny the existence of truth is itself an affirmation of truth. In other words, attempts to eliminate truth are unsuccessful because they depend on truth in the first place, as Augustine indicates in this epilogue's epigraph. Similarly, I argue here that the very attempt to deny Critical Race Theory's permanence thesis as represented in the work of Bell is an affirmation of that very thesis. I attempt to make this point in two ways: propositionally and poetically (or, dare I say, analytically and continentally!). My aim here is to juxtapose *logos* and *mythos*, demonstrating that on either account, the permanence of racism in America, in both reason and story, is beyond the reach of our attempts to eliminate it. The upshot is that since it cannot be eliminated, we must, as Bell himself argued, commit our moral energies to resisting it. I now turn to the propositional, logical, and analytic articulation of Critical Race Theory as paradox.

II.

One may reconstruct the above epigraph from Augustine as making the following argument about the nature of truth:

(1) Truth does not exist.

(2) (1) is true.

Therefore, from (2), in contradiction to (1), truth exists.

Augustine makes this argument to show that the person who claims that truth does not exist undermines that very claim because in making that claim, one must accept that premise (1) itself is true. Premise (2) has a certain intuitive force and does not beg the question precisely because of the very nature of truth itself, which, the argument goes, is presupposed at (1). In denying truth, then, one puts oneself in the paradoxical position of assuming the existence of the truth—the very thing that one is claiming does not exist.

I argue here that a similar problem exists for the denier of racism:

(1) Racism does not exist in America.

(2) (1) is a racist statement.

Therefore, from (2) in contradiction to (1), racism exists.

As with Augustine's argument about the fallacy in the truth denier's claim, my argument aims to show that one who claims that racism does not exist undermines that very claim because the claim that racism does not exist in America is itself a racist statement (by "racist statement" I mean a statement that enables racism). This is because the very racism that is denied at (1) is essential for the claim about the nonexistence of racism, similar to how the truth that is denied is essential for the claim about the nonexistence of truth. Now, to avoid begging the question, one needs to cogently argue for the truth of (2), which I intend to do here. In support of (2), in addition to the above examples from recent history at the beginning and the end of the Trump administration, there is a sordid history of such denials in American history that have strengthened racism rather than eliminated it—a history of denials of racism extending back much further into American history than the Trump administration. Such historical denials, I argue, are representative of the claim made at (1) and thus demonstrate the truth of the claim made at (2). Consider the following.

Denying racism was especially prevalent during the Reconstruction era. Social theorist W.E.B. Du Bois, in his treatise *Black Reconstruction in America* discusses this problem in the final chapter titled "The Propaganda of History." Here, Du Bois chronicles the various falsehoods being told in "current textbooks." He discusses three such falsehoods: (1) All Negroes were ignorant, (2) All Negroes were lazy, dishonest, and extravagant, and (3) Negroes were responsible for bad government during Reconstruction.[2] These three claims were offered to show that the South did not have a race problem, but instead was justified in its hostility toward newly freed slaves, not because they were Black, but rather because they were ignorant, lazy, and incompetent to govern. But in this denial of having a race problem, the South resorted to racist stereotypes about Black people. This is akin to the denial of racism in the interest of perpetuating it: within each denial of a Southern hostility toward Blacks because of their race is an abiding hostility toward Blacks because of their race. Bolstering such sociological denials of racism in American history was a series of Supreme Court decisions in the post-Reconstruction era that ensured a status for African Americans as near to chattel slavery as possible for almost a century. As I pointed out in the introduction, beginning with the *Slaughterhouse Cases* and through *Plessy v. Ferguson*, the Supreme Court ensured that whatever rights newly freed slaves had were to provide unnecessary protection from the federal government (*Slaughterhouse Cases*) and a frightening vulnerability to southern state governments (*Civil Rights Cases* and *United States v. Cruikshank*). Protection from the federal government was unnecessary because the federal government was actively aiding newly freed slaves, whereas vulnerability to southern states was frightening because southern states were actively targeting newly freed slaves for social and political oppression (Black Codes, Jim Crow, disenfranchisement, and lynching). Again, the Supreme Court enabled this state of affairs, resulting in a ninety-five-year chasm between the ratification of the Fifteenth Amendment of the United States Constitution (which, on paper, granted suffrage to newly freed slaves) in 1870 and the Voting Rights Act of 1965, which gave the Fifteenth Amendment meaning. Add to this history the Supreme Court's contemporary Equal Protection jurisprudence, which, beginning with *Regents of the University of California v. Bakke* and continuing with *City of Richmond v. J.A. Croson Company*, renders even the most benign, remedial, race-based statutory classifications unconstitutional in the name of an extreme abstract, ahistorical notion of equality in the liberal political tradition, and African Americans face a world in which, according to Chief Justice John Roberts, "the only way to stop discriminating on the basis of race is to stop discriminating on the basis of race."[3] Such a world is racist, then, because of its denial of race and racism. So it is that with each denial of racism (or race itself), racism is affirmed, even as with each denial of truth, truth is affirmed.

Considering this sociological and legal history, I would conclude that (2) of the above argument has been sufficiently proven, and thus (1), which claims that racism does not exist is actually itself a racist statement. Therefore, (2) contradicts (1), meaning that racism exists. But more importantly than simply defeating the racism denier's claim, it shows that the claim itself depends on racism, which it purports to deny.

THE PARADOX OF RACISM AS POETIC

As a fitting tribute to Bell, I now turn to a fictional, narrative mode of expression to show how recent and current historical events embody the Augustinian insight that the affirmation of truth is found in its denial. The takeaway from this brief and hopefully insightful work of short fiction is the following principle, a correlate of the permanence thesis of Racial Realism, which I articulated in the previous section propositionally: *claims that racism does not exist are themselves racist because they ignore history in the interest of avoiding a just redress of historical wrongs done against*

Black people. So, claims that racism does not exist are ultimately racist in that they affirm the continued vitality of the thing they aim to eliminate. As I argued in the last chapter of this book, there is something valuable about the nature of indirect communication: it brings with it more than just a logical clarity; it brings with it a demand for moral action. There is a risk whenever a philosopher ventures away from *logos* to *mythos*. Plato did, after all, fail as a tragic poet. But, in the words of Nietzsche, I resolve to "live dangerously."[4] In what follows, however, like Bell, I weave factual events with fictional narrative to indicate how denials of racism are themselves racist.

The "Racism" that Racism Destroyed

Monday, October 25, 2020

"Gooooooooooooooooooood morning, Philly, and welcome to your news source for all things related to the Black community! I'm your host, Solomon Wells and today, we're talking about a recent move from the Trump administration to ban the teaching of Critical Race Theory in any federally funded diversity training program. To offer us some perspective on this issue is our weekly guest, Dr. Marshall Houston, critical race theorist, lawyer, and philosopher. Marshall joins us each week from Melbourne College, a small, Christian college in southwestern New Mexico, where he is professor of philosophy, legal studies program coordinator, and founder of the Barbara Jordan Institute for Law and Public Policy. For more than twenty years, he was a criminal defense attorney in Philadelphia and in the federal courts. Marshall, good morning!"

Marshall had to clear his throat to make sure he didn't sound as if he just woke up. He was, after all, two hours behind Philly time, so although it was 9 a.m. Philly time, it was just 7 a.m. for him. He did his best to warm up his voice before Solomon finished his introduction. "Good morning, Solomon! So good to be with you this morning. And good morning to your listening audience, too!" Solomon replied, "Thank you, Marshall, for joining us. The pleasure is mine." "Now," said Solomon, "let's get down to it. Marshall, can you tell us exactly what is going on with the Trump administration attempting to eliminate Critical Race Theory from federally funded diversity education programs?" As Marshall prepared to answer, Solomon continued, "First of all, Marshall, what is Critical Race

Theory? And second, why would President Trump want to eliminate any reference to it in federally funded diversity education programs?"

Marshall answered, "Well, Solomon, Critical Race Theory is a legal theory grounded in African American social and political thought that is centered on three basic principles. The first of these principles is that race and racism are not peripheral but are central to American life. The second principle is that of interest convergence, which is the notion that so-called civil rights "gains" only happen because the hopes and dreams of African Americans coincidentally merge with interests that whites see as more important. And third, there is a commitment to fictional narrative and storytelling, merged with historical events. From the first two principles, legal theorist Derrick Bell argues his thesis of Racial Realism, which is that racism is permanent. And through welding historical events into fictional narrative, Bell helps inspire his reader to resist racism in American social and political life. Critical Race Theory became a formal, academic legal theory because of the work of Bell and Richard Delgado, two law professors who saw the Supreme Court reversing certain gains in anti-discrimination law that prior generations of civil rights legal advocates like Thurgood Marshall, Constance Baker Motley, and Charles Hamilton Houston fought so hard to win. Bell argued, like Ralph Bunche before him, that African Americans should not put their hopes for liberation in civil rights litigation because courts resort too quickly to abstractions in ways that lead them to rule against the legal interests of African Americans and thus maintain rather than eradicate racial discrimination."

"Wow," said Solomon. And Marshall continued, "Well, Solomon, that's what Critical Race Theory is. Here's why I think the Trump administration would oppose it. The opposition to Critical Race Theory is an opposition that is based on an evasion of history. History has been around a lot longer than Critical Race Theory, so there is plenty of precedent for Trump's desire to avoid it." "How so?" asked Solomon. Marshall replied, "Well, the desire to avoid truth as it relates to the mistreatment of African Americans goes back at least as far as chattel slavery. After all, Frederick Douglass writes in his 1845 autobiography that slaves were encouraged to falsely claim that they were being treated well, which was part of a southern pro-slavery propaganda machine that sought to minimize the mistreatment of slaves in opposition to intense criticism from abolitionists.[5] And as if that weren't enough, the lies continued during reconstruction. W.E.B Du Bois writes about these lies in the final chapter of his important book *Black Reconstruction in America*. There, Du Bois points out that the southern propaganda machine resorted to stereotypical depictions of newly freed slaves as illiterate, ignorant, lazy, and criminal to justify Jim Crow and Black Codes. In denying that they were racist, southern whites resorted to racist tactics! So when Trump opposes the teaching of Critical Race Theory for federally funded diversity education programs, he essentially wants to deny certain aspects of American history and thus follows a long tradition of racism denial that is, itself, racist."

Solomon replied with an emphatic "Have mercy!" He continued, "So Marshall, it sounds like Critical Race Theory is being vilified because it forces whites to confront a history that they'd rather ignore." Marshall interjected, "Yes, that's right, Solomon."

Solomon spoke up again. "Marshall, I want to go back to something you said about how the courts decide cases, according to Critical Race Theory. You said that according to Bell and other Black legal theorists like Ralph Bunche, civil rights litigation is likely to disappoint the Black community because courts reason too abstractly. As we approach what many hope is the end of the Trump presidency, I'm reminded of an initiative of his at the beginning of his presidency in 2017 that makes Bell's point about the courts. It was a crazy and scary move by the Department of Justice. The *Washington Post* reported in the early days of the Trump presidency that then Attorney General Jeff Sessions sought to nullify consent decrees put in place by President Obama to facilitate police reform. What happened was that in the wake of the police killings of three unarmed Black suspects—Michael Brown in Ferguson, Missouri, in 2014, Laquan McDonald in Chicago, Illinois, also in 2014, and Freddie Gray in Baltimore, Maryland, in 2015—Eric Holder, the Attorney General of the United States, ordered a Department of Justice investigation into the practices of the Baltimore Police Department and it was discovered that numerous areas needed reform. So the Department of Justice sat down with Baltimore PD brass and came to an agreement that was binding on both sides as a consent decree in federal court. This decree would facilitate Department of Justice oversight of the Baltimore PD as it implements the DOJ recommendations. Jeff Sessions actually sought to get the consent decrees overturned in federal court, while also going to court to bring an end to race-based college admissions at Ivy League universities. It's almost as if the courtroom is fertile ground for the oppression of African Americans because, as you said, courts will always ignore history, be it the recent history of police killings of Black people or the more longstanding history that justifies race-based college admissions."

"Well, Solomon," Marshall replied, "That's exactly the point. After all, the first problem with the consent decrees is the natural result of the 'Blue Lives Matter' campaign that began not long after the shooting death of Michael Brown in Ferguson, Missouri." Solomon interrupted: "Can you elaborate on that for us, Marshall?" "Sure," Marshall replied. "As is often the case when Black people assert their humanity in resistance to dehumanizing, racist tactics like police shootings of unarmed Black people, white people find a way to shift the discussion away from race to some other topic that's, frankly, well, irrelevant to the oppression of Black people. And all the while, they claim that the instance of injustice complained of has nothing to do with the specifics of race or America's racist past, but instead has more to do with some broader, more general and abstract issue that prevents us from seeing the harm that the injustice has done to Black people. In this way, white people can deny that the situation is racist and in that very denial, perpetuate the racism that they deny." Solomon inquired, "Explain that further, can you, Marshall?" Marshall said, "Sure, Solomon. It's sort of like when someone says 'The truth does not exist.' Well, in order for this statement to be accurate, it must be true—the very thing that it denies. So truth is a necessary presupposition that contradicts its denial. In other words, truth cannot be denied without being assumed. The same goes for Critical Race Theory. Attempts to eliminate Critical Race Theory from our academic, social, and political lives actually end up strengthening its thesis about the permanence of racism in that each attempt to eliminate it demonstrates an effort to erase a history that keeps us vigilant in the fight against racism. So, just as any attempt to eliminate the truth must assume its existence, any attempt to eliminate Critical Race Theory ends up strengthening the central claim of Critical Race Theory itself. This sort of argument is doomed to failure. So in this situation, after the failure to indict Officer Darren Wilson of the Ferguson Police Department for the shooting death of Michael Brown, Black people were understandably tired of the lack of accountability. Remember that Michael Brown's death occurred after the killing of Eric Garner in New York, who, just about a month earlier, repeatedly exclaimed that he couldn't breathe some eleven times while the police choked him on camera. And, just two days before the grand jury in Ferguson, Missouri, failed to indict Wilson, Cleveland Police shot and killed twelve-year-old Tamir Rice, who was playing with a toy gun in a park in broad daylight. These three deaths were—and are—a source of great trauma for Black people, and the ongoing lack of accountability led them to believe, justifiably so, that Black life didn't matter. The deaths of these three unarmed Black men in 2014 aggravated frustrations in the Black community that began two years earlier with George Zimmerman's 2013 acquittal for the 2012 vigilante killing of Trayvon Martin, an unarmed Black teen. Hence the slogan, 'Black Lives Matter,' which began as a hashtag '#BlackLivesMatter' shortly after the Trayvon Martin killing and became a rallying cry for justice that began in 2013, and that, by the end of 2014, became a full-fledged social and political movement."

Solomon politely interrupted: "Yeah, Marshall, those deaths really hurt, man. I think we all felt those. And what hurt even more was the lack of accountability." "Indeed," Marshall replied. Marshall continued: "And then, of course, it worsened with the deaths of Sandra Bland while in police custody in Texas, and the killing of Breonna Taylor while at home sleeping in Louisville, Kentucky, and Atatiana Jefferson, who was at home playing video games with her nephew, also in Texas. It seems that the old claims of social conservatives for Black people to 'pull up their pants' and 'be respectful of the police' simply don't apply because in so many of these situations, especially Breonna Taylor and Atatiana Jefferson, Black people are involved in ordinary, everyday circumstances in the privacy of their own homes. Not to mention Botham Jean, who was shot and killed while sitting at home eating a bowl of ice cream. It's really scary."

"Yes, Marshall, it really is scary," Solomon said. "Well, Marshall, where do we go from here?"

This question was always a difficult question for Marshall, but he knew it was an opportunity to leave Solomon's listening audience with some sense of hope. But it couldn't be a pie-in-the-sky hope; it had to be a sobering sense of fortitude and endurance that would keep people vigilant in the struggle against racism. Marshall seized the opportunity: "Good question, Solomon. Like Bell, I think we must realize that our hope is not in winning the fight against racism but rather in never ceasing to resist it. Our hope thus lies not in overcoming racism but instead in not allowing racism to overcome us—to resolve to resist racism at every turn. The courts may not bring us liberation, but we must still fight within the legal system as one weapon among many. In addition, protest movements with strong, identifiable leadership and clear public policy objectives; voting in local, state, and national elections; serving in community groups; and serving on juries are among the many tools we have at our disposal to keep fighting. Not necessarily fighting to win but fighting to stay in the fight. The day we stop fighting is the day we've lost."

"Wow, Marshall, that's encouraging, brother. Thank you for being on our show today. Talk with you next week."

"Thank you, Solomon," said Marshall.

Marshall hung up his phone and pensively stared at the portrait of Thurgood Marshall hanging on the wall of his home office. Marshall surrounded himself with portraits of great Black men and women, inspiring biblical messages and a sublime icon of justice. To his left was Thurgood Marshall; to his right, Paul Robeson; behind him was Charles Hamilton Houston; and in front of him were portraits of Ida B. Wells, Barbara Jordan, Shirley Chisolm, and a statue of Themis, the Greek goddess of justice, blindfolded and holding scales. Also behind him was a lithograph of a Bible passage from Deuteronomy chapter 16, verse 20, that read in Hebrew and English, "Justice, justice shalt thou pursue." Marshall hoped that being amidst images of such great Black people and such a strong moral imperative would inspire him. And it did, for Marshall panned the walls of his home office after he hung up the phone at the end of his weekly radio commentary with Solomon, looked down at his desk, and saw an image of a young Frederick Douglass on the cover of his recently published book on Douglass and Christian theology. Inspired by the spirit of those forbears who hung on his walls and their pursuit of justice, and that icon directly in front of him which represented a principle of justice that was ever so elusive, Marshall then said to himself, "Fighting to stay in the fight. Yup. I need that strength today and always. God help me." Marshall had a long day ahead of him.

Notes

1. Augustine, *Soliloquies*, trans. Rose Elizabeth Cleveland (Boston: Little, Brown, and Company, 1910), 55.

2. W.E.B. Du Bois, *Black Reconstruction in America* (New York: Oxford University Press, 2007), 582–583.

3. See *Parents Involved in Community Schools v. Seattle School District No. 1*, 551 U.S. 701 (2007).

4. Friedrich Nietzsche, *The Gay Science*, trans. Walter Kaufmann (New York: Vintage Books), 237.

5. Frederick Douglass, *Narrative of the Life of Frederick Douglass* (Mineola, NY: Dover, 1999), 11, 12.

Works Cited

Augustine, *Soliloquies*. Translated by Rose Elizabeth Cleveland. Boston: Little, Brown, and Company, 1910.
City of Richmond v. J.A. Croson Company, 488 U.S. 469 (1989).
Civil Rights Cases, 109 U.S. 3 (1883).
Douglass, Frederick. *Narrative of the Life of Frederick Douglass*. Mineola, NY: Dover, 1999.
Du Bois, W.E.B. *Black Reconstruction in America*. New York: Oxford University Press, 2007.
Nietzsche, Friedrich. *The Gay Science*. Translated by Walter Kaufmann. New York: Vintage Books.
Parents Involved in Community Schools v. Seattle School District No. 1, 551 U.S. 701 (2007).
Plessy v. Ferguson, 163 U.S. 537 (1896).
Regents of the University of California v. Bakke, 438 U.S. 265 (1978).
Slaughterhouse Cases, 83 U.S. 36 (1873).
United States v. Cruikshank, 92 U.S. 542 (1876).

Contributors

Tommy J. Curry (Foreword) is Professor of Philosophy at the University of Edinburgh. He holds a Personal Chair in Africana Philosophy and Black Male Studies. He is the author of *The Man-Not: Race, Class, Genre, and the Dilemma of Black Manhood* (Temple University Press, 2017), which won the 2018 American Book Award, and *Another white Man's Burden: Josiah Royce's Quest for a Philosophy of white Racial Empire* (SUNY Press, 2018), which won the 2020 The Josiah Royce Prize in American Idealist Thought. He is also the editor of *The Philosophical Treatise of William H. Ferris: Selected Readings from The African Abroad, or his Evolution in Western Civilization* (Rowman and Littlefield, 2016). His research interests are 19th Century Ethnology, Critical Race Theory, Anti-Colonial Theory, and Black Male Studies.

Keri Day is Associate Professor of Constructive Theology and African American religion at Princeton Theological Seminary. She works in womanist and feminist theologies, social critical theory, cultural studies, economics, and Afro-Pentecostalism. Her books are *Unfinished Business: Black Women, The Black Church, and the Struggle to Thrive in America*, (Orbis Books, 2012), *Religious Resistance to Neoliberalism: Womanist and Black Feminist Perspectives*, (Palgrave Macmillan, 2016), *Notes of a Native Daughter: Testifying in Theological Education* (Eerdmans, 2021), and *Azusa Reimagined: A Radical Vision of Religious and Democratic Belonging* (Stanford University Press, 2022).

Timothy J. Golden (Editor) is Professor of Philosophy and director of the Legal Studies/Pre-Law Program at Walla Walla University. He works in

African American Philosophy, Jurisprudence, Nineteenth and Twentieth century European philosophy, and philosophical theology. His books are *Frederick Douglass and the Philosophy of Religion: An Interpretation of Narrative, Art, and the Political* (Lexington Books, 2022), and *Reason's Dilemma: Subjectivity, Transcendence, and the Problem of Ontotheology* (Palgrave MacMillan, 2022). His book chapters include "German Chocolate: Why Philosophy is so Personal," in *Philosophy and the Mixed-Race Experience*, ed. Tina Fernandes Botts, (Lexington Books, 2016), and "Theory, Epistemic Failure, and the Problem of (Hue)Man Suffering: A Phenomenology of Breathlessness," in *Black Men from Behind the Veil: Ontological Interrogations*, ed. George Yancy, (Lexington Books, 2022).

Bill E. Lawson is Emeritus Professor of Philosophy from the University of Memphis. His work is in African American philosophy from 1619 to the present and includes *Pictures and Power*, co-edited with Celeste Bernier (Liverpool University Press, 2018), "Douglass among the Romantics," *The Cambridge Companion to Frederick Douglass* (Cambridge University Press, 2009), *Frederick Douglass: A Critical Reader*, co-edited with Frank M. Kirkland, (Blackwell, 1999), and the co-authored book with Howard McGary, *Between Slavery and Freedom: Philosophy and American Slavery*, (Indiana University Press, 1992). He was a 2011-12 Fulbright Fellow at the University of Liverpool, Liverpool, UK. He has also testified before a United States Congressional Subcommittee on the issue of welfare reform.

Vincent Lloyd is Associate Professor of Theology and Religious Studies at Villanova University, where he also directs the Africana Studies Program. He works in political theology and his books include *Law and Transcendence: On the Unfinished Project of Gillian Rose* (Palgrave Macmillan, 2009), *The Problem with Grace: Reconfiguring Political Theology* (Stanford University Press, 2011), *Black Natural Law*, (Oxford University Press, 2016), and the co-authored *Break Every Yoke: Religion, Justice, and the Abolition of Prisons* (Oxford University Press, 2020).

Desirée H. Melton is a philosophy professor and associate chair of liberal arts at Savannah College of Art & Design. She specializes in critical philosophy of race, Black feminist thought and social and political philosophy. An academic and public philosopher, her work has appeared in scholarly books and in diverse publications such as *The Black Scholar*, *The Washington Post*, *Aeon*, and *Psyche*.

Audra Lyn Savage is Assistant Professor of Law at Wake Forest University School of Law and a McDonald Distinguished Fellow with the Center for the Study of Law and Religion, Emory University School of Law. Her work examines race and law by engaging several different fields of study, including critical race theory, business law, and law and religion. Her publications include "Aunt Jemima's Resignation Letter," *Columbia Law Review Forum* (2021); "The Religion of Race: The Supreme Court as Priests of Racial Politics," *Utah Law Review* (2021); and "Turning the Other Cheek: The Persecution of the Christian Minority," *Florida Journal of International Law* (2014).

George Taylor is Emeritus Professor of Law at the University of Pittsburgh School of Law. He concentrates his research and writing on evaluating the methods by which judges and lawyers interpret statutory and constitutional law and writes particularly on hermeneutics and legal hermeneutics. His publications include: "Ricoeur, Narrative, and Legal Indeterminacy," in *Reading Ricoeur Through Law* (Lexington Books, 2022), "Addressing Contemporary Challenges to Hermeneutics," Études *Ricoeuriennes/Ricoeur Studies* (2021), "Reenvisioning Justice," in *The Ambiguity of Justice: New Perspectives on Paul Ricoeur's Approach to Justice* (Brill 2020), "No Reasonable Person" (co-author), in *Justice Scalia: Rhetoric and the Rule of Law* (2019), "The Practice of Hermeneutics: The Legal Text and Beyond," *Budhi: Journal of Culture and Ideas* (2016), "The Object of Diversity," *University of Pittsburgh Law Review* (2015), "Derrick Bell's Narratives as Parables," *New York University Review of Law and Social Change* (2007), and "Racism as 'the Nation's Crucial Sin': Theology and Derrick Bell," *Michigan Journal of Race and* Law (2004), republished in The Derrick Bell Reader (2005).

Index

abortion, 147, 163–64. See also *Roe v. Wade*
Abrams, Kathryn, 148
abstraction, 94–95, 103–4, 114–15, 217–19, 223–26, 229–31, 233–35, 237, 245, 259
ACA (Affordable Care Act), 92, 152
Ackerman, Bruce, 153
adjudication, 86, 88–92, 95–97, 100–102, 106, 110n1, 113n48, 114n74, 132, 151, 224
affirmative action, 93, 203; Douglass on, 58
Affordable Care Act. *See* ACA
Africa, 56, 134; ancestry, 61, 64, 105
Africans, 58; enslaved, 75, 101
"The Afrolantica Awakening," 233, 240–43
AIRFA (American Indian Religious Freedom Act), 127–28
Alexander, Michelle, 13, 24
Allen, Anita, 181
ALR (American Legal Realism): and adjudication, 106; and Legal Formalism, 87–88, 90; as political movement, 113n38; purpose of, 86; and Racial Realism, 89, 95, 102
An American Dilemma, 68–69

American Indian Religious Freedom Act (AIRFA). *See* AIRFA (American Indian Religious Freedom Act)
Amish, 128
Anderson, Victor, 208
And We Are Not Saved, 201
anomaly thesis, 69
apocalyptic eschatology, 198
Aristotelian logic, 217, 220
Atwood, Margaret, 108, 243
Augustine, Saint, 255–57

Baker-Fletcher, Karen, 198–99
Bakke v. Board of Regents of the University of California, 89, 93–94, 99–100, 102, 108, 188n20, 223–24, 233, 257
Balkin, Jack M., 104–5
Bell: Derrick, and abstraction, 219, 224, 229, 235; Derrick, and ALR, 87, 113n38; Derrick, on *Bakke*, 93, 101; Derrick, and Biona MacDonald, 22, 107, 150, 227–29; Derrick, on *Brown*, 12, 68, 99–100, 133, 164, 239; Derrick, on Camus, 44; Derrick, on Christianity, 7, 31; Derrick, on civil rights movement, 71; Derrick, and CLS, 111n10; Derrick, on color-

269

Bell *(continued)*
blindness, 236; Derrick, on *Coppage v. Kansas*, 91; Derrick, critique of liberalism, 15; Derrick, on defiance, 207; Derrick, on *Dred Scott*, 8; Derrick, on education, 29, 40–41, 202; Derrick, on empiricism, 98–99; Derrick, on eradication, 205; Derrick, on faith, 42; Derrick, on Fanon, 226; Derrick, on federalism, 13; Derrick, and the Franklins, 179–80; Derrick, and gender injustice, 206; Derrick, and indirect communication, 219, 230–31, 236–37, 239; Derrick, and interest convergence, 102, 133; Derrick, and Jewel Hairston Bell, 179; Derrick, and juridical vs. theological hope, 147, 149; Derrick, on law's dependence on racism, 5; Derrick, and Legal Formalism, 88; Derrick, on Legal Formalism, 97; Derrick, on marriage, 179–80; Derrick, on Myrdal, 20, 68–71; Derrick, on Obama, 2; Derrick, and paradox, 219, 223, 225, 227–28, 247n18; Derrick, and Patricia Williams, 31; Derrick, and permanence of racism, 103, 177, 204, 207, 217, 226; Derrick, on *Plessy v. Ferguson*, 65–67, 99–100; Derrick, on racial symbols, 21, 146; Derrick, on racist faith, 33–34; Derrick, and religion, 30–32, 35; Derrick, resistance thesis, 195, 241–42; Derrick, on the role of law, 37–41; Derrick, and spiritual reformation, 36; Derrick, on statistical data, 110; Derrick, on struggle, 72; Derrick, on subordination, 171, 184; Derrick, themes of Racial Realism, 111n17, 112n17; Derrick, on theological hope, 148, 150–51; Derrick, on Thurgood Marshall, 108; Derrick, and use of fiction, 20, 216, 218, 231–33, 240, 242–43, 245, 248n53, 258; Derrick, and womanism, 200–201; Jewel Hairston, 36, 179

Bennett, Lerone, 65
Berry, Mary Frances, 11–14
"Beyond Despair," 145, 151
Biden, Joe, 24n20
Black, Galen, 119–20
black codes, 4, 6–7, 22, 104, 257, 260
Blackmun, Harry, 163–64
Black Reconstruction in America, 256, 260
Black Resistance White Law, 11, 13
Black Skin White Masks, 226, 246
black subjectivity, 88, 103, 105
Bland, Sandra, 262
Bowen v. Roy, 128
Bowers v. Hardwick, 147
Boxill, Bernard, 72
Braunfeld v. Brown, 130
Brown, John, 234, 237
Brown, Michael, 209, 261
Brown, Oliver, 178
Brown v. Board of Education, 37, 42, 89, 95, 100, 102, 108, 146–47, 152–53, 160–61, 163, 235, 239; Bell on, 37–41, 68, 99, 133; as failure, 164; and juridical hope, 152, 159; and *Plessy*, 154–55; and theological hope, 148; and Warren, 156–58
Brown v. Board of Education, Brown II, 68
Brown vs. Board of Education, as rhetorical trope, 147
Bunche, Ralph, 6, 12–13, 102, 106, 260
Bush v. Gore, 152

Camus, Albert, 44, 226
Cantwell v. Connecticut, 126
Cardozo, Benjamin, 90
Cartesian thought, 96, 217
Catholicism, 121, 129, 134; and slavery, 32

children, as rhetorical figures, 147, 153, 156, 158–59, 161–62
Christianity, 34–35, 119–20, 217–20, 222, 229, 245, 246n17, 263; and conversion of slaves, 125; Derrick Bell on, 7, 31–32; preferential treatment for, 121, 124, 129; and racism, 30, 32–33, 48n47; and slavery, 32; theology, 153; and womanism, 209
Church of the Lukumi Babalu Aye Inc. v. City of Hialeah, 132–37
citizenship, 56–57, 60–61, 64, 67, 71, 73; and slaves, 122
City of Richmond v. J.A. Croson Co., 89, 233, 257
civil rights, 5, 8, 11–12, 61, 67, 69, 218, 223, 235, 238, 259
Civil Rights Act (1875), 7
Civil Rights Act (1964), 7, 9, 178, 217
Civil Rights Cases, 6–8, 223, 257
civil rights movement, 32, 75, 201, 223; Bell on, 71; Biona MacDonald, 107–8; strategies, 90, 201, 204–5
Civil War, 46, 55–56, 61, 75; and Reunification, 57
Climacus, Johannes, 220–23, 227–28, 230, 246n17. See also Søren Kierkegaard
CLS (Critical Legal Studies), 45n11, 87, 94, 102, 104
Cold War, effect on legislation, 136, 178. See also Communism
Coleman, Monica, 198
Colfax massacre, 7
color-blindness, 103, 218, 223–24, 229, 233, 236, 245, 247n17
The Color Purple, 198
Communism, 133, 136, 178. See also Cold War
Concluding Unscientific Postscript, 230, 246n17
Constitution: and citizenship, 73; Commerce clause, 92; drafting, 121–22; Fifteenth Amendment, 6; First Amendment, 119, 127, 132; ratification, 124; and religion, 124, 126, 137, 138n16; and segregation, 100; and slavery, 56, 61, 122–24, 248n53; and Three-Fifths Compromise, 122
Constitutional Convention, 11, 121–23, 248n53
Cooper, Anna Julia, 75, 199
Coppage v. Kansas, 91–93, 102
criminalization, 62–63
criminal justice, 13–14
Critical Legal Studies. See CLS
Critical Race Theory (CRT), 30, 104, 165, 196, 232, 258, 261; bans on teaching, 254, 259–60; and Bell, 111n12; Curry on, 105–6; and permanence of racism, 255; and religion, 31, 121
cultralogics, 105–6
Curry, Tommy J., 103–6

Davis, Angela, 211n4
defiance, 100, 107, 150, 195–96, 201, 207–8; and Christianity, 209–10; and womanism, 209–10
Delany, Martin, 241
Delgado, Richard, 23, 259
Department of Justice, founding purpose, 13
Descartes, René, 216–17, 245
desegregation, 201; schools, 106
disparity: education, 173, 175–76; employment, 173; financial, 174; health, 172–74; housing, 175–76
"Divining a Racial Realism Theory," 233–38
Douglas, William O., 160–62
Douglass, Frederick, 58, 73, 114n80, 115n84, 241, 259
Dred Scott v. Sandford, 8, 61, 89, 153, 178

Du Bois, W.E.B., 11, 20, 67–68, 89, 106, 259; on education, 37; on federalism, 11–12; on Reconstruction, 256, 260; on slavery, 11–12
Due Process clause, 162

Edelman, Lee, 159
education: Bell on, 40–41, 101, 202; and *Brown*, 155; disparity, 173, 175–76; Du Bois on, 37; funding, 41; and integration, 100; King on, 71; and segregation, 37, 154; as solution to racism, 202–3; Warren on, 156
Electoral College, creation of, 123
Emancipation Proclamation, 2, 178; Douglass on, 58
empiricism, 97–99
Employment Div. Dept. of Human Resources of Ore. v. Smith, 120, 126–29, 132, 134–35
Enforcement Act of 1870, 7
Enlightenment, 34, 42
Equal Protection jurisprudence, 88, 90, 97, 154, 161
eradication, 195–96, 200–201, 207–8
eschatology: apocalyptic, 198; realized, 198–200, 211n6
Ethical Ambition, 30, 32, 179
Euthyphro Dilemma, 216
Evers, Medgar, 9
Ewing, Quincy, 58–59

Faces at the Bottom of the Well, 89, 94, 145, 151, 201–3, 206, 225, 234
faith: originating, 38–39; racist, 29, 34, 42; and religious structure, 34–36; and spirit, 35–36
Fanon, Frantz, 225–26
federalism, 6, 10; Berry on, 11–12; and criminal justice, 13–14; Du Bois on, 11; as philosophical tool, 12; significance of, 11; and white supremacy, 12–13
fiction: as critique of abstraction, 218; and legal tradition, 232–33; and narrative, 231, 233, 240
Fifteenth Amendment, 6, 10, 14, 56, 247n31, 257
First Amendment, 119, 121, 124–27, 130–31, 134, 137, 138n23
folk psychology, 88, 95, 100–102, 106, 113n38, 114n74
Foner, Eric, 7
forced sterilization, 160–63. See also *Skinner v. Oklahoma*
Fortune, T. Thomas, 8, 23
Fourteenth Amendment, 6–7, 9, 56, 65–66, 91–93, 126, 131–32, 154–55, 157, 161, 247n31; Due Process clause, 91; "Liberty" clause, 92
Frankfurter, Felix, 157
Franklin: Aurelia Whittington, 179–80; John Hope, 66, 179–80
Frazee v. Illinois Department of Employment Security, 129
free exercise rights, 120, 125–27, 129–32, 134–35
fugitive slave clauses, 123

Gallagher v. Crown Kosher Super Market of Massachusetts, 130, 135
Garner, Eric, 261
Garvey, Marcus, 241
gender injustice, 205–6
gerrymandering, 62
Ginsburg, Ruth Bader, 9
Goldman v. Weinberger, 130, 135
Goodloe, H.H., 57
Gordon, Lewis, 115n84
Gospel Choirs, 30, 45, 206
Gray, Freddie, 260
Grutter v. Bollinger, 89, 102

Hackney, James Jr., 68
The Handmaid's Tale, 108
Haufneinsis, Vigilius, 220
Hayes, Rutherford B., 56
Hayes-Tilden Compromise, 56, 60–61
health disparities, 172
Hegel, Friedrich, 220, 229
heuristics, 43
Higginbotham, A. Leon, 60, 75–76
Hobbie v. Unemployment Appeals Commission of Florida, 129
Hochschild, Jennifer, 69
Holder, Eric, 260
Hollandsworth, James G., 56–57
Hollow Hope, 164
homophobia, 162–63
hooks, bell, 211n5
Houston, Charles Hamilton, 244, 259

indirect communication, 113, 215–16, 218–19, 221, 230–31, 236–37, 239, 258
individual racism, 180
inferiority. *See* racial inferiority
institutional racism, 13, 171, 180–81, 185, 187
integration, 37, 39–41, 43, 147, 157, 227–28; schools, 68, 99–100
integrationism, 226–27
interest convergence: and *Brown*, 12, 38, 102, 146, 178; and Communism, 133, 136; and CRT, 259; and *Hialeah*, 135–37; and minority groups, 133–34; and Obama election, 4; and organizing, 44; and racial bonding, 69; and racial realism, 202–3; and racial symbols, 2, 217–18; and religion, 132; and white privilege, 41, 43
interracial marriage, 154, 180–81
intersectionality, 197, 206
intersectional oppression, 197–98

Iredell, James, 123–24
Islam, 45, 125, 131. *See also* Muslims

Jean, Botham, 262
Jefferson, Atatiana, 262
Jehovah's Witnesses, 131
Jews, 46, 120, 127, 129–30, 132, 135–36, 220. *See also* Judaism
Jim Crow laws, 6–7, 9, 13, 22, 24n20, 55, 61, 64, 177–78, 181, 257, 260
John Lewis Voting Rights Advancement Act, 14
Johnson, Lyndon B., 9
Judaism, 125, 129–30, 134–35, 149, 220. *See also* Jews
judicial hope. *See* juridical hope
juridical hope, 152, 163; vs. theological hope, 146–47
"Justice Marshall and the Handmaid's Tale," 233, 243–45

Kant, Immanuel, 228
Karst, Kenneth, 158–59
Kazantzakis, Nikos, 34–35
Kelsey, George, 32–33
Kennedy, Anthony, 162
Keren, Hila, 148
Kierkegaard, Søren: and abstraction, 218–19, 225, 229; and indirect communication, 218–19, 230–31, 237; and paradox, 219–23; and subjectivity, 218; and use of fiction, 217, 231, 233, 240, 245; use of pseudonyms, 220–21
King, Martin Luther Jr., 3, 32, 71, 74, 217
King v. Burwell, 92
Klarman, Michael, 155, 157, 167n39
Krieger, Nancy, 174

labor unions, 91

Langdell, Christopher Columbus, 90, 92; and adjudication, 91; and Legal Formalism, 110
The Last Temptation of Christ, 34–35
Lawrence v. Texas, 147, 162, 168n45
Leahy, Patrick, 14
learner's paradox, 221–22
Legal Formalism: and abstraction, 104, 224; and ALR, 90; Bell's critique of, 87–88; definition, 90–92
legal indeterminacy, 86
legal subject, 103–5
Leiter, Brian, 90–91, 110n1, 112n37; and ALR, 106, 110n1, 113n48; and CLS, 86–87, 111n10; and CRT, 111n12; on folk psychology, 100–102; on folk theories of adjudication, 97; on *Knight*, 92; on legal indeterminacy, 86; on naturalized jurisprudence, 95; on Quine, 86–87; on Racial Realism, 96
liberalism, Bell's critique of, 15
Lloyd, Vincent, 208, 210
Logan, Rayford, 55, 57, 61
Lorde, Audre, 211n5
Loving v. Virginia, 180
lynching, 7, 9, 22, 61, 71, 257
Lyng v. Northwest Indian Cemetery Protective Association, 128

MacDonald, Biona, 22, 88, 107–9, 150–51, 228–29
Marietta, Morgan, 72–73
Marshall, Thurgood, 108, 244–45, 250n111; on resistance, 109
Martensen, Hans, 220
Martin, Trayvon, 262
mass incarceration, 9, 13, 22, 24n20, 63, 183
McCain, John, 2–3
McClintock, Anne, 211n3
McWhorter, Ladelle, 60

Meditations on First Philosophy, 216
Meno, 221
Miller, Samuel Freeman, 7
Mills, Charles, 104, 114n79, 224
Mormons, 131, 135, 138n23
motherhood, as legal symbol, 163–64
Muhammad, Khalil Gibran, 62–63
multipositionality, 196–98
Muslims, 120, 127, 130–32, 136. *See also* Islam
Mynster, Jakob Peter, 219–20
Myrdal, Gunnar, 56, 68–69

NAACP, Legal Defense Fund, 37, 223
National Federation of Independent Business v. Sebelius, 152
Native Americans: church, 119, 128; and religion, 120, 125, 127–29, 132, 135–36
Naturalizing Jurisprudence, 85–87
"Negro Problem": Douglass on, 58; Du Bois on, 68; Ewing on, 58–59; Goodloe on, 57; Myrdal on, 69; origin of phrase, 56; and permanence of racism, 55; and *Plessy*, 65–67; vs. race problem, 58; and segregation, 61–62, 70; and views on inferiority, 56–57, 59–60
The Negro Problem Solved, 56
Noonan, John T. Jr., 46n18
Nunn, Kenneth, 103, 105

Obama, Barack, 2–5, 159, 230, 254
O'Connor, Sandra Day, 244–45
O'Lone v. Estate of Shabazz, 130–31
originating faith, 38–39
otherization, 63, 65

paradox: in Bell and Kierkegaard, 35, 149, 200, 204, 218–23, 225, 227–30, 233, 245, 255; learner's, 221–22
Peller, Gary, 226–27

permanence of racism: and civil rights movement, 204; and CRT, 261; as inferiority problem, 71, 74; and integrationism, 226; and the "Negro Problem," 55; and objectivity, 227; and Racial Realism, 87, 103, 106, 110, 149, 201, 207, 228; reasons for, 14; and resistance, 242
Philadelphia Convention. *See* Constitutional Convention
Philosophical Fragments, 220–22, 227
Plato, 216–17, 221, 245, 258
Plessy v. Ferguson, 9, 39–40, 56, 65–66, 89, 178, 256; Bell on, 99–100; and *Brown*, 154–55; as rhetorical trope, 147
polygamy, 131, 140n53
Poole, Mary, 63
porno-tropics, 211n3
post-racialism, 4–5, 41, 223
prison populations, 9, 13, 22, 63, 183

Quine, Willard Van Orman, 86–88; and epistemology, 106, 113n48; on first philosophy, 95; and logical positivism, 110n1; on naturalized epistemology, 96

race: as biological construct, 60–62; and crime statistics, 63; and criminalization, 62–63; and disparity, 172; language of, 64
Race, Racism, and American Law, 1, 4, 6
racial bonding, 69
racial equality, 3, 6, 38–39, 41, 132–33, 172, 177, 179, 183, 185, 187, 233–34, 244, 250n111
racial identity, 103, 105
racial inferiority, 59, 62–63, 65, 70, 74, 76; and *Brown*, 59, 61–62, 71, 73, 75, 186; as legal concept, 61; and segregation, 67

racialized subjects, 105, 196–97
racial justice, 30, 39, 42, 44, 115n80, 146, 171–72, 175, 177–78, 183, 185, 201–2, 205–7
"The Racial Preference Licensing Act," 233, 238–40
"Racial Realism," 90, 94, 97, 103, 106, 228
Racial Realism (RR): and ALR, 87, 89–90, 95, 102; and black subjectivity, 103–6; and *Brown*, 39; and despair, 172; and education, 41; and eradication, 201; and fictional narrative, 233; and interest convergence, 202–3; and interracial relationships, 172, 181–87; and jurisprudence, 88–89, 110, 147; and Legal Realism, 177; limits of, 205; and the "Negro Problem," 55; and paradox, 223, 225, 229, 253; and permanence, 103, 254, 257, 259; and pessimism, 179; as pragmatic approach, 172; and racist faith, 43; and religious freedom, 132; and womanism, 196, 200–201, 207
racial-religious minority: and basis of oppression, 121; definition, 127; vs. racial minority, 120–21
racial stratification, 63
racial subjectivity, 60
racial symbol, 2, 4, 21, 23, 24n20, 146, 217
racism: and Christianity, 32–33; and defiance, 208; denial of, 257; and education, 202–3; as faith, 29, 32–34, 42; individual, 180; institutional, 13, 171, 180–81, 185, 187; and integrationism, 226; permanence, 14, 227; religious basis for, 33; and science, 62; structural, 99, 195–97, 200, 202, 205–8, 226; systemic, 172, 186

Racism and the Christian Understanding of Man, 32
"Racism's Secret Bonding," 202
racist faith, 29, 34, 40–42
Ragland, Byron, 5
Rawls, John, 104, 114n80, 224
Read, Hollis, 56
Reagan, Ronald, 23n20, 24n20
realized eschatology, 198–200, 211n6
Reconstruction, 4, 7, 9, 55, 61, 69, 256, 259
Reconstruction Amendments, 8–10, 22
religious freedom, 119–20, 124–26, 135, 137, 138n16
Religious Freedom Restoration Act (RFRA). *See* RFRA (Religious Freedom Restoration Act)
religious minorities, 131–32; definition, 121
Replacement Naturalism, 96, 110
Republic, 216
resistance, 106–8, 110, 151, 172, 183, 195–96, 200–201; Marshall on, 109
resistance thesis, 21, 24, 103, 240–42, 250
reunification, 57, 61
Reynolds v. U.S., 126
RFRA (Religious Freedom Restoration Act), 127, 135–37
Roberts, John, 9–11, 92, 224–25, 257
Robeson, Paul, 106
Roe v. Wade, 147, 152, 163–64, 167n40
Roithmayr, Daria, 175
Rosenberg, Gerald, 164

Santeria, 132, 134–37
Schmitt, John, 173
secular hope, 148, 153, 159
segregation: and *Brown*, 39–40, 62, 100, 133, 163–64, 178; and children, 155; Du Bois on, 37; Frankfurter on, 157; justification for, 60; and *Plessy*, 65–67; and Reconstruction, 61; schools, 37, 99, 177–78; Warren on, 156, 158

Semple, Jesse B., 2, 206
"separate but equal" doctrine, 9, 37, 39–40, 66, 95, 99, 177
Sessions, Jeff, 254, 260
Shange, Ntozake, 206
Shelby County Alabama v. Holder, 9, 13–14, 23, 23n20, 224, 247n31, 247, 248n31, 248
Sherbert v. Verner, 126, 129–30, 135
Silent Covenants, 29, 39–40, 66, 73, 99–100, 177
Sisyphus, myth of, 44
Sivulka, Juliann, 61
Skinner, Jack T., 160
Skinner v. Oklahoma, 147, 160–61
Slaughterhouse Cases, 6–7, 10, 256–57
slavery: biblical references, 45n16, 46n16, 46n17, 46n20; and Christianity, 48, 125; and Constitution, 122–24; and dehumanization, 234; and *Dred Scott*, 178; and equality, 172; and eradication, 208; and federalism, 6, 11–12; fugitive slave clauses, 123; justifications for, 123, 175; and permanence of racism, 72–73, 120; and racial bonding, 69; religious justification for, 32; and sexual violence, 197–98, 211n3; and theories of inferiority, 11, 61, 65; and the War Amendments, 56; and women, 211n4
slaves, 46n20; Bell on, 151; and citizenship, 122; fugitive slave clause, 123; and religion, 125; and Three-Fifths Compromise, 121
Social Gospel, 199
Socrates, 216–17, 221–23, 245
Sotomayor, Sonia, 165
"Space Traders," 203, 205
spirit, vs. structure, 35, 37
spiritual reformation, 36, 42
statistical data, 98–100, 110; as catalyst for reform, 101

sterilization, forced, 160–63. See also *Skinner v. Oklahoma*
Stone, Harlan, 161–62
structural racism, 99, 195–97, 200, 202, 205–8, 226
struggle for equality, 72, 103, 109
subordination, 121, 178–79, 183–84, 186, 243
Sunday blue laws, 129, 135
sundown towns, 61–62
Supreme Court: and adjudication, 151; *Brown*, 37, 68, 147, 178; and color-blindness, 225, 236; *Coppage*, 91; Equal Protection jurisprudence, 88, 97; and federalism, 6; Fifteenth Amendment, 257; First Amendment, 127–28, 131; Fortune on, 8; free exercise cases, 126; *Hialeah*, 132, 134, 137; *King*, 92; *Plessy*, 9, 39, 65–66, 99–100, 256; and Racial Realism, 89; and Reconstruction, 7; religious rulings, 119–20; *Shelby County*, 247n31; *Sherbert*, 130; and voting rights, 10, 12

Taney, Roger B., 8, 61, 153
Taylor, Breonna, 262
Taylor, George, 149, 225
Tenth Amendment, 247n31
theological hope, 159; aim of, 149; vs. juridical hope, 146–47; vs. law, 151–52
A Theory of Justice, 224
Thirteenth Amendment, 6–7, 56, 75
Thomas, Clarence, 102
Thomas v. Review Board, 129
Three-Fifths Compromise, 121–23
Thurman, Howard, 32, 35, 48n47
Tilden, Samuel, 56
Trump, Donald, 183, 254, 256, 258–60

unemployment, 172–73

United States v. Cruikshank, 6–7, 257
United States v. E.C. Knight Co., 92–93

voter fraud, 56
voter registration, 10
voter suppression, 14, 22
voting rights, 5–6, 10–11, 13–14, 123
Voting Rights Act (1965), 9–10, 14, 217, 247n31, 257

Wagner Act, 112n26
Walker, Alice, 198, 206, 211n5
War Amendments, 56, 61
Warren, Earl, 153–58
Washington, Sylvia Hood, 64
Wells, Ida B., 199
whiteness: definitions of, 64; as property right, 32–33
white privilege, 43
white supremacy: and abstraction, 103; and affirmative action, 203; and Equal Rights Protection jurisprudence, 88; and federalism, 12; and Fifteenth Amendment, 14; and intersectional oppression, 185; and Legal Formalism, 236; and liberalism, 15; and permanence, 5, 148, 253; and structural racism, 202, 205
Williams, Delores, 198–99, 211n6
Williams, Patricia, 31, 42, 45n11
womanism: and black liberation, 196; and defiance, 209–10; and hope, 195, 200; and imperialism, 211; and intersectional oppression, 197–98; and realized eschatology, 199–200
"Women to the Rescue," 206
Woodson, Carter G., 89
World War II, 133

yellow dog contracts, 91

www.ingramcontent.com/pod-product-compliance
Lightning Source LLC
Chambersburg PA
CBHW021652230426
43668CB00008B/594